CARE FOR OLDER ADULTS IN INDIA
Living Arrangements and Quality of Life

Edited by
Ajay Bailey, Martin Hyde and K. S. James

First published in Great Britain in 2024 by

Policy Press, an imprint of
Bristol University Press
University of Bristol
1-9 Old Park Hill
Bristol
BS2 8BB
UK
t: +44 (0)117 374 6645
e: bup-info@bristol.ac.uk

Details of international sales and distribution partners are available at
policy.bristoluniversitypress.co.uk

FSC
www.fsc.org
MIX
Paper | Supporting
responsible forestry
FSC® C013604

Contents

List of figures and tables

Figures

Tables

Notes on the editors

Ajay Bailey is Professor of Social Urban Transitions at the International Development Studies Group at the Department of Human Geography and Spatial Planning, Utrecht University. He leads the research line Global Migration, Culture and Place, working at the interface of anthropology, geography, demography and public health. He holds the prestigious Dr T. M. A. Pai Endowed Chair in Qualitative Methods at Manipal University, India, named after Dr Tonse Madhav Ananth, the founder of the university. With his Chair, Dr Bailey co-ordinates the Transdisciplinary Center for Qualitative Methods. To develop this research line Professor Bailey has been awarded more than €1.5 million in grant funding by a number of organisations, such as NWO/Dutch Organisation for Scientific Research, ZONMW, Ubbo Emmius Foundation, among others. As an anthropologist and a cultural demographer, Professor Bailey has produced 45+ top peer-reviewed international publications; one highly cited monograph; and has supervised 12 PhD researchers. His work significantly contributes to expanding the field of transnational mobilities, ageing, intergenerational relations, health systems research, health services and reducing barriers to care, while establishing meaningful North–South and South–South collaborations.

Martin Hyde is an Associate Professor in Gerontology at Swansea University. His main research interests are ageing and later life and he has published on a wide range of topics including quality of life, work and retirement, health inequalities and globalisation. He has published over 40 papers in peer-reviewed journals, numerous reports and book chapters, as well as three books. He has been involved in a number of large-scale studies including the English Longitudinal Study of Ageing (ELSA), the Survey for Health, Retirement and Ageing in Europe (SHARE) and the Swedish Longitudinal Occupational Study of Health (SLOSH). He is heavily involved in a number of international professional organisations. He is on the Executive Committee of the British Society of Gerontology (BSG), the President of BSG Cymru, a Member at Large of the Sociology of Ageing (RC11) committee of the International Sociological Association and a Fellow of the Gerontological Society of America. He is also the Chair of the Ministerial Advisory Forum on Ageing group on Preparing for the Future, and the Chair of the BSG Work and Retirement Group. He is a Deputy Editor for *Ageing & Society* and on the editorial boards of the *International Journal of Social Research Methodology* and *Quality in Ageing and Older Adults*.

K. S. James is currently the Director and Senior Professor, International Institute for Population Sciences (IIPS), Mumbai, India. Prior to this he was Professor of Population Studies at the Centre for the Study of Regional Development, Jawaharlal Nehru University, New Delhi, and also a Professor at the Population Research Centre, Institute for Social and Economic Change, Bengaluru. He works extensively on demographic changes with focus on population and development and ageing issues. His areas of interest include demographic changes, health transition, ageing issues and migration. He has published widely on demographic transition and demographic dividend in India in journals such as *Science, BMC Public Health, Ageing International, Brown Journal of World Affairs, Maternal and Child Health Journal, Economic and Political Weekly* and many more. He has been a visiting fellow at many prestigious institutes and universities including Harvard University, USA; London School of Economics, UK; University of Southampton, UK; University of Groningen, the Netherlands, and the International Institute of Applied System Analysis (IIASA), Austria.

List of contributors

Vanessa Burholt is Chair in Gerontology in the Faculty of Medical and Health Sciences jointly in the School of Nursing and School of Population Health, University of Auckland.

Anindita Datta is Professor at the Department of Geography, Delhi School of Economics, University of Delhi.

Jyoti S. Hallad is Director of the Population Research Centre, JSS Institute of Economic Research, Dharwad Karnataka.

Inge Hutter is Rector of the International Institute of Social Studies, The Hague, of Erasmus University Rotterdam, and Professor of Participatory and Qualitative Research in Population and Development, at the International Institute of Social Studies, Erasmus University, Rotterdam.

Selim Jahangir is a post-doctoral researcher at the Manipal Academy of Higher Education, Manipal.

Sebastian Joseph is DRDO Psychologist (Retd), Services Selection Board, Ministry of Defence, Bengaluru.

Sanjay Kumar is National Programme Officer at UNFPA – India.

Carol A. Maddock is Research Officer at the Centre for Innovative Ageing, Swansea University.

R. Maruthakutti is Professor of Sociology at the Department of Sociology Manonmaniam Sundaranar University Tirunelveli, Tamil Nadu.

Nikhil Pazhoothundathil is a doctoral candidate at the University of Groningen and a Research Associate and Manipal Academy of Higher Education, Manipal.

S. Irudaya Rajan is Chair of the Ministry of Overseas Indian Affairs (MOIA) Research Unit on International Migration at the Centre for Development Studies, Thiruvananthapuram, Kerala.

S. Siva Raju is Professor at the Centre for Excellence in CSR Tata Institute of Social Sciences, Mumbai.

S. Sunitha is Research Manager at the International Institute of Migration and Development, Thiruvananthapuram, Kerala.

T. S. Syamala is Associate Professor and Head of the Population Research Centre, Institute for Social and Economic Change, Nagarbhavi Post, Bengaluru.

Allen P. Ugargol is Associate Professor of Practice and Public Policy at the Indian Institute of Management, Bengaluru.

Supriya Verma is a Programme Officer at the Population Council, New Delhi.

Acknowledgements

To put a book together on ageing in India is a daunting task due to the range of complex social issues, the regional demographic variations, the sheer diversity of cultures and inequalities that shape everyday life for older adults. This book provides key insights into how we have learned, debated and experienced ageing and care in India. We have benefited greatly from the discussions with the authors and learnt so much from the rich empirical material they present.

Many of the chapters in this book are a result of the Indian–European Research Networking Grant: Ageing and Well-Being in a Globalising World, funded by NWO-ESRC-ICSSR (Project Number: 465-11-009). The participating institutions in this network included the Institute for Social and Economic Change, Bangalore, India; Center for Development Studies, Trivandrum, India; Population Research Centre, University of Groningen, The Netherlands and the University of Southampton, United Kingdom. The network grant allowed us to build capacity and create a community of academics working on ageing issues in India. The chapters in this book are a testament to this community we have been able foster.

Producing a book at any time is a trying task. However, doing so during a global pandemic has taken a near heroic effort on behalf of everyone involved. As editors we must acknowledge the tremendous efforts and hard work put in by the contributors to this book. Many of them were working under extreme lock down conditions which often prevented them from even going to their offices to access their materials. We have also been incredibly fortunate to be working with such an understanding and infinitely patient team at Policy Press. Their practical and moral support at various key junctures during this process has been essential in getting this book over the line. While we are grateful for all the support from Policy Press, we would like to thank Laura Vickers-Rendall, Millie Prekop, Phylicia Ulibarri-Eglite, Zoe Forbes and Alice Greaves in particular for all their hard work, guidance and support at the various stages of the process. Without them this would have been a much harder and much less enjoyable experience. We would also like to thank the anonymous reviewers whose comments, on the proposal and the draft, were insightful and constructive.

We are also extremely grateful to Tom Scharf, Toni Calasanti and Chris Phillipson, the *Ageing in a Global Context* series editors, who worked with us to help us realise our vision for the book and ensure that it was accessible to a wide audience. Above all else, we could not have done this without the generosity of the participants in the various studies that make up this book. We are extremely grateful that you have given your time to share your experiences and opinions with the researchers. We hope that in producing this book we are able to represent them fairly and share them with the world. Finally, we could not have done this without the support of our families and friends. We are incredibly fortunate to have such caring, understanding and supportive personal networks.

Series editors' preface

Chris Phillipson (University of Manchester, UK)
Toni Calasanti (Virginia, Tech, USA)
Thomas Scharf (University of Newcastle, UK)

As the global older population continues to expand, new issues and concerns arise for consideration by academics, policy makers, and health and social care professionals worldwide. *Ageing in a Global Context* is a series of books, published by Policy Press in association with the British Society of Gerontology, which aims to influence and transform debates in what has become a fast-moving field in research and policy. The series seeks to achieve this in three main ways: first, through publishing books which rethink the key questions shaping debates in the study of ageing. This has become especially important given the re-structuring of welfare states, alongside the complex nature of population change, both of these elements opening up the need to explore themes which go beyond traditional perspectives in social gerontology. Second, the series represents a response to the impact of globalisation and related processes, these contributing to the erosion of the national boundaries which originally framed the study of ageing. From this has come the emergence of issues explored in various contributions to the series, for example: the impact of cultural diversity, changing patterns of working life, new forms of inequality, the role of ethnicity in later life and related concerns. Third, a key concern of the series is to explore interdisciplinary connections in gerontology. Contributions to the series provide a critical assessment of the disciplinary boundaries and territories influencing later life, creating, in the process, new perspectives and approaches relevant to the twenty-first century.

Given these broad aims, this very comprehensive study of the care of older people in India is to be especially welcomed. The editors are surely right in their assessment of the importance of a better understanding of the Indian context, given both the size of the country's population and also its immense cultural, demographic and social diversity. Indeed, the key conclusion to be drawn from the various chapters is precisely the variety of living arrangements of older adults, set within the continued importance of the traditional family structure within India. The book is of particular importance in the way it draws together a wealth of material, based upon both quantitative and qualitative data, looking at trends across India and individual states. The study also provides significant evidence of the importance of gender and socio-economic inequalities in the provision of care, as well critical issues relating to the various systems of support targeted at older adults. The book will certainly be a key resource for academics, NGOs and policy makers more generally. It should also stimulate further research and policy discussion about the future of care and welfare in a country with a rapidly expanding older population.

Map of India

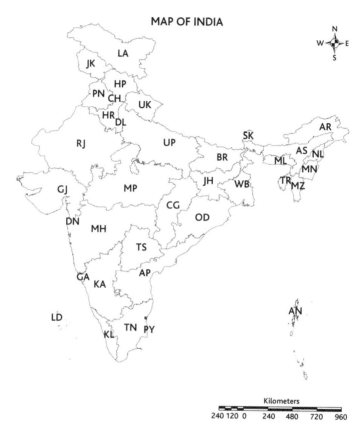

MAP OF INDIA

State name	Abbreviation	State name	Abbreviation
Arunachal Pradesh	AR	Lakshadweep	LD
Assam	AS	Odisha	OD
Chandigarh	CH	Dadra and Nagar Haveli and Daman and Diu	DN
Karnataka	KA		
Manipur	MN	Ladakh	LA
Meghalaya	ML	Jammu and Kashmir	JK
Mizoram	MZ	Chhattisgarh	CG
Nagaland	NL	Delhi	DL
Punjab	PN	Goa	GA
Rajasthan	RJ	Haryana	HR
Sikkim	SK	Himachal Pradesh	HP
Tripura	TR	Jharkhand	JH
Uttarakhand	UK	Tamil Nadu	TN
Telangana	TS	Uttar Pradesh	UP
Bihar	BR	West Bengal	WB
Kerala	KL	Andhra Pradesh	AP
Madhya Pradesh	MP	Puducherry	PY
Andaman and Nicobar	AN	Maharashtra	MH
Gujarat	GJ		

Introduction: Living arrangements and care in India

Ajay Bailey, Martin Hyde and K. S. James

Introduction

India has one of the most rapidly ageing populations on the planet. Given the change in the size and nature of the older population in India it is imperative that we better understand the situation of older people in India. However, India is a complex and diverse country made up of different states, castes, cultures, and ethnic groups. India's older adult population has now risen to 8.57 per cent, however in states such as Goa and Kerala the percentage of older adults is as high as 11.20 per cent and 12.55 per cent respectively (Census, 2011). Recent data from the Longitudinal Ageing Study in India (LASI) show that nearly 12 per cent of older adults were 60+ and that the states of Kerala, Himachal Pradesh, and Tamil Nadu had a higher proportion of older adults (IIPS, 2020). India had, in the past, a predominantly family-based elder care system. However, rapid population ageing, the decline of extended families coupled with decreasing fertility rates, increasing life expectancy, widowhood, singlehood or strained intergenerational relationships, have all raised concerns that an increasing number of older adults in India live alone. These concerns are amplified as India, like many other lower- and middle-income countries, is still struggling in setting up social security and pensions systems (Arokiasamy and Yadav, 2014; Giridhar et al, 2014; Bloom et al, 2015). However, as we show throughout this edited volume, the demographic picture is not uniform as Indian states are at surprisingly diverse levels of demographic transition and vary to a great extent in their cultural practices, social norms and socio-political contexts.

This chapter provides a general introduction to the topic by situating the subsequent chapters within the broad demographic trends already mentioned and gives an outline of the structure and chapters of the book. This chapter introduces the need for focus on living arrangements and care. It highlights the social, economic and cultural contexts that shape the provision of care for older adults. We link the different studies presented and explore the consequences of changing living arrangements on long-term care, and the economic, physical, social and psychological well-being of older people.

Demographic changes and modernisation

Societies across the world are ageing and it is increasingly the case that people are living longer. The UN population division reports that in 2019 there were 703 million people aged 65 and over and in 2050 the number is predicted to reach 1.5 billion (UN, 2019). With this demographic transition we see societies rapidly moving to below-replacement fertility levels and a larger share of the population who are older adults. However, for large countries such as India, there are multiple transitions, with some states such as Kerala experiencing this situation for more than two decades, whereas states such as Uttar Pradesh still has high fertility rates. Modernisation, availability of education for lower socio-economic groups, and urbanisation have weakened some of the earlier traditional structures whereby older adults had more control of the resources and decision-making in the households. For Cowgill and Holmes (1972) modernisation represented a shift from the natural rhythms of 'family' time, in which older people were venerated, to the artificial, impersonal dictates of 'industrial' time, which privileges the young. They argued that the spread of new technologies would also disadvantage older people by devaluing their skills and experiences, developed during a different time, and creating new jobs for which they are ill equipped. This change in status and a reduced ability to contribute economically – to the family and wider society – means that older adults have shifted from being valued members of the community to being seen as burden and pushed to the margins of society.

Family care, gender and support

Family still remains the primary source of care for older adults. The family composition in modern India has gone through multiple transitions. While moving from primarily agrarian livelihoods to industrialisation and the service economy, household composition has also undergone changes due to migration and reducing fertility. The popular image of a crumbling joint family system is not necessarily true for India as whole. Breton (2021) observes that states in the Indo-Gangetic plain and central India have more joint families, while in states in South India (except Karnataka) such households are rare. Nuclear families are an outcome of rural–urban migration, education and aspiration for non-agrarian livelihoods. Irrespective of the family composition, patriarchal norms have in the past and to the present day influenced the provision of care within the family. In the Western context, adult daughters are more likely to provide filial care compared to adult sons. Campbell and Matthews (2003) note that the type of care and its linkage to traditional gender roles determines who provides more care. In the Indian context the burden of care falls primarily on the daughter-in-law or spouse (Ghosh et al, 2017; Ugargol and Bailey, 2018; Bhan et al, 2020). As is the case for almost every country in the world, women in India outlive men. Asaria et al (2019) observe that life expectancy at birth for women was found to be higher than for men in every wealth quintile across both urban and rural households. However, in terms of morbidity, women also experience worse health than men (Balchandaran and James, 2019). Moreover, women in India often experience discrimination and neglect as they age, which can be exacerbated by widowhood and dependence on others (Kalavar and Jamuna, 2011; Samanta et al, 2015; Perkins et al, 2016). Loss of spouse in later life can result in greater vulnerability. This is true for both sexes, but it is more frequent for women than men. Census data shows that among older men, 82 per cent are currently married while among older women the figure is only 50 per cent. About 48 per cent of older women are widowed while only 15 per cent of older men are. There are other life course factors that impact this, too. Women in India are much less likely than men to be engaged in employment and, where they are, they are much more likely to be in informal and vulnerable employment (Ladusingh, 2018). This clearly has important implications for access to resources and the receipt of care in later life. To add further to the complexity, India is now witnessing alarming attrition of the few women who do enter the labour market. Chatterjee and colleagues (2018) and Sarkar and colleagues (2019) attribute this to increase in wealth and income of other members of the household, leading to higher chances that women leave jobs.

Urbanisation, migration and ageing

As predicted by the World Cities Report of 2020 (UN Habitat, 2020), the world will further urbanise over the next decade, from 56.2 per cent of the global population today to 60.4 per cent by 2030. Some 96 per cent of urban growth will occur in the less-developed regions of East Asia, South Asia, and Africa with three countries – India, China, and Nigeria – accounting for 35 per cent of the total increase in global urban population from 2018 to 2050. Urban growth is largely fuelled by increasing job opportunities, improvement in education and the inability of rural areas to provide employment opportunities for the young. The reduction in farming- and agriculture-related profits has led to many agrarian families sending their children to work or study in urban areas, hoping that they would enter the service economy (Datta, 2018; Singh and Basu, 2020). Reducing fertility, internal migration, and lack of job opportunities in rural areas has led to smaller family sizes both in the rural and urban centres. The networks created by migration to urban areas often encourage new waves of migration from rural and semi-urban areas (Chandrasekhar and Mitra, 2019). Cities are often projected as spaces of growth, individualisation and modernisation, but due to different spatial and socio-economic inequalities many urban residents remain in islands of poverty and disadvantage. The WHO (2007) defines 'age-friendly cities' as spaces where older adults continue to live in security, enjoy good health and participate fully in society. This goal, however, is more challenging to achieve in low- and middle-income countries that are marked with rising socio-economic inequalities. Studies on ageing in cities in India show a lack of green spaces (Subramanian and Jana, 2018; Adlakha et al, 2021), high rates of crime and abuse (Mishra and Patel, 2013; Shankardass and Rajan, 2018), social isolation (Pilania et al, 2019) and a lack of subsidised housing (Brijnath, 2012; Datta, 2018).

Living arrangements and care

Despite the fact that many of the tenets of modernisation and ageing theory (Cowgill and Holmes, 1972) have been questioned and often fail to stand up to empirical enquiry, interest in and concern about the living arrangements of older people have proved to be remarkably enduring features of much gerontological research. However, there is a dual discourse on the living arrangements of older people around the world. In the advanced welfare economies of Europe and North America the focus is on supporting independent living in later life, as opposed to the institutionalisation of older people, while when looking at the developing world commentators express increasing concern about the deterioration of traditional, multi-generational family structures. This reflects the fact that the family is often the main, if not the sole, provider of welfare for older people in low- and middle-income countries (Aldous 1962; Nyangweso 1998; Mba, 2007). Hence, any change or challenge to family as an institution has an impact on the welfare of older people.

According to the recent LASI study 41 per cent of older adults aged 60 and above live with their spouses and children. More than a quarter of the older adults live with their children without a spouse and around 6 per cent of older adults live alone (IIPS, 2020). The household composition of older adults also varies across the states: households with members aged 60 and above are higher than the national average in the states of Kerala (56 per cent), Lakshadweep (53 per cent), Puducherry (53 per cent), Tamil Nadu (49 per cent), Himachal Pradesh (49 per cent), Punjab (48 per cent), Rajasthan (45per cent) and Uttarakhand (50 per cent). However, the proportion of households with only members less than 60 years of age is comparatively higher than the national average in the states of Assam (65 per cent), Haryana (58 per cent), Jammu and Kashmir (59 per cent), Chhattisgarh (65 per cent), Dadra and Nagar Haveli (70per cent), Andhra Pradesh (58 per cent) and Karnataka (58 per cent) (IIPS, 2020, p 45). This pattern again reflects the differential demographic transition and migration patterns both within and between the states.

The chapters

Chapter 2 explores the ways in which living arrangements and the provision of care for older people in India have been affected by migration. In this chapter we examine both internal and international migration to understand how families establish, maintain, and retain transnational and transregional care relations. In this chapter we situate migration as part of the life course. The life-course approach focuses on life events and transitions of individuals and the ways in which these events define their life trajectories (Elder, 1985). In particular, we will draw on the concept of 'linked-lives' to show how older people's life course transitions, for example into care, are linked to the migration decisions of their offspring. With increasing urbanisation and migration we will see emerging trends of global and transregional chains of care to supplant and complement care deficits for vulnerable populations left behind, especially older adults.

Chapter 3 examines the various living arrangements of older adults in India, the various factors that motivate this choice of living arrangement, and the welfare implications of living arrangement patterns on older adults. This chapter combines unique datasets from the United National Fund for Population Activities (UNFPA), the India-sponsored research project on 'Building Knowledge Base on Population Ageing in India' (BKPAI), the National Family Health Surveys, and the Longitudinal Ageing Study of India (LASI). These data reveal that 1) there is an increasing incidence of older people living independently, that is not co-residing with their adult children or grandchildren, in India; 2) older adults who live alone have lower standard of living compared to older adults who live with children, spouses or with others; and 3) living arrangement pattern has no bearing on the subjective well-being of the older persons. No effect of living arrangement on subjective well-being indicates that living alone is not necessarily seen as a burden by older people. Such analysis is new and problematises the cultural norm of co-residence as a pathway to well-being.

Chapter 4 aims to understand the patterns of living arrangements, living arrangement preferences, and the concordance in living arrangements among Indian older adults. The authors apply Person–Environment Fit theories to examine the impact of concordance of living arrangement preferences on the health and well-being of older adults. In this chapter the concordance is defined as the correspondence between the actual and the preferred living arrangement of older adults. The chapter uses BKPAI data and provides new insights into the role of preference and its impact on the health of older adults. One of the key findings is that approximately one third of Indian older adults preferred independent living in comparison to co-residence. Of real interest, however, are the results which show that living arrangement concordance did not appear to be a significant predictor of self-rated health or better mental health status. This suggests that the Person–Environment Fit model might need to be adapted for use in the context of living arrangements in India.

Chapter 5 takes a longitudinal perspective to ageing and focuses on Kerala. Kerala was the frontrunner in terms of demographic changes and population ageing. Using an extensive longitudinal panel (2004 to 2019) of older adults, this chapter explores how living arrangements have changed among older adults in Kerala and how changes in family size influence living arrangements, and studies if this change in living arrangements or household size is associated with changes in the health and survival status of older adults. The results show that a high proportion of the population aged 60 and over in Kerala still live with their family members. The study also found that older persons who live with one other person had a lower chance of dying whilst those who lived with five or more household members had an increased risk of mortality. This finding remained even after adjusting for daily living activities score, health perception, sex and age. These results are interesting and raise some crucial questions about the assumptions around the impact of demographic change on older adults in Kerala and India more widely.

Chapter 6 applies a qualitative approach to study the evolving nature of care frameworks for older adults in the Indian context through examining the changing household living arrangements and complexities that exist in identifying caregiving motives and primary caregivers to older adults, especially in an emigration context where older adults are left behind. This chapter serves to initiate dialogue on the negotiated intergenerational contract that seems to have evolved in the background of changing family situations and modernisation. Findings from this study indicate that adult children from emigrant households are responsive to parental needs of support and find ways to effect supportive exchanges and care arrangements. The intergenerational care arrangements reflect the emigration event-led adaptation of family and household structure to retain traditional familial ties and enable mutually supportive exchanges between adult children and their parents.

Chapter 7 investigates how life-course obligations, expectations and practices are linked to older adults' sense of well-being. It takes a life-course approach with a specific focus on linked lives, recognising that life trajectories of individuals are socially embedded and closely linked to the transitions of significant others such as family members. Moreover, linked lives are translocal as they include older adults in migrant households, their adult children (co-residing or migrant children), grandchildren, caregivers and non-kin social networks. To explore these issues, qualitative in-depth interviews were conducted with 37 older adults. The participants included couples, widows and widowers. Participants in this study include both older adults co-residing with kin and older adults residing on their own. The interviews reveal that life stages and expectations of successful transition from one stage to the next was perceived as crucial for the offspring and for the older adults. The chapter observes that economic security, social support, health and better living conditions aid in realising the life course obligations and contribute towards the overall well-being of the older adults.

Chapter 8 contributes to existing debates in the geographies of care by exploring different forms of care for older men received both at home and in care homes. The research is based on 79 in-depth interviews of older men and their caregivers, collected from homes as well as care homes in Delhi and Kolkata. The analysis reveals that older men's care needs, which ranged from personal and economic health to emotional, were perceived to be inadequately addressed in rapidly transforming societies and family structures. However, the practice of intergenerational reciprocal care is strongly gendered and involves inequalities of power. The care relationships between older men and their caregivers are situated within wider socio-economic relations which influence the power of each other. The caring relationships in the Indian context are deeply rooted in filial obligation and intergenerational dependence, where older adults are entitled to receive care from their children in exchange for the care they had provided to them growing up.

Chapter 9 examines home ownership, residential changes and the meaning home has for older adults in Kerala. The chapter addresses three questions: 1) What motivates older adults to retain their (previous) home while currently residing in retirement homes? 2) How do older adults maintain their previous homes? And 3) how do these motivations help to maintain place attachment? Using a unique set of qualitative interviews with residents of care homes, the authors show that health issues, a need for assistance, a lack of security, migration of children, loneliness due to loss of a spouse and a wish to live independently are the major reasons for older adults to seek an alternative source of residence in the form of a retirement home. Cultural schemas of care and obligations towards next generations motivate older adults in retaining and maintaining homes.

Chapter 10 draws on data from 30 in-depth interviews with older male and female residents of nine care homes in three districts of Tamil Nadu and addresses the following questions: 1) What are the decision-making routes leading to relocation to a care home? And 2) How does culture and the political economy influence the care choices available to older people? The chapter states that a majority of care home residents had families that deviated from the social ideal of the 'traditional' joint family. Cultural norms prevented some participants from drawing on support from daughters or other relatives. The chapter suggests that amendments to social protection, the provision of a carers' allowance, accessible and affordable health and community care would ease pressures on family assistance where this is available and provide alternatives for older people without filial support.

Chapters 3 to 10 present empirical evidence of the different experiences of living arrangements, and their impacts, for older adults. However, it is crucial to understand the broader welfare structures, or lack thereof, in which these demographic changes are occurring. In Chapter 11 the author enumerates the various schemes provided by the Government of India for older adults and other schemes open for older adults. In addition to listing these issues, the chapter goes a step further to discuss the barriers in accessing these schemes. The multiplicity of schemes has resulted in wastage of resources and failure to achieve synergies. The chapter also reports that various evaluation studies have highlighted leakages, inefficiencies and ineffectiveness of programme design.

Chapter 12 draws together the main issues and findings from the wealth of information presented in the previous chapters and reflects on what this means for researchers, social care providers and policy makers in India and elsewhere. Although each chapter makes a unique contribution to our understanding of the impact of the changing living arrangements on the care for older people in India, there are a number of common themes that connect them. The narrative that emerges across these chapters is one that challenges the assumed wisdom about the demographic, industrial and social change on older adults. The chapters in this book tell us a much more complex story about living arrangements and care for older adults in India. Rather than being a single, linear narrative, it is a story about the heterogeneity of families, care and migration experiences.

References

Adlakha, D., Chandra, M., Krishna, M., Smith, L. and Tully, M. A. (2021) 'Designing age-friendly communities: exploring qualitative perspectives on urban green spaces and ageing in two Indian megacities', *International Journal of Environmental Research and Public Health*, 18(4): 1491.

Aldous, J. (1962) 'Urbanization, the extended family, and kinship ties in West Africa', *Social Forces*, 41(1): 6–12.

Arokiasamy, P. and Yadav, S. (2014) 'Changing age patterns of morbidity vis-à-vis mortality in India', *Journal of Biosocial Science*, 46(4): 462–79.

Asaria, M., Mazumdar, S., Chowdhury, S., Mazumdar, P., Mukhopadhyay, A. and Gupta, I. (2019) 'Socioeconomic inequality in life expectancy in India', *BMJ Global Health*, 4(3): e001445.

Balachandran, A. and James, K. S. (2019) 'A multi-dimensional measure of population ageing accounting for quantum and quality in life years: an application of selected countries in Europe and Asia', *SSM-Population Health*, 7: 100330.

Balachandran, A. and James, K. S. (2021) 'A multi-dimensional perspective on the gender gap in health among older adults in India and China: application of a new ageing measure', *Ageing and Society*, 41(5): 1000–20. doi:10.1017/S0144686X19001521

Bhan, N., Rao, N. and Raj, A. (2020) 'Gender differences in the associations between informal caregiving and wellbeing in low-and middle-income countries', *Journal of Women's Health*, 29(10): 1328–8.

Bloom, D. E., Chatterji, S., Kowal, P., Lloyd-Sherlock, P., McKee, M., Rechel, B. and Smith, J. P. (2015) 'Macroeconomic implications of population ageing and selected policy responses', *The Lancet*, 385(9968): 649–57.

Breton, E. (2021) 'Modernisation, demographic change and state-level variations in household composition in India', *Asian Population Studies*, 17(3): 225–49.

Brijnath, B. (2012) 'Why does institutionalised care not appeal to Indian families? Legislative and social answers from urban India', *Ageing and Society*, 32(4): 697–717.

Campbell, L. D. and Martin-Matthews, A. (2003) 'The gendered nature of men's filial care', *The Journals of Gerontology Series B: Psychological Sciences and Social Sciences*, 58(6): S350–S358.

Census (2011) Census of India 2011, Provisional Population Totals, Government of India: New Delhi.

Chandrasekhar, S. and Mitra, A. (2019) 'Migration, caste and livelihood: evidence from Indian city-slums', *Urban Research and Practice*, 12(2): 156–72.

Chatterjee, E., Desai, S. and Vanneman, R. (2018) 'Indian paradox: rising education, declining women's employment', *Demographic Research*, 38: 855–78.

Cowgill, D. O. and Holmes, L. (eds) (1972) *Aging and Modernization*, New York: Appleton-Century-Crofts.

Datta, A. (2018) 'Pride and shame in the city: young people's experiences of rural–urban migration in India', *Children's Geographies*, 16(6): 654–65.

Elder, G. H. Jr., (1985) 'Perspectives on the life course', in G. H. Elder (ed), *Life Course Dynamics: Trajectories and Transitions 1968–1980*, Ithaca, NY: Cornell University Press, pp 23–49.

Ghosh, S., Capistrant, B. and Friedemann-Sánchez, G. (2017) 'Who will care for the elder caregiver? Outlining theoretical approaches and future research questions', in T. Samanta (ed) *Cross-Cultural and Cross-Disciplinary Perspectives in Social Gerontology*, Singapore: Springer, pp 23–43.

Giridhar, G., Sathyanarayana, K. M., Kumar, S., James, K. S. and Alam, M. (eds) (2014) *Population Ageing in India*, Cambridge: Cambridge University Press.

IIPS (International Institute for Population Sciences) (2020) *Longitudinal Ageing Study in India (LASI) Wave 1, 2017-18, India Report*, International Institute for Population Sciences: Mumbai.

Kalavar, J. M. and Jamuna, D. (2011) 'Aging of Indian women in India: the experience of older women in formal care homes', *Journal of Women and Aging*, 23(3): 203–15.

Mba, C. J. (2007) 'Gender disparities in living arrangements of older people in Ghana: evidence from the 2003 Ghana demographic and health survey', *Journal of International Women's Studies*, 9(1): 153–66.

Mishra, A. J. and Patel, A. B. (2013) 'Crimes against the elderly in India: a content analysis on factors causing fear of crime', *International Journal of Criminal Justice Sciences*, 8(1): 13–23.

Nyangweso, M. A. (1998) 'Transformations of care of the aged among Africans-a study of the Kenyan situation', *Aging & Mental Health*, 2(3): 181–5.

Perkins, J. M., Lee, H. Y., James, K. S., Oh, J., Krishna, A., Heo, J. and Subramanian, S. V. (2016) 'Marital status, widowhood duration, gender and health outcomes: a cross-sectional study among older adults in India', *BMC Public Health*, 16(1): 1–12.

Pilania, M., Yadav, V., Bairwa, M., Behera, P., Gupta, S.D., Khurana, H. and Poongothai, S. J. B. P. H. (2019) 'Prevalence of depression among the elderly (60 years and above) population in India, 1997–2016: a systematic review and meta-analysis', *BMC Public Health*, 19(1): 1–18.

Samanta, T., Chen, F. and Vanneman, R. (2015) 'Living arrangements and health of older adults in India', *Journals of Gerontology Series B: Psychological Sciences and Social Sciences*, 70(6): 937–47.

Sarkar, S., Sahoo, S. and Klasen, S. (2019) 'Employment transitions of women in India: a panel analysis', *World Development*, 115: 291–309.

Shankardass, M. K. and Rajan, S. I. (eds) (2018) *Abuse and Neglect of the Elderly in India*, Singapore: Springer.

Singh, C. and Basu, R. (2020) 'Moving in and out of vulnerability: interrogating migration as an adaptation strategy along a rural–urban continuum in India', *The Geographical Journal*, 186(1): 87–102.

Subramanian, D. and Jana, A. (2018) 'Assessing urban recreational open spaces for the elderly: a case of three Indian cities', *Urban Forestry and Urban Greening*, 35: 115–28.

Ugargol, A. P. and Bailey, A. (2018) 'Family caregiving for older adults: gendered roles and caregiver burden in emigrant households of Kerala, India', *Asian Population Studies*, 14(2): 194–210.

UNDESA (United Nations, Department of Economic and Social Affairs, Population Division) (2019) 'World Population Ageing 2019: Highlights (ST/ESA/SER.A/430), https://www.un.org/development/desa/pd/content/world-population-ageing-2019-highlights

UN Habitat (2020) *World Cities Report 2020: The Value of Sustainable Urbanization*, Kenya: United Nations.

World Health Organization (2007) 'Global age-friendly cities: a guide'. World Health Organization, https://apps.who.int/iris/handle/10665/43755.

2

Theorising care and relationships in the age of migration

Ajay Bailey and Martin Hyde

Introduction

This chapter provides a theoretical framework to understand the ways in which living arrangements and the provision of care for older people in India have been affected by migration. According to the United Nations, as of 2020 nearly 18 million Indians were living outside their country of origin. Indians are the largest diaspora groups followed by Mexican, Russian and Chinese diasporas (UNDESA, 2020). The largest concentration of Indian international migrants is in the Gulf region. The international migration from India prior to 2000 was largely low skilled and more focused towards the Middle East. After 2000 rapid globalisation increased the migration of skilled workers to the developed countries. Much of this skilled migration was among middle-class households and followed a trajectory where education and employment mobility to cities fuelled further migration plans to other countries. Indian migrants also contribute a large portion of their incomes as remittances. According to the World Bank, India received close to $US84 billion as remittances in 2019, close to 2.8 per cent of its GDP. Due to the COVID pandemic the World Bank estimates that remittances could drop by between 7 and 9 per cent (Ratha et al, 2020).

However, as eye-catching as these figures are, it is important to remember that the number of internal migrants within India is far greater than those who migrate abroad. Increasing urbanisation, improvement of travel and access to travel, coupled with greater educational opportunities, has led to widespread migration within India. Migration to the cities is driven by a combination of labour migration, which can be both temporary and circular, educational mobility and marriage migration. Bhagat's (2016) analysis of the 2011 census data shows that nearly 30 per cent of the Indian population moved internally. De (2019) reports that there were 450 million internal migrants in India and much of this migration was intra-state migration. See Chapter 3 by James and Kumar on the impact of migration on living arrangements of older adults in India. The lower levels of inter-state migration could potentially be due to the non-transferability of social security entitlements across state borders (Kone et al 2018). Migration to urban areas is largely due to lack of employment opportunities in rural and semi-urban areas. Cities often provide informal work opportunities which attract low- and semi-skilled workers from the peripheral rural regions. The ILO (2021) estimates that in 2011–12 nearly 92 per cent of the workforce were employed in the informal sector. Boyden (2013) observes that increasing educational opportunities for poor and disadvantaged groups has meant that more children can have access to schools and boarding facilities outside their villages and more often in urban areas, thus creating new forms of educational migration.

Migration (internal and international) needs to be seen as a stepwise approach. Internal migration increasingly precedes international migration. For example, migration for education to cities can often lead to onward migration to larger metropolitan areas for work and create opportunities for international migration. As King and Skeldon (2010) argue, both internal and international migration form an integrated system, where the neglect of one leads to a partial interpretation of the total picture. Through examining these patterns, different chapters in this book (see Chapters 6, 7 and 9) explore the relationship between these two forms of migration and examine the potential consequences for care relationships in India both between household members and across family members separated by distance.

The chapters employ the notion of 'global householding' developed by Douglass (2009, 2014). This includes marriage, child bearing and rearing, adoption, hiring foreign domestic helpers and caregiving to older adults. In Chapter 6 and Chapter 7 the authors examine the impact of international migration on everyday experiences of ageing. These dimensions are the new motives for transnational movements and linkages among people. The linked lives in global householding include: 1) for marriage: Indian spouses in foreign countries, parents/siblings arranging marriages in India; 2) for childcare: grandparents providing culturally appropriate care; 3) care for older adults: traditionally the cultural duty of the adults' children but now more non-kin helpers in India. Through these householding tasks and linkages, the global Indian household emerges.

Care and family caregiving in India

Because India does not have a comprehensive social security system (see Chapter 11 by S. Siva Raju) and the majority of the workforce are in the informal economy (Hyde, George and Kumar, 2019), the family remains the primary source of care for older adults. However, families are changing. Living arrangements in India have moved from being primarily joint families to nuclear and extended families with more and more evidence of multi-generational households living under one roof. Co-residence in the Indian context is the expected norm. However, this is more often due to a lack of alternative forms of living arrangements for older adults. The reciprocity of care or care exchange between generations binds families together. With an increasing numbers of men and women entering the labour force, the availability of caregivers within the household has changed and the traditional caregiving patterns and expectations have also undergone considerable changes in urban areas. Various studies report that primary caregivers are often younger female members of the household (Jamuna, 2000; Raju, 2014; Ugargol et al, 2016). It is argued that this is due to patriarchal norms and traditions which hold that the daughter-in-law should provide the necessary care. In situations where there are no younger members in the household, older women bear a larger share of the care burden, often not only for their spouses but also for other older adults within the household. Bloom et al (2010) observe that increased longevity in India has meant that taking care of older adults has become more expensive due to increases in chronic health conditions. Moreover, falling fertility rates have further reduced the intergenerational care network. See Chapters 8 and 10 on how older adults seek different forms of care and the challenges in accessing such care. With the migration of adult children, the tasks of caregiving are left to the aged spouse or to hired non-kin caregivers.

Transnational households also exchange care through financial, social and reverse remittances. Levitt (2001) coined the term social remittances to call attention to the fact that, in addition to the money that migrants send home, they also export ideas and behaviours. She observed four types of social remittances: norms, practices, identities and social capital. Levitt acknowledges that social remittances are inherently cultural and circulate between sending and receiving countries (Levitt and Lamba-Nieves, 2011). Crucial life transitions draw on care from family members. Care can then be seen as one of these social remittances (Mazzucato, 2011). Childcare is perceived as one of the 'cultural duties' that Indian parents often perform by migrating internationally to provide care (see Chapter 7 for a more detailed example on such mobilities) for the offspring of their children (Glick and van Hook, 2002). In addition to care giving and receiving, reverse remittances of material culture in the form of food, religious artifacts, clothes and other personal/familial objects reflect the objectification of norms, values and practices (Miller, 1998). Baldassar and Merla (2014, p 25) developed the concept of 'care circulation' as the reciprocal, multi-directional and asymmetrical exchange of care that fluctuates over the life course within the transnational family networks and is subject to political, economic, cultural and social contexts of both sending and receiving countries. The norms and values that underlie these exchanges are subject to multiple interpretations as many of the migrants combine traditional and modern lifestyles to create spaces where intergenerational care and exchange is possible. The concept of 'co-presence' (Campos-Castillo and Hitlin, 2013) best captures these reverse remittances between households, where individuals try to maintain links across geographically dispersed households.

Cultural norms and expectations between generations form the basis for care provision. Many of the chapters in this book (see Chapters 6–10) examine the underlying cultural meaning system and the cultural schemas that motivate people to be part of care relationships. d'Andrade, Shweder and Le Vine (1984, p 116) define culture as 'learned systems of meaning, communicated by means of natural language and other symbol systems … Cultural meaning systems can be treated as a very large diverse pool of knowledge, or partially shared cluster of norms, or as intersubjectively shared, symbolically created realities.' With increasing migration, such cultural meaning systems also experience change. Ali (2007) observes how emigration is seen as a necessary step to cross into successful adulthood. The norms of intergenerational care provision also change with a different set of expectations and obligations that are required of both older adults and the adult children living abroad.

Life course, linked lives and migration

The life-course approach aids in situating life events and trajectories over time in specific social contexts (see Elder, 1985, 1994; Kulu and Milewski, 2007; Wingens et al, 2011). Various crucial life transitions (Elder, 1985; Dykstra and Van Wissen, 1999) such as graduating, entering the labor market or having a child significantly alter the family and employment status. According to Elder (1985), the life-course approach focuses on life events and transitions of individuals and the ways in which these events define their life trajectories. He provides a framework with three key components. The first 'lives in time and space' deals with the historical, geographical and cultural contexts that influence life paths of individuals. The second component is 'timing of lives'; here the focus is on the occurrence, sequence and duration of transitions. The timing of events is connected to the timing of other individuals in the family. Linked lives emphasises the interrelatedness between the timing of life paths of people in social relationships. The third component is 'human agency' which, in line with the previous components, shows how individuals create their own life paths based on the choices they make (Elder, 1975, 1994).

Migration decisions are inextricably bound up with events and experiences in other life-course trajectories. The life-course approach focuses on life events, transitions of individuals and the ways in which these events define their life trajectories (Elder, 1985). Several chapters in this book draw on the concept of 'linked-lives' to show how older people's life-course transitions, for example going into care, are linked to the migration decisions of their offspring. However, Hagestad and Dannefer (2001) have criticised the life-course approaches in migration studies for their 'microfication' and recommend that researchers take a broader view to include the asymmetry of power relations both within and beyond national borders. From this perspective, caregiving and receipt by family members often act as countermeasures to the lack of access to formal welfare. As family members move across borders to provide care, these mobilities of caregiving become new motives for onward/return migration (Kõu and Bailey 2014; Bailey, 2017). Research in this field needs to pay attention to the heterogeneity of the experience of migration.

In terms of transitions and relocations, Rossi (1968) discusses the life cycle approach as a predetermined set of events that individuals undergo. This set of events, for example marriage, having children, divorce, widowhood and retirement, are major reasons for relocations. This model however assumes a linear sequence and a patriarchal assumption that all individuals will follow these paths. Despite this, the model does provide a structure to see how one transition can have an effect on the life status of a fellow family member. The life paths that individuals choose or are forced to choose due to limited supply of employment opportunities can change the family composition and aspirations of other members of the household. In the Indian context we see that migration for education and employment is more the norm for men and often difficult for women. Traditionally, women's migration was linked to marriage and relocation to a patrilocal residence. However, recent evidence shows the increasing independent migration of women for education and employment (Rugunanan, 2017; Manohar, 2019; Thompson and Walton-Roberts, 2019). With international migration, there is blurring on migration motives between education and employment. Raghuram (2012) notes that skilled migrants could have multiple identities and motives during their stay abroad. For example, some educational programmes require students to gain work experience as part of their educational trajectory. The status change often occurs when work permits have to be organised by the employer.

The USA has been the main destination for skilled Indian migrants since the 1990s, followed by Canada, Australia, the United Kingdom and the Netherlands (Banerjee, 2006; Shachar, 2006; Cerna, 2011). The European Union introduced the 'Blue Card' to further improve mobility and transferability of skills across its member states. There is much competition to attract young and highly skilled men and women to fill gaps created by population ageing and specifically an ageing workforce. Compared to other immigrant groups, the highly skilled migrants (HSMs) have easier entry both for themselves and their linked movers. The ability of spouses to work, obtain long-term visas, reduce taxes and the imposition of integration rules has led to specific corridors for the swift mobility of professionals. Though skilled migration programmes are keen to have the best and brightest from the Global South, this invitation for mobility is often restricted to the spouse and children. Previously the USA and Canada allowed for the green cards to be issued to parents to facilitate family reunification. With changing immigration policies and strengthening of conservative politics, the ability of older adults to seamlessly move between transnational households is curtailed (Braedley, Côté-Boucher and Przednowek, 2019). With the lack of opportunities for permanent stay, older (able-bodied) adults often travel between home and host countries to maintain family networks.

However, not all older adults are able to or want to emigrate with their children. In the popular, and policy, imagination, these older adults are seen as 'left behind'. This evokes a sense that the older adults have been isolated from or even abandoned by their family. Older adults with a stable income and good living situations may choose to stay behind (Jónsson, 2011). The decision to stay and not co-migrate (internally or internationally) is linked to the social networks and bonds established by the older adults which they are often reluctant to let go of. In the Western context, the choice to stay could be linked to the wishes to live independently and cultural norms that do not stress on co-residence. Whereas, in the non-Western context, the decision to stay is much more complex and is often linked to immigration policies that deter co-migration of older adults, the strong familial and community bonds that extend beyond the immediate family and the fear to leave behind social capital accumulated over the life course to make a fresh start in a new country. As immigrant populations age, we will see more *pendular migration* (Fokkema, Cela and Witter, 2016) between countries of origin and destinations. With the onset of ill-health and disability, these mobilites become rare (De Silva, 2017).

The impact of migration on older adults who are 'left behind' depends on a range of factors, family relationships, financial status, immigration politics, bordering and legality of mobilities (see Chapter 6, 7 and 9 on asymmetrical care relations). Among low-income families or families where older adults were employed in manual work, remittances provide them with reprieve (Chyi and Mao, 2011; Böhme, Persian and Stöhr, 2015). Older adults also face emotional costs of migration. Older adults in rural China reported more depression and lower life satisfaction (Guo, Aranda and Silverstein, 2009). Due to smaller family sizes, older women may face a greater care burden, often caring for fellow older adults and any left behind grandchildren (Ugargol and Bailey, 2018, 2021; Harling, 2020. To better understand the impact of migration we need to first understand the social and economic status before the migration of adult children and the contribution of remittances has made to their overall well-being.

Global chains of care

From this perspective one, can see the global/translocal Indian household as a node in an (emerging) global/translocal chain of (elder) care. The 'global care chain' concept refers to the 'series of personal links between people across the globe based on the paid or unpaid work of caring' (Hochschild, 2000, p 131). In Hochschild's model wealthier families in the Global North were able to buy-in care from poorer women from the Global South to supplement or supplant the (child) care that was required. She defined a global care chain as typically entailing:

> an older daughter from a poor family who cares for her siblings while her mother works as a nanny caring for the children of a migrating nanny who, in turn, cares for the child of a family in a rich country. (Hochschild, 2000, p 131)

In so doing Hochschild shone a light on the then emerging interactions (and inequalities) between care and globalisation. In the 21st century, there is growing literature covering a wide range of issues and groups involved in these global chains of care (Yeates, 2012). For example, research has looked at the experiences of migrant Filipina domestic workers (Ling and Chang, 2000; Parrenas, 2000), female Ethiopian domestic workers in the Gulf countries (Fernandez, 2011) and Thai 'marriage migrants' in Belgium (Fresnoza-Flot and Merla, 2018). Other studies have looked at the role that brokers or employment agencies play in these global chains (Fudge, 2011) or the role of the nation-state itself as a labour broker (Rodriguez, 2008)

However, there appears to be relatively little work on the place of India or the Indian diaspora in these global chains of care. This could be, as Yeates (2012, p 372) notes, that the original model was based on 'a particular group of migrant care workers – namely childcare workers in contemporary, individualized social care settings'. As Indian female migrants are more likely to work in health care settings in host countries, for example nursing, rather than domestic care, they have not received as much attention as other groups who more closely fit the original model (Walton-Roberts, 2012, 2016). Another reason for this is that, as the name suggests, researchers on global chains of care have tended to take 'the "global" as the most appropriate level for analysing care' (Raghuram, 2012, p 155). Yet, as we have already shown, internal migration far outstrips international migration in India. According to the official statistics in India, there are 4.75 million domestic workers. However, this is thought to be a significant underestimation and the true number could be somewhere between 20 million to 80 million workers (ILO, 2021). However, the overwhelming majority of these are either intra-state migrants, usually moving from rural to urban areas, or intra-state migrants, migrating from poorer states such as Jharkhand, Bihar and Odisha to wealthier states in search of employment (Agarwala and Saha, 2018; ILO, 2021). Although there is a growing awareness of the heterogenous employment relationships of care (see Duffy, 2005), there does not appear to be any research on the proportion of those domestic workers who provide care for older adults as opposed to childcare or other domestic work, for example cleaning, gardening and so on. Yet, as the chapters in this book explore, if living arrangements in India are changing in a way that has an impact on the availability of family-based care, that is the decline in co-residence with adult children, then it is likely that there will be a growing demand for paid carers for older adults. Aside from how these issues would be managed in the home, this raises issues for those migrant domestic workers. As Agarwala and Saha (2018) point out, there is very little legal protection for these workers, particularly for 'in-house' workers, in India. Domestic workers, who tend to be poorer, illiterate and uneducated women, are often in very precarious and low-paid employment. Moreover, any future rise in rural migrant workers to care for the needs of urban older population raises questions about who will provide care for older adults who remain in rural towns and villages.

This chapter has shown that migration, both internal and international, bring about major changes in living arrangements for older adults and their family members. Migration in this context does not disrupt the household, but the household gets linked both transregionally and transnationally, where care is exchanged between different family members. The change in the family composition and the application of the life-course approach supplies us new insights into situating how decisions around migration or other life-course decisions have a significant role to play. In understanding the exchange of care, the availability of resources and the satisfaction people experience by being part of these family care networks is crucial for their wellbeing. What we have shown through these different theories and concepts is that migration and its impact is much more complex in the sense that it has differential impact depending on the context in which people live. For example, households with low socio-economic backgrounds and who are dependent on the financial will face greater challenges when associated with reduction in the receipt of remittances. In contrast, migrants who would move for aspirational reasons come from middle or upper-middleclass families for whom migration is not an economic motive, but an aspirational one – for these groups, social capital is placed above financial incentives. What we soon will see in different states of India going through rapid demographic changes is that movement out of the household of family caregivers will lead to the arrival of non-family caregivers who care for the older adults. There needs to be much more in-depth understanding about how older adults arrange, negotiate, appropriate and reciprocate care for better well-being both for themselves and for their family members. Notably, male and female older adults may experience the impact of migration differently; women often share a larger burden or face a larger burden of care, so the migration of young male family members puts undue pressure on left behind female members, especially older women in the family. In the rest of the chapters of this book, the authors discuss how gender, age and family composition create new forms of living arrangements and how older adults evaluate the benefit or the satisfaction that is associated with these living arrangements.

References

Agarwala, R. and Saha, S. (2018) 'The employment relationship and movement strategies among domestic workers in India', *Critical Sociology*, 44(7–8): 1207–23.

Ali, S. (2007) '"Go West young man": The culture of migration among Muslims in Hyderabad, India', *Journal of Ethnic and Migrations Studies*, 33: 37–58.

Bailey, A. (2017) 'The migrant suitcase: food, belonging and commensality among Indian migrants in The Netherlands', *Appetite*, 110: 51–60.

Baldassar, L. and Merla, L. (eds) (2014) *Transnational Families, Migration and the Circulation of Care: Understanding Mobility and Absence in Family Life*, New York: Routledge.

Banerjee, P. (2006) 'Indian information technology workers in the United States: the H-1B visa, flexible production, and the racialization of labor', *Critical Sociology*, 32(2–3): 425–45.

Bhagat, R. B. (2016) 'Changing pattern of internal migration in India', in C. Guilmoto and G. Jones (eds) *Contemporary demographic transformations in China, India and Indonesia*, Cham: Springer, pp 239–54.

Bloom, D. E., Canning, D., Hu, L., Liu, Y., Mahal, A. and Yip, W. (2010) 'The contribution of population health and demographic change to economic growth in China and India', *Journal of Comparative Economics*, 38(1): 17–33.

Böhme, M. H., Persian, R., Stöhr, T. (2015) 'Alone but better off? Adult child migration and health of elderly parents in Moldova', *Journal of Health Economics*, 39: 211–27.

Boyden, J. (2013) '"We're not going to suffer like this in the mud": Educational aspirations, social mobility and independent child migration among populations living in poverty', *Compare: A Journal of Comparative and International Education*, 43(5): 580–600.

Braedley, S., Côté-Boucher, K. and Przednowek, A. (2019) 'Old and dangerous: bordering older migrants' mobilities, rejuvenating the post-welfare state', *Social Politics: International Studies in Gender, State and Society*, 28(1): 24–46.

Campos-Castillo, C. and Hitlin, S. (2013) 'Copresence: revisiting a building block for social interaction theories', *Sociological Theory*, 31(2): 168–92.

Cerna, L. (2011) 'Selecting the Best and the Brightest'. Oxford: Policy Primer, University of Oxford.

Chyi, H. and Mao, S. (2011) 'The determinants of happiness of China's elderly population', *Journal of Happiness Studies*, 13: 167–85.

d'Andrade, R. G., Shweder, R. A. and Le Vine, R. A. (1984) 'Cultural meaning systems', *Behavioral and Social Science Research: A National Resource: Part II*, 197–236.

De, S. (2019) 'Internal migration in India grows, but inter-state movements remain low'. https://blogs.worldbank.org/peoplemove/internal-migration-india-grows-inter-state-movements-remain-low

De Silva, M. (2017) 'The care pentagon: older adults within Sri Lankan-Australian transnational families and their landscapes of care', *Population, Space and Place*, 23(8): e2061.

Douglass, M. (2009) 'Global householding in Pacific Asia', *International Development Planning Review*, 28: 421–46.

Douglass, M. (2014) 'Afterword: global householding and social reproduction in Asia', *Geoforum*, 51: 313–16.

Duffy, M. (2005) 'Reproducing labor inequalities: challenges for feminists conceptualizing care at the intersections of gender, race, and class', *Gender and Society*, 19(1): 66–82.

Dykstra, P. A. and van Wissen, L. J. G. (1999) 'Introduction: the life course approach as an interdisciplinary framework for population studies', in L. J. G. van Wissen and P. A. Dykstra (eds) *Population Issues: An Interdisciplinary Focus*, New York: Kluwer Academic/Plenum Publishers, pp 1–22.

Elder, G. H. (1975) 'Age differentiation and the life course', *Annual Review of Sociology*, 1(1): 165–90.

Elder, G. H., Jr. (1985) 'Perspectives on the Life Course', in G. H. Elder, Jr., (ed) *Life Course Dynamics: Trajectories and Transitions, 1968–1980*, Ithaca, NY: Cornell University Press, pp 23–49.

Elder, G. H., Jr. (1994) 'Time, human agency, and social-change: perspectives on the life-course', *Social Psychology Quarterly*, 57(1): 4–15.

Fernandez, B. (2011) 'Household help? Ethiopian women domestic workers' labor migration to the Gulf countries', *Asian and Pacific Migration Journal*, 20(3–4): 433–57.

Fokkema, T., Cela, E. and Witter, Y. (2016) 'Pendular migration of older adults: misconceptions and nuances', in V. Horn and C. Schweppe (eds) *Transnational Aging: Current Insights and Future Challenges*, London: Routledge, pp 141–61.

Fresnoza-Flot, A. and Merla L. (2018) '"Global Householding" in mixed families: the case of Thai migrant women in Belgium', in I. Crespi, S. Giada Meda and L. Merla (eds) *Making Multicultural Families in Europe. Palgrave Macmillan Studies in Family and Intimate Life*, Cham: Palgrave Macmillan, pp 23–37.

Fudge, J. (2011) 'Global care chains, employment agencies, and the conundrum of jurisdiction: Decent work for domestic workers in Canada', *Canadian Journal of Women and the Law*, 23(1): 235–64.

Glick, J. E. and Van Hook, J. (2002) 'Parents' coresidence with adult children: can immigration explain racial and ethnic variation?', *Journal of Marriage and Family*, 64: 240–53.

Guo, M., Aranda, M. P. and Silverstein, M. (2009) 'The impact of out-migration on the inter-generational support and psychological wellbeing of older adults in rural China', *Ageing and Society*, 29: 1085–104.

Hagestad, G. O. and Dannefer, D. (2001) 'Concepts and theories of aging: beyond microfication in social science approaches', *Handbook of Aging and the Social Sciences*, 5: 3–21.

Harling, G., Kobayashi, L. C., Farrell, M. T., Wagner, R. G., Tollman, S. and Berkman, L. (2020) 'Social contact, social support, and cognitive health in a population-based study of middle-aged and older men and women in rural South Africa', *Social Science and Medicine*, 260: 113167.

Hochschild, A. R. (2000) 'Global care chains and emotional surplus value', in W. Hutton and A. Giddens (eds) *On the Edge: Living with Global Capitalism*, London: Jonathan Cape, 130–46.

Hyde, M., George, S. and Kumar, V. (2019) 'Trends in work and employment in rapidly developing countries', in U. Bültmann and J. Siegrist (eds) *Handbook of Disability, Work and Health*. Handbook Series in Occupational Health Sciences, vol 1. Cham: Springer, pp 33–52.

ILO (2021) 'About domestic work', https://www.ilo.org/newdelhi/areasofwork/WCMS_141187/lang--en/index.htm

Jamuna, D. (2000) 'Ageing in India: some key issues', *Ageing International*, 25(4): 16–31.

Jónsson, G. (2011) 'Non-migrant, sedentary, immobile, or "left behind"? Reflections on the absence of migration', IMI Working Paper No 39, Oxford: The International Migration Institute.

King, R. and Skeldon, R. (2010) '"Mind the gap!" Integrating approaches to internal and international migration', *Journal of Ethnic and Migration Studies*, 36(10): 1619–46.

Kone, Z. L., Liu, M. Y., Mattoo, A., Ozden, C. and Sharma, S. (2018) 'Internal borders and migration in India', *Journal of Economic Geography*, 18(4): 729–59.

Kõu, A. and Bailey, A. (2014) '"Movement is a constant feature in my life": contextualising migration processes of highly skilled Indians', *Geoforum*, 52: 113–22.

Kulu, H. and Milewski, N. (2007) 'Family change and migration in the life course: an introduction', *Demographic Research*, 17: 567–90.

Levitt, P. (2001) *The Transnational Villagers*, Berkeley: University of California Press.

Levitt, P. and Lamba-Nieves, D. (2011) 'Social remittances revisited', *Journal of Ethnic and Migration Studies*, 37(1): 1–22.

Ling, L. and Chang, K. (2000) 'Globalization and its intimate other: Filipina domestics in Hong Kong', in *Gender and Global Restructuring: Sightings, Sites and Resistances*, Abingdon: Routledge.

Manohar, N. N. (2019) 'Gendered agency in skilled migration: the case of Indian women in the United States', *Gender and Society*, 33(6): 935–60.

Mazzucato, V. (2011) 'Reverse remittances in the migration-development nexus: two-way flows between Ghana and the Netherlands', *Population, Space and Place*, 17: 454–68.

Miller, D. (Ed.) (1998) *Material Cultures: Why Some Things Matter*, Chicago: University of Chicago Press.

Parrenas, R. (2000) 'Migrant Filipina domestic workers and the international division of reproductive labor', *Gender and Society*, 14(4): 560–80.

Raghuram, P. (2012) 'Global care, local configurations–challenges to conceptualizations of care', *Global Networks*, 12(2): 155–74.

Raju, S. S. (2014) 'Studies on ageing in India: a review', in G. Giridhar, K. M. Sathyanarayana, S. Kumar, K. S. James and M. Alam (eds) *Population Ageing in India*, Cambridge: Cambridge University Press.

Ratha, D., De, S., Kim, E.J ., Plaza, S., Seshan, G. and Yameogo, N. D. (2020) 'Migration and Development Brief 33: Phase II: COVID-19 Crisis through a Migration Lens', KNOMAD-World Bank, Washington, DC.

Rodriguez, R. M. (2008) 'The labor brokerage state and the globalization of Filipina care workers', *Signs: Journal of Women in Culture and Society*, 33(4): 794–800.

Rossi, A. S. (1968) 'Transition to parenthood', *Journal of Marriage and the Family*, 30(1): 26–39.

Rugunanan, P. (2017) '"fitting in": social cohesion among skilled migrant Indian women and host diasporic communities in South Africa', *Alternation Journal*, 24(1): 170–96.

Shachar, A. (2006) 'Race for talent: highly skilled migrants and competitive immigration regimes', *The New York University Law Review*, 81: 148–206.

Thompson, M. and Walton-Roberts, M. (2019) 'International nurse migration from India and the Philippines: the challenge of meeting the sustainable development goals in training, orderly migration and healthcare worker retention', *Journal of Ethnic and Migration Studies*, 45(14): 2583–99.

Ugargol, A. P. and Bailey, A. (2018) 'Family caregiving for older adults: gendered roles and caregiver burden in emigrant households of Kerala, India', *Asian Population Studies*, 14(2): 194–210.

Ugargol, A. P. and Bailey, A. (2021) 'Reciprocity between older adults and their care-givers in emigrant households of Kerala, India', *Ageing and Society*, 41(8): 1699–725.

Ugargol, A. P., Hutter, I., James, K. S. and Bailey, A. (2016) 'Care needs and caregivers: associations and effects of living arrangements on caregiving to older adults in India', *Ageing international*, 41(2): 193–213.

UNDESA (United Nations Department of Economic and Social Affairs, Population Division) (2020) 'International Migration 2020 Highlights (ST/ESA/SER.A/452)', https://www.un.org/development/desa/pd/sites/www.un.org.development.desa.pd/files/undesa_pd_2020_international_migration_highlights.pdf

Walton-Roberts, M. (2012) 'Contextualizing the global nursing care chain: international migration and the status of nursing in Kerala, India', *Global Networks*, 12(2): 175–94.

Walton-Roberts, M. (2016) 'Transnational health institutions, global nursing care chains, and the internationalization of nurse education in Punjab', in V. J. Varghese, S. Irudaya Rajan and Aswini Kumar Nanda (eds) *Migration, Mobility and Multiple Affiliations*, Cambridge: Cambridge University Press, pp 296–318.

Wingens, M., de Valk, H., Windzio, M., Aybek, C. (2011) 'The sociological life course approach and research on migration and integration', in M. Wingens, M. Windzio, H. de Valk, C. Aybek (eds) *A Life-Course Perspective on Migration and Integration*, Dordrecht: Springer, https://doi.org/10.1007/978-94-007-1545-5_1

Yeates, N. (2012) 'Global care chains: a state-of-the-art review and future directions in care transnationalization research', *Global Networks*, 12(2): 135–54.

3

Emerging living arrangements of older adults in India: patterns and welfare implications

K. S. James and Sanjay Kumar

Introduction

In India, the pattern of living arrangements of older adults is of immense significance as families are seen as the major source of care and support. Hence, any changes in family structure are assumed to have potentially serious consequences for the well-being of older adults. Living arrangements have significant consequences on long-term care, economic, physical, social and psychological well-being of older adults. It is increasingly recognised that the intersections between various forces of development have had an impact on older adults in India. Two major forces of development of significance are i) demographic and epidemiological transitions, such as reduction in fertility and increase in life expectancy of adults, and ii) migration, both domestic and international. Although there is wide-spread speculation that these forces of development are responsible for bringing about changes in family structure, primarily in the living arrangements of the older adults in India, the findings have not been empirically supported. However, if the claim is indeed true, it has significant consequences, as the family has been historically thought of as the primary place in which to age. This chapter is a step towards exploring the various living arrangements of older adults in India. The second aim is to assess the various factors associated with these living arrangements. Further, the chapter also looks at possible welfare implications of patterns of living arrangements of older adults.

This chapter draws on data from the UNFPA, India-sponsored research project on 'Building Knowledge Base on Population Ageing in India' (BKPAI). This project was coordinated by the Population Research Centre (PRC) at the Institute for Social and Economic Change (ISEC), Bangalore, the Institute of Economic Growth (IEG), Delhi, and the Tata Institute of Social Sciences, Mumbai. As part of this study, a survey was carried out in seven states – Himachal Pradesh, Kerala, Maharashtra, Odisha, Punjab, Tamil Nadu and West Bengal – which have a higher percentage of the population aged 60 years and above compared to the national average. The survey collected information on 9,852 people aged 60 years and above drawn from 8,329 households. The minimum criteria for selecting a household was that at least one older person was living in the household. It was the first time that a comprehensive knowledge base has been made available exclusively on older persons in India. The field work was carried out from May to September 2011. The chapter also draws insights from the National Family Health Survey (NFHS) for various rounds which is equivalent to the Demographic Household Surveys (DHS) carried out in many countries, as well as the data from Longitudinal Ageing Study of India (LASI) Wave I conducted in 2017–18.

Type and composition of living arrangements

The survey statistics from BKPAI-2011 show that the majority of older people are co-residing, 16 per cent are living with their spouse only and 6 per cent are living alone (Table 3.1). The third and fourth round of National Family Health Surveys (NFHS) conducted during 2005–06 and 2015–16 respectively provide information on demographic and health parameters and the patterns of living arrangements. The LASI wave 1 provides information on the living arrangement of older adults in 2017– 18. The analysis of the living arrangement patterns of older adults from NFHS (2015–16) shows that about 4 per cent and 13 per cent of older adults are living alone or with only their spouse (Figure 3.1). It does not show much of a change from 2005–06. However, the LASI survey conducted in 2017–18 shows a slight increase in the percentage of older adults living alone – 5.7 per cent – but a substantially larger increase in the proportion who are living with their spouse only, to 20.3 per cent. This increase in the pattern of older adults living alone is in line with the findings of other studies (Sathyanarayana et al, 2014). Statistics from NFHS may underestimate the percentage of older adults living alone; if older adults ordinarily live with their children but their children are staying elsewhere, for example working in another city, they are still classified as living with children. Because of this data limitation, there are differences in the percentage of older adults who are reported as living alone between the NFHS and BKPAI estimates. Since BKPAI survey is conducted only in states with a higher proportion of older adults, it is expected that the survey gives higher estimates of older persons living alone. This indicates the likely future pattern of living arrangements with the proportion of older adults increasing in the country. It is possible that some level of

Figure 3.1: Types of living arrangement for those aged 60+ in India 2005/06–2017/18

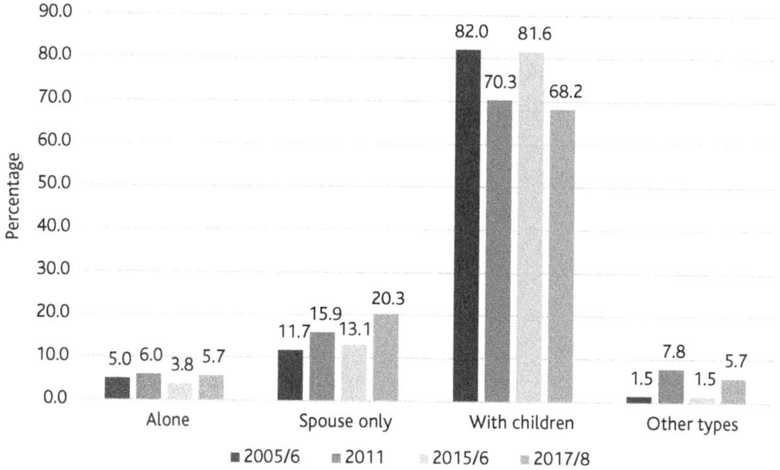

Source: Computed from NFHS 2005–06 & 2015–16, BKPAI 2011 and LASI 2017–18

Table 3.1: Percentage distribution of older persons by type of living arrangement according to place of residence and sex, 2011

	Rural			Urban			Total		
	Men	Women	Total	Men	Women	Total	Men	Women	Total
Alone	2.1	9.3	5.9	1.7	10.5	6.5	2.0	9.6	6.0
Spouse only	21.6	12.9	17.1	19.2	7.1	12.7	21.0	11.3	15.9
Spouse, children and grandchildren	57.6	25.7	41.0	59.3	22.5	39.3	58.1	24.9	40.6
Children and grandchildren	12.4	43.6	28.6	11.3	50.6	32.7	12.1	45.5	29.7
Others	6.2	8.5	7.4	8.5	9.3	9.0	6.8	8.7	7.8

Source: Alam et al (2012)

variation across these different type of surveys with different objectives are due to the survey design effect.

The evidence from the BKPAI survey (Alam et al, 2012) interestingly shows that there are no significant differences across urban and rural areas on the percentage of living alone or only with their spouse despite the demographic transition and migration being more common in urban areas (Table 3.1). On the contrary, the major differences were found between men and women. A higher proportion of older women (10 per cent) than older men (2 per cent) live alone. Perhaps marital status, particularly widowhood, could be an underlying factor. Earlier evidence from the 52nd round of the National Sample Survey (NSS) also shows that older women are more likely to be living alone as compared to their male counterparts (Gupta and Sankar, 2002; Chaudhuri and Roy, 2009). If we combine the number of older adults either living alone or with spouse only, the data from India Human Development Survey conducted during 2004–05 have also shown similar results that about one-fifth of the older population are either living alone or living with spouses only, but they want to stay with their children (Golandaj et al, 2013). Evidence from Orissa, in the east of India, suggests that the age, sex and number of living children of older people have significant effects on their living arrangements (Panigrahi, 2009).

One of the striking patterns observed in the data has been the differences in the living arrangements of older adults in different states in India (Table 3.2). The states are at various stages of the demographic transition and economic development. Tamil Nadu and Kerala are more advanced while states such as Odisha are lagging behind. The southern Indian states in general have relatively higher proportions of older adults who are living alone. For instance, about 6 per cent of older people are living alone in Tamil Nadu. As Tamil Nadu has undergone rapid demographic changes in recent years, it is tempting to assume that this has impacted on the living arrangements of older adults. Interestingly, however, Kerala has a much lower proportion of older adults living alone compared to its neighbours, with only around 3 per cent in such living arrangements, yet it was one of the first states in India to undergo the demographic transition and has the highest level of out migration in the country (see Chapter 4 in this volume).

In addition to looking at the living arrangements of older adults, it is also possible to look at what proportion of households are haracterized by different living arrangements. Table 3.3 presents the composition of older members within the households.

These figures show that around 15 per cent of households in India are occupied solely by older adults, of which nearly half are occupied by a single older person. This suggests that, for the 7 per cent of older households in India, there is no immediate physical support available in case of necessity. This number is expected to increase in the future which could have serious implications if it becomes necessary to provide immediate care and attention for older adults.

The proportion of older adults in India living alone is in line with other Asian countries, particularly those in East Asia. East Asia has also witnessed drastic demographic changes in the second half of the last century and resulted in considerable changes in family composition and patterns of living arrangements. It appears that India is also progressing towards that pattern, although it is a long way off from the patterns seen in either the

Table 3.2: Percentage of older adults by type of living arrangement by state

	NFHS-3 (2004/5)		BKPAI (2011)		NFHS-4 (2014/15)	
	Alone	Spouse only	Alone	Spouse only	Alone	Spouse only
Andhra Pradesh	7.9	20.3			6.3	21.1
Arunachal Pradesh	4.2	3.6			4.2	12.1
Assam	2.1	4.3			2.8	6.6
Bihar	4.0	10.2			2.3	10.6
Chhattisgarh	5.7	12.5			5.0	13.8
Delhi	2.8	8.7			2.1	9.7
Goa	4.6	7.0			4.6	11.6
Gujarat	4.8	12.6			3.9	14.7
Haryana	2.6	5.3			1.2	8.2
Himachal Pradesh	4.6	10.3	4.0	18.5	2.8	12.0
Jammu & Kashmir	1.3	4.8			0.8	6.4
Jharkhand	2.2	8.4			3.1	12.7
Karnataka	5.2	7.3			4.3	10.8
Kerala	2.7	7.6	3.6	11.1	2.8	16.4
Madhya Pradesh	5.6	12.7			3.6	13.7
Maharashtra	4.7	11.3	5.7	14.0	4.2	11.9
Manipur	2.4	4.8			1.9	5.0
Meghalaya	7.4	8.0			4.4	5.5
Mizoram	2.3	4.4			2.6	4.9
Nagaland	10.1	15.2			6.1	16.4
Orissa	4.3	10.3	2.8	16.5	3.4	14.3
Punjab	2.2	7.7	3.3	13.2	1.8	8.3
Rajasthan	3.1	13.5			3.0	12.6
Sikkim	2.3	5.0			1.1	5.7
Tamil Nadu	13.5	27.6	16.2	27.7	6.3	19.0
Tripura	3.9	7.3			3.5	10.6
Uttar Pradesh	3.7	8.9			3.7	11.3
Uttaranchal	5.6	9.6			5.2	13.9
West Bengal	3.9	7.4	6.3	9.1	2.9	11.5
Telangana	—	—			6.4	21.6

Note: In NFHS-3, Andhra Pradesh includes the sample of Telangana; the percentage of older adults who are living with their children/grandchildren/others were not presented in this table.

Table 3.3: Percentage of households with living composition, 2011

Household composition	Percentage of households
One older adult living alone	6.8
Two or more older adults living without children or anyone else	8.1
Older adult/s living with children or grandchildren and with other relatives	85.1
Total number of households	8329

Source: Computed from household level micro data of BKPAI Survey, (2011)

Table 3.4: Percentage of those aged 60 or over living alone in selected countries

Country	Living alone (%)
USA	25.1
France	31.2
Netherlands	31.1
Philippines	5.4
China	8.2
Thailand	6.0
Vietnam	9.4
Japan	15.5
Mexico	11.3
Brazil	13.3

Source: UNDESA (2017)

USA or Europe. Table 3.4 gives figures of the proportion of older adults living alone in different countries.

The data also shows the older adults who live alone are disproportionately drawn from the poor sections of society. Not only is there a significant gender gap, but it is the poor women who are destined to live alone. Tables 3.5 and 3.6 present some key characteristics of older persons by living arrangement from BKPAI (2011) and NFHS (2005–06 and 2015–16).

The evidence from both the BKPAI (2011) and the NFHS (2005–06 and 2015–16) provide a clear understanding of the characteristics of older adults living alone or with a spouse. The proportion living alone decreases with increasing levels of education while the proportion living with spouses only increases with increasing levels of education. Perhaps children of higher-educated parents are staying outside of their home, leaving their parents at home. It is those in the lowest wealth quintiles and widows that have the highest proportions of older adults who are living

Table 3.5: Percentage distribution of older adults by type of living arrangement, 2011

	Alone	Spouse only	Spouse, children and grandchildren	Children and grandchildren	Others	N
Married	0.5	26.2	67.3	0.0	6.1	5,847
Widowed	14.4	0.0	0.0	76.8	8.8	3,768
Other	15.5	4.7	0.0	44.1	35.8	237
No education	7.4	14.1	32.6	38.2	7.7	4,528
1–4 years education	4.5	13.9	43.3	30.0	8.2	1,258
5–7 years education	5.8	14.0	46.8	25.9	7.5	1,324
8+ years education	4.1	22.1	53.0	12.8	8.0	2,682
Scheduled caste/tribe	6.2	15.6	39.8	31.2	7.4	2,383
Other backward class	7.6	16.9	39.1	29.4	6.9	3,353
Other tribe/caste	3.9	15.2	43.4	28.6	9.0	3,868
Lowest wealth quintile	13.6	22.4	29.5	27.9	6.6	1,954
Second wealth quintile	6.8	17.9	39.0	29.4	7.0	1,974
Middle wealth quintile	4.0	13.6	43.1	31.4	7.9	1,938
Fourth wealth quintile	1.2	11.7	47.2	31.0	8.9	1,962
Highest wealth quintile	1.3	10.7	49.4	29.1	9.5	2,018
Total	6.0	16.0	40.6	29.7	7.8	9,852

Source: Computed from household level micro data of BKPAI Survey, 2011

alone. Wealth, perhaps, has the largest effect on living alone. The wealth index is a composite measure of the household's cumulative living standard computed using amenities and possessions within the household. A recent study citing the evidence from the 71st round of NSS shows that the share of older adults who are living alone is higher in the poorest households in empowered action group (EAG) states than that of the non-EAG states (Kumar and Kumar, 2019).[1]

Implications of living arrangements for older adults

It is clear that there is an increasing trend towards older adults living alone, even in a developing country such as India. It is also true that the majority of those living alone are females and drawn from socio-economically poor sections of the society. Therefore, it is important to ask another question on

Table 3.6: Percentage distribution of older people by type of living arrangement according to background characteristics in India, 2005–06 and 2015–16

	NFHS-3			NFHS-4		
	Alone	Spouse only	N	Alone	Spouse only	N
Married	0.6	18.9	26875	0.6	19.7	189355
Widowed	11.5	—	15730	9.8	—	88157
Others	18.1	1.3	959	13.8	2.1	6136
No education	6.0	10.8	25336	4.6	11.2	164092
Primary education	3.3	13.3	7383	3.1	13.9	49625
Secondary education	2.6	11.7	8277	2.3	15.0	57794
Higher education	4.1	20.5	2340	2.4	23.5	12137
Scheduled caste/tribe	5.7	12.9	11592	4.4	13.1	91011
Other socially disadvantaged groups	5.5	12.8	13677	3.7	13.0	110697
Other tribe/caste	3.8	9.4	18295	3.3	13.3	81940
Lowest wealth quintile	9.9	17.6	5840	8.9	20.0	59371
Second wealth quintile	6.2	12.6	6593	4.3	13.5	57735
Middle wealth quintile	4.3	10.7	8169	2.7	10.8	55764
Fourth wealth quintile	2.9	8.1	9305	2.1	10.5	52520
Highest wealth quintile	1.6	9.2	13657	1.2	11.1	58258
Total	5.0	11.7	43564	3.8	13.1	283648

Note: The percentage of older persons who are living with their children/grandchildren/others were not presented in this table.

what the welfare implications are for those living alone. In order to answer this question, we have used some selected information gathered from the BKPAI survey on older adults. Figure 3.2 shows the economic contribution of older adults to the households by living arrangement.

The results show that 68 per cent of older adults who live alone contribute economically to the household and 57 per cent of older adults who live in households with two or more older adults contribute economically to the household. This indicated that the contribution of children is not significant once they leave households. Hence, older adults continue to pay for their needs, for example food and so on.

Figure 3.3 shows the level of economic dependency of older adults in different types of households by their living arrangement. These figures reveal that around 80 per cent of older adults living with children and others depend on their children for their economic needs; however, this is far less in those households where only older adults live. This reconfirms

Figure 3.2: Economic contribution by older adults to the household by living arrangement, 2011

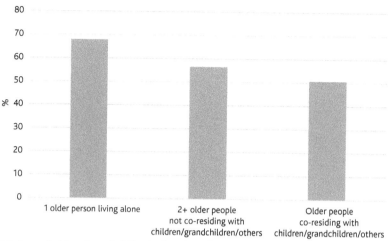

Source: Computed from household level micro data of BKPAI Survey (2011)

Figure 3.3: Percentage of older adults who are economically dependent on their children by living arrangement type, 2011

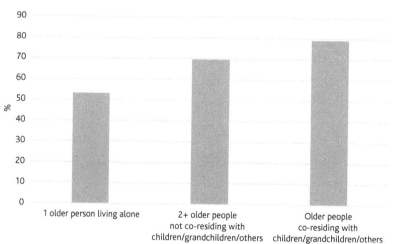

Source: Computed from household level micro data of BKPAI Survey (2011)

the earlier finding that older people who live alone meet their economic needs through their own income, savings or pension rather than depending on children.

As per the cultural context in India, sons are supposed to provide support to their parents as they age, while daughters are married away and it is not culturally acceptable to receive financial support from them. To explore

Figure 3.4: Percentage of older adults who are economically dependent on their son by living arrangement type, 2011

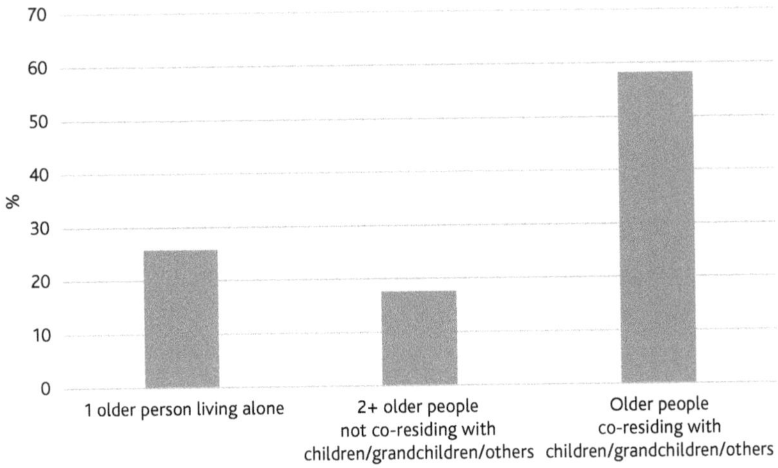

Source: Computed from household level micro data of BKPAI Survey (2011)

this, we have analysed the transfer of money from the son (as they have the obligations to support their parents) to the older person depending upon the household type. The findings, in Figure 3.4, show that only 26 per cent of older adults who live alone receive a financial transfer from their son, while around 58 per cent do in households where older adults live with children or others.

Health-related factors

We next assess health-related factors that are associated with the household living arrangements of older adults. In the earlier study, the results from NFHS-2 shows that older adults who live alone are more likely to suffer chronic and acute illnesses compared with those who are living with others (Agrawal, 2012). The data from the 52nd round of the NSS also show that older adults in poor economic conditions are more vulnerable in terms of health outcomes (Gupta and Sankar, 2002). A study using the 60th round of NSS data revealed that older adults who live alone are more likely to have morbidity and less likely to seek treatment compared with those who are staying with children or other relatives (Paul and Verma, 2016). Another study using the data from IHDS conducted during 2004–05 revealed that solitary living is closely associated with short-term morbidity among older adults (Samanta et al, 2015).

We first look at the disability status of older adults in the household. The relationship between child and older adult on the transfer of money, as well

34

Figure 3.5: Percentage of older adults with a disability by living arrangement pattern, 2011

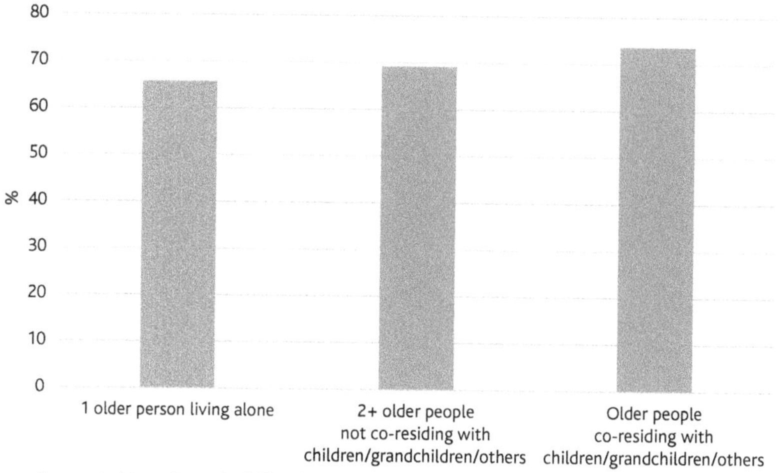

Source: Computed from household level micro data of BKPAI Survey (2011)

as the decision to live alone, could potentially be mediated by disability. Therefore, it is important to discover whether those living alone are healthier than the rest of the older population. Figure 3.5 presents the percentage of older people with any disability by living arrangement type.

The results show a slight gradient in the proportion of older adults with disabilities across the different types of living arrangement. Those who are living alone have the lowest rates of disability (66 per cent) and those living with children and/or grandchildren have the highest rate (74 per cent). These figures show that, while there is a significant minority of older adults who live alone are healthy and able to live independently, this is not the case for the majority. The concern is that these people may need help with their condition and that there is no-one living with them who can provide this. The higher rates of disability among those living with children and/or grandchildren indicates that, as older adults acquire health problems, they move in with family members or family members move in with them to provide support.

We also analysed the same disability figures separately for women and men, as more older women are found to live alone than men. The results are almost identical for older women (Figure 3.6) as those for the general older population (probably as women make up a large proportion of the older population). However, the results for men (Figure 3.7) are quite different. Here, there is no real difference in the rates of disability among men in different living arrangements. This suggests that older men living alone might have higher (unmet) care needs than older women who live alone.

Figure 3.6: Percentage of older women with disability by living arrangement pattern, 2011

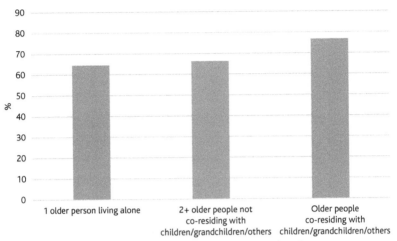

Source: Computed from household level micro data of BKPAI Survey (2011)

Figure 3.7: Percentage of older men with disability by living arrangement pattern, 2011

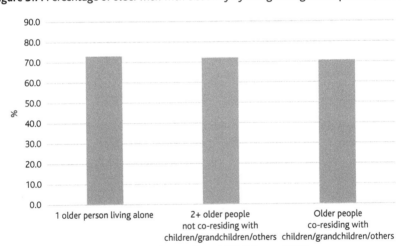

Source: Computed from household level micro data of BKPAI Survey (2011)

Implications of living arrangements on the well-being of older people

To understand the potential impact that living arrangements could have on the well-being of older people, we conducted a multivariate regression analysis (Table 3.7). We chose to look at subjective well-being as the outcome as this provides an indicator of a person's evaluation of their overall life

Table 3.7: The results from the linear regression model: beta coefficients of subjective well-being among older adults in India, 2011

	Beta coefficients (95%CI)
Living alone (Ref.)	
Living with spouse only	0.01 (-0.35–0.38)
Living with others	-0.27 (-0.59–0.05)
Receives money transfers from children (Ref.)	
Does not receive money transfers from children	**0.19 (0–0.37)**
No child/Missing	**0.64 (0.33–0.96)**
Does not have daily or weekly communication with children (Ref.)	
Has daily or weekly communication with children	**0.68 (0.52–0.84)**
1 living child (Ref.)	
2–3 living children	0.24 (-0.04–0.51)
4+ living children	0.14 (-0.16–0.43)
No living children	-0.36 (-0.75–0.03)
Married (Ref.)	
Widowed	**-0.72 (-0.89—0.55)**
Other marital status	-0.32 (-0.80–0.16)
No education (Ref.)	
<5 years of education	**0.50 (0.28–0.72)**
5–7 years of education	**0.86 (0.63–1.08)**
8+ years of education	**1.14 (0.94–1.34)**
Scheduled Caste/Tribe (Ref.)	
Other socially disadvantaged groups	0.05 (-0.14–0.23)
Other tribe/caste	-0.01 (-0.20–0.18)
Lowest wealth quintile (Ref.)	
Second wealth quintile	**0.99 (0.78–1.20)**
Middle wealth quintile	**1.78 (1.56–2.00)**
Fourth wealth quintile	**2.42 (2.18–2.66)**
Highest wealth quintile	**3.69 (3.42–3.95)**
Constant	5.68
Number of observations	9,852
F(19, 9832)	
R-squared	0.1819
Adjusted R-squared	0.1804
Root MSE	3.5085

Source: Computed from household level micro data of BKPAI Survey (2011)
Note: Figures in **bold** are statistically significant at the p<.05 level.

satisfaction, as well as one's experience of pleasant and unpleasant emotions (Moore et al, 2005). The subjective well-being score is based on the responses to nine questions.[2] Before preparing the score, each response was classified as: two for 'very much satisfied', one for 'moderately satisfied' and zero for 'not satisfied', and the sum total of all nine items was calculated. Thus, the subjective well-being score ranges from 0 to 18 with a higher score indicating higher subjective well-being. Since the score pattern follows the normal distribution function, the linear regression model was applied for the multivariate analyses.

The results reveal that the living arrangement of older adults does not affect subjective well-being. It is generally argued that co-residence with children enhances the well-being of older people in India as it is the expected norm. However, that does not appear to be true. The analysis shows that living arrangements do not have any effect on the well-being, indicating that living alone does not necessarily reduce the well-being of older adults in the country. On the other hand, communication with children has significant effects on enhancing well-being. Even money transfers from children to older parents have very little effect on subjective well-being. It appears that the reporting of good well-being might depend upon having good relationships and communication with children and family. Aside from these factors, the level of education and wealth status of the households play an important role in the subjective well-being of older people in India. The reporting of subjective well-being improves with increasing levels of education and wealth.

Discussion

This paper brings up several important dimensions of the changing living arrangements of older persons in India. The analysis indicates that we might need to rethink some of the assumptions around older adults who are living alone. The important question to be answered is whether changing living arrangements among older persons in India reflect the fundamental change in family structure, driven by demographic changes and economic transformation, that is observed in many other countries. Alternatively, is living alone a reflection of mere necessity in which the children migrate for better opportunities but keep the ties and relationship with the family intact? The findings from this chapter provide an important clue to these questions and finds that the latter explanation is more relevant in the Indian context.

We found that the direction of relationship between demographic changes and older persons living alone are not clear cut. This indicates that living arrangements among older adults are primarily motivated by the migration of children due to a lack of employment opportunities in the current place of residence. Living alone has some connection with the migration patterns across states. This may provide some lead towards the motivation for living alone that it is merely by chance and not by choice. Thus, the argument of structural changes in society leading to higher incidences of living alone appears not to be a correct reflection of living alone in the country.

This hypothesis is supported when one considers that the major changes in the living arrangements of older persons are more clearly visible among those living with a spouse only, rather than those living alone. The children have migrated due to employment and educational needs but the older persons live with their spouse. Thus, individualism – as depicted in the second demographic transition theories (Lesthaeghe, 2010) – due to structural changes in the society are not visible in the context of India.

At the same time, the striking difference in the pattern of living alone has been between males and females with large numbers of older women living alone. Undoubtedly it shows the age differences in marriage in India as well as the advantage of women in life expectancy. According to the NFHS data in 2015–16, the average age difference between spouses is around 5 years in the country, with women invariably younger than men. Both these factors result in many women bound to live alone consequent to the death of the spouse. With children away due to employment reasons, the women continue to live alone until they are unable to take care of the daily activities by themselves.

Interestingly, however, living arrangements have considerable economic gradient in India, with a higher proportion of the poor living alone compared with the richer sections of society. This is contrary to the expectation that living arrangements are driven by economic progress and that those who are more economically advanced are more likely to live alone. The pattern observed here reconfirms the argument of this paper that living alone is more accidental than intentional in India. Evidence from elsewhere on patterns of migration shows that those from poorer sections migrate more than those from richer sections due to the lack of availability of work in the rural areas (Malhotra and Devi, 2014). Therefore, it is natural that the number of people living alone is higher among the poorer sections, with large migration to the urban informal sector.

Finally, although discussions about changing living arrangements among older people in India are framed within a vulnerability paradigm (Rajan et al, 1995; Rajan and Kumar, 2003; Agarwal, 2012; Samanta et al, 2015), our results suggest that neither the current living arrangement pattern nor its trend necessarily reflect a serious vulnerability but is the result of economic necessity. The analysis demonstrates that living alone does not mean that the older persons are compromising on their subjective well-being. Migration is a necessary condition for the economic advancement of the household and, perhaps, the older persons are happy with such arrangements. Thus, it is important to develop alternative perspectives from current literature on the living arrangements in India.

Conclusion

The demographic transition has a direct impact on population ageing. Changing household structures and migration due to demographic change have significant effects on the living arrangement of older adults. In this context, it is important to understand the pattern of living arrangements among the older population in India and their association with well-being or satisfaction of life. The summary of findings is as follows: first, there is increasing incidences of older people in India not co-residing with their children. However, this is mostly driven by the increase in the proportion of older adults who live with their spouse only. Second, living arrangements vastly differ by state. Tamil Nadu has the lowest proportion of older adults who live with their children. A quarter of the older population who live alone have the lowest wealth quintile, showing lower standard of living compared with older adults who live with children, spouses or with others. Third, older adults, irrespective of living with their children, contribute to household expenses. But the rate of contribution varies by living arrangement pattern. Those older adults who live alone contribute more to their households. Fourth, economic dependency on children, specifically on the son, is highest among adults who live with their children and the lowest among households where they live alone. Fifth, the living arrangement pattern has no bearing on the subjective well-being of the older persons. As living with children is an expected norm in India, living alone is often considered to affect the subjective well-being of older people considerably. No effect of living arrangement on subjective well-being indicates that living alone is not necessarily seen as a burden by older person; living alone is motivated by the migration of children for better opportunities which provides them good satisfaction.

Notes

[1] In India, the eight low socio-economically states of Bihar, Chhattisgarh, Jharkhand, Madhya Pradesh, Orissa, Rajasthan, Uttaranchal and Uttar Pradesh, referred to as the Empowered Action Group (EAG) states, lag behind in the demographic transition and have the highest infant mortality rates in the country.

[2] The items included are feeling life is interesting; how is present life compared to past; happiness with the kind of work one has been doing in recent years; achieved expected standard of living and social status; the extent to which one achieves success; accomplishment; managing situations even when they do not turn out to be expected; feeling confident in being able to handle a crisis situation; and feeling confident in coping with one's future based on the current trajectory.

References

Agrawal, S. (2012) 'Effect of living arrangement on the health status of elderly in India: findings from a national cross sectional survey', *Asian Population Studies*, 8(1): 87–101.

Alam, M., James, K. S., Giridhar, G., Sathyanarayana, K. M., Kumar, S., Raju, S. S., Syamala, T. S., Subaiya, L. and Bansod, S. (2012) Report on the Status of Elderly in Slet Sates of India, November 2011, New Delhi: UNFPA India.

Chaudhuri, A. and Roy, K. (2009) 'Gender differences in living arrangements among older persons in India', *Journal of Asian and African Studies*, 44(3): 259–77.

Golandaj, J. A., Goli, S. and Das, K. C. (2013) 'Living arrangements among older population and perceptions on old age assistance among adult population in India', *International Journal of Sociology and Social Policy*, 33(5): 367–79.

Gupta, I. and Sankar, D. (2002) 'Health of the elderly in India: a multivariate analysis', *Discussion Paper 46*, Institute of Economic Growth.

Kumar, S. and Kumar, K. A. (2019) 'Living arrangement and economic dependency among the elderly in India: a comparative analysis of EAG and non EAG states', *Ageing International*, 44(4): 352–70.

Lesthaeghe, R. (2010) 'The unfolding story of the second demographic transition', *Population and Development Review*, 36(2): 55–81.

Malhotra, N. and Devi, P. (2014) 'Trend, pattern and determinants of internal migration in India', *Indian Journal of Regional Science*, 46(2): 41–50.

Moore, S. E., Leslie, H. Y. and Lavis, C. A. (2005) 'Subjective well-being and life satisfaction in the Kingdom of Tonga', *Social Indicators Research*, 70: 287–311.

Panigrahi, A. K. (2009) 'Living arrangements preferences of elderly: evidence from field study in Orissa', *Indian Journal of Gerontology*, 23(4): 478–99.

Paul, A. and Verma, R. K. (2016) 'Does living arrangement affect work status, morbidity, and treatment seeking of the elderly population? A study of south Indian states', *SAGE Open*, 6(3): 2158244016659528.

Rajan, I. S. and Kumar, S. (2003) 'Living arrangements among Indian elderly: new evidence from the National Family Health Survey', *Economic and Political Weekly*, 38: 75–80.

Rajan, I. S., Mishra, U. S. and Sarma, P. S. (1995) 'Living arrangement among the Indian elderly', *Hongkong Journal of Gerontology*, 9(2): 20–8.

Raju, S. S. (2014) 'Studies on ageing in India: a review', in G. Giridhar, K. M. Sathyanarayana, S. Kumar, K. S. James and M. Alam (eds) *Population Ageing in India*, New Delhi: Cambridge University Press, pp 180–214.

Samanta, T., Chen, F. and Vanneman, R. (2015) 'Living arrangements and health of older adults in India', *Journals of Gerontology Series B: Psychological Sciences and Social Sciences*, 70(6): 937–47.

Sathyanarayana, K. M., Kumar, S. and James, K. S. (2014) 'Living arrangements of elderly in India: policy and programmatic implications', in G. Giridhar, K. M. Sathyanarayana, S. Kumar, K. S. James and M. Alam (eds) *Population Ageing in India*, New Delhi: Cambridge University Press, pp 74–95.

4

Living arrangement concordance and the well-being of older persons in India

T. S. Syamala, Supriya Verma and Sebastian Joseph

Introduction

It has been postulated that individuals are more likely to experience control and a sense of positive adjustment when their abilities, resources and needs are in consonance with the demands of the environment. If older adults live in an environment of their preference and choice, it is expected that they will have more positive attitudes towards life, greater capabilities for adjustment and improved realisation of welfare among them as compared with others who cannot abide in environments they prefer (Wahl and Gersdorf, 2020). This should also hold true for living arrangements, for example, if older adults have the sort of living arrangements that they want, they should have better health and well-being than if they did not. However, as of 2022, there is relatively little research on the living arrangement concordance (the correspondence between the actual and preferred living arrangement) among the older adults in lower- and middle-income countries. This chapter seeks to redress that by exploring living arrangement concordance and the well-being of older adults in India.

The Congruence Theory of Person-Environment Fit, drawn from Lewin's (1935, 1951) field theory, postulates that behaviour (B) is a function of the person (P) and the (psychosocial) environment (E), expressed as $B=f(P, E)$. This assumes that behavioural outcomes result from interaction between individuals and their environment and a good fit typically results in positive outcomes for the individual (Edwards, 1991; Kristof, 1996). At its core, fit theory holds that individuals seek environments that match best with their unique personal attributes in accordance with their individual differences in attributes. It also argues that the alignment between a person's characteristics and their environment results in positive outcomes and the individual often strives to maximise concordance between needs and environment (Kahana, 1975; Kahana et al, 1980). Conversely, Festinger (1957) proposed that people holding inconsistent beliefs, termed as dissonant cognitions, experience an unpleasant tension-state. Hence, they are constantly motivated to reduce or resolve this inconsistency. Furthermore, fit theory holds that both a deficiency (wherein the environmental attributes become less than the personal attributes) and an excess (wherein the environmental attributes become greater than the personal attributes) are harmful for individuals at extreme levels as not getting what one greatly desires is as detrimental as getting what one detests (van Vianen, 2018).

The concept of press-competence (Lawton and Nahemow, 1973), defined as the dynamic between a person's functional competence (or capacities) and the environmental press (or stress) that surround them, has its roots in Murray's (1938) personology theory in which the needs (the resultant forces emanating from the individual) and press (the significant determinants of behaviour in the environment) combine to constitute a thema (the dynamic interactive behavioural unit). However, this has been criticised for its passive stance on the role of the person within the environment. The environmental docility hypothesis (Lawton and Simon, 1968) contends that those with fewer resources will be more greatly affected by environmental factors. However, this has also been criticised for placing too much emphasis on the person as a passive receiver of the environment rather than an active, dynamic and engaged contributor. In response to these issues, Kahana (1982) has proposed the seven-dimensional model of P–E congruence, or the existence of a mutual relationship between people and their environments, that can be person-specific or environment-specific. What is postulated by the congruence concept is that the arousal of human behaviour is due to the environment meeting the needs of a person rather than from the person's competence controlling the demands of the environment. Thus, congruence aligns more with the perceived indicators of P–E fit and represents a departure from a primary focus on the physical environment. In arguing for a heightened focus on a person's perceptions of the salience and relevance of the environment as an essential component of P–E fit, Carp and Carp (1984) extended Kahana's (1982) congruence model by introducing the interactive component in the P–E fit equation, namely the concept of PcE, or the conditions of the person and the environment, with a reshaping of Lewis's field theory to, $B = f(P, E, PcE)$, and highlighting thereby the P–E interaction.

The P–E fit model in the Indian context needs to also consider the cultural dimension of co-residence of generations and the role of others in facilitating or providing for basic and the higher-order needs. In addition to the personal choice of the older adults on living arrangements, there is also the larger societal discourse which discusses the preference to multi-generational co-residence and cultural norms on filial piety (Zhang Gu and Luo, 2014). A study in Hong Kong using the P–E fit model on older persons included filial piety as an important cultural feature in their model. Family support was still seen to be an important element in the lives of older persons in Hong Kong (Phillips et al, 2010). Bongaarts and Zimmer (2002), who compared the living arrangements of older adults in 43 developing countries, found that females are more likely to live alone compared with males and co-residence with adult children, particularly with sons rather than daughters, was more common in Asia.

Living arrangement concordance among older adults has been defined here as the correspondence between the actual and the preferred living arrangement. When the actual place of stay of older adults matches their preferred place of stay, the older adult is said to be in concordance with their living arrangements. Any difference between the actual and the preferred place of stay indicates non-concordance or discordance in living arrangements. Living arrangement concordance can be an important indicator for understanding the welfare of older adults. In situations where there is discordance in living arrangements, some older persons find ways to cope, often through indirect means such as rationalisation, denial or passivity (Yung et al, 2017). It is also necessary to understand that older persons are active agents in adapting to the environment they live in. The coping behaviour can have many forms whereby they might either move to live apart from the traditional household, live in a different part of the house or, in cases where they live alone, they might find other ways that can still meet their basic and higher-order needs.

In most developing countries, including India, living arrangements of older adults were never an issue a few decades back as it was customary for families to take care of their older relatives. However, issues concerning household structure and support for older persons in developing countries are becoming increasingly important as the ageing population is making its presence more felt in many of these countries. Along with the population ageing, these countries are also experiencing socio-economic changes. The complex effects of these changes on families, households, kin-networks and the support of older persons are not well documented. It is generally felt that the size and relationship complexity of the households decrease with industrialisation and urbanisation. Families remained more extended in traditional rural societies than in modern urbanised society, with more independent nuclear families. Extended kinship ties began to weaken, and the nuclear family became an independent unit in urban areas. This weakening of filial linkages has reduced the intimacy of social interaction and the timely financial and physical support due for the older generation. As countries develop, the preference for separate living arrangements for the different generations is gathering momentum and is becoming prevalent. The issues of living arrangements among the older adults in this context therefore need attention as the welfare of the older adults greatly depend on it.

Studies on the pattern of living arrangements of older adults in developing countries have shown that the proportion of older adults living alone is on the rise, although the family is still the primary care provider for older adults (see Chapter 3 in this volume for the figures for India). A complex set of social, economic and cultural factors shape the choice of living arrangements. The present understanding of these factors in India is unclear. While living arrangements form a potentially important constituent of the well-being of older adults, relatively little is known about it in the context of the developing countries. Studies on living arrangements have generally presumed that there is a convergence between preferred place of stay and the actual residence in any society. However, the information available on the preferences in living arrangements among older adults is scarce, especially in the Indian context. Although information on actual living arrangement patterns and their determinants exist, it is not clear what kind of existing living arrangements older adults in India prefer and to what level these living arrangement preferences match their actual circumstances.

It is generally argued that older adult's living arrangement preferences are primarily governed by the changing need for privacy versus the value placed on co-residence with family members, as well as by the need for financial, physical and emotional support from their children. However, it is likely that the impact of privacy will vary by the demographic and socio-economic characteristics of the individual. Needs and resources are determined by economic and health status besides kin availability. Research on living arrangement preferences in the West initially focused on the need for privacy and living alone. However, subsequent research on living arrangements elsewhere challenged this assumption considering large ethnic differentials in living arrangement preferences, even after controlling the other confounding factors. These differentials in preferences have been interpreted as stemming from cultural values, family roles and filial responsibility (Lai et al, 2007; Thomas and Wister, 1984). Since preference is embedded in societal norms and cultural values concerning parent–child co-residence and arrangements for the care of older dependents, greater value on family cohesiveness may encourage co-residence while strong emphasis on privacy may yield independent living arrangements (Goldscheider and Goldscheider, 1989). However, the ideal living arrangement in India is assumed to be the co-residence of multiple generations. With the ongoing social and economic changes, modernisation and industrialisation, multi-generational co-residence is predicted to decline and an increasing number of older adults may have to live alone or with their spouse in the future. Any decline in co-residence may generate intriguing questions about the attitudes and preferences of older people in relation to their living arrangement. A key question will be whether the increase in older adults living alone is a reflection of their preference for independent living, or whether it is due to factors which have forced this situation on them, for example the migration of their children. It would therefore be meaningful to analyse the preference of older persons for different types of living arrangements.

The observed increase in older adults not co-residing with children in many developed and developing countries has generally been attributed to the apparent improvement in their economic resources that has enabled them to opt for independent living. It is presumed that, even in the developing countries, there is a shift in the preference for independent living over co-residence and this change in preference has been attributed to the observed increase in the desire for living independently. The socio-economic and demographic characteristics of older adults can shape their living arrangement preferences (Domingo and Asis, 1995; Elman and Uhlenberg, 1995; Chan and Davanzo, 1996; Kim and Rhee, 1997). Studies from both the developed and the developing countries have indicated that living arrangement preferences among the elderly vary with age, gender, marital status and number of surviving children. Gender differentials in living arrangement preferences have been noted by many researchers, from both the developed and the developing countries (Rudkin, 1993; Shah et al, 2002). Studies have generally shown that a higher proportion of females prefer to live alone whereas a higher proportion of males prefer co-residence. However, mixed results have been seen in the developing countries. A few studies have shown that elderly females in developing countries prefer co-residence while the elderly males prefer to live alone (Zimmer and Kim, 2001). Other studies show quite contrary findings: more elderly females prefer to live alone while males prefer co-residence. The reason for this was mainly due to the fact that a majority of the elderly males were not able to perform household jobs such as cooking, cleaning and so on by themselves and are therefore not able to maintain their house without external help (Zimmer and Kim, 2001).

The level of concordance or discordance between older adults and their living arrangements depends greatly on their ability to specify a preference. It is also likely that they might be making an objective assessment of their constraints/opportunities based on their present circumstances before indicating a preference. An older adult who is economically dependent on their children, for example, would surely hesitate to state a preference for independent living as their financial dependency constrains that person from achieving that preference. Similarly, indicating a preference for co-residence with children would be difficult for those older persons who do not have children. Given this situation, it is likely that many older adults in India might be rationalising their actual living arrangement as their preference. This may be true especially for those who are already in co-residence as co-residence with children is the culturally accepted pattern of living arrangement for older adults in India. Indicating a preference for independent living among those who co-reside would have to be based on a careful analysis of both their economic and emotional constraints. The same might be true for those who live independently. Indicating a preference for co-residence involves an objective assessment of their circumstances in terms of kin availability and the possibility of residing with them. Therefore, a match between the actual and the preferred living arrangements may depend on the extent to which preferences depend on economic constraints and their cultural context. Further, certain abilities/resources are also required to indicate a preference that would differ from their actual circumstance. These abilities/resources could be in terms of education, the financial situation of the household, the economic independence of the individual and so on. In such circumstances it is possible that the older persons who are educated or those with better financial situations would be more empowered to indicate a preference that is different from the actual living arrangement with an anticipation that they might be able to adhere to the preference sometime in the future. In such a situation, those who are better endowed with skills and resources might be more at discordance than those who are not. Hence, it would be of interest to explore the dynamics of living arrangement concordance in India and to study what factors are associated with concordance. The literature from the West and also from countries such as China and Taiwan has shown that older persons who are financially better off and those who are better educated are more in concordance with their living arrangements because they are able to exercise a choice and live in their preferred place of stay. However, in countries such as India where the care for older adults is primarily the responsibility of the family, ascertaining what really determines the concordance in the Indian context would be interesting.

Several factors can determine the living arrangement concordance among older adults. Adherence to the preferred living arrangement can only happen when the older adults make the choice on their own. Older adults are often seen as a vulnerable group in the Indian context and exercising choices in their later years of life can be problematic. The actual and preferred place of residence can vary for two main reasons. As has been commonly observed, inadequate social security measures and poor financial potentials deprive older adults of any chance to express their preference for their place of residence (the challenges for older adults in accessing social benefits is covered in Chapter 11). Secondly, considerable differences in the mind-set of the older and the younger generations regarding the care of the older adults are also likely. While the older generation may still prefer to stay with their children, the younger generation might see older adults as a burden, and would therefore be unwilling to take care of them (Asis et al, 1995; Domingo and Asis 1995). Hence, the actual and the preferred place of residence in this context too might vary, not because of economic reasons but due to the changing cultural norms (Burr and Mutchler, 1992; Lee et al, 1995). Studies of the concordance of living arrangements among the older adults are limited. Studies that have dealt with this issue have come mainly from

Taiwan and China (Logan and Bian, 1999; Hermalin and Yang, 2004) and such studies are virtually absent in the Indian context. Besides, there are only few studies that pertain to the preference of older adults with respect to their living arrangement and draw on comparisons between the actual and the preferred place of stay. Any information on the living arrangement preferences and on the concordance in living arrangements therefore would offer a clearer understanding of the welfare needs of older adults.

The major objective of this chapter is to understand the patterns of living arrangements, living arrangement preferences and the concordance in living arrangement among older adults in India. The chapter will also examine the socio-economic and demographic factors that affect the living arrangement concordance in India. Finally, the chapter will explore the linkages between living arrangement concordance and the health of the older adults in India.

Data and methods

The data for this study are from 'Building Knowledge Base on Population Ageing in India' (BKPAI) conducted by Institute for Social and Economic Change (ISEC), Bangalore, in collaboration with UNFPA, Institute for Economic Growth, Delhi and Tata Institute for Social Sciences, Mumbai. This cross-sectional survey, conducted in seven states in India, covered 9,852 older adults. The seven states covered in this survey – Kerala, Tamil Nadu, Maharashtra, Himachal Pradesh, Punjab, Odisha and West Bengal – were selected as they had a higher percentage of the population that was aged 60 and over compared to the national average. The sample was split equally between urban and rural areas, irrespective of the proportion of urban and rural population. Eighty Primary Sampling Units (villages or urban wards, 40 in each urban and rural) were selected and within each of these 16 households in which there was an older person living were sampled.

In this chapter, concordance is defined as the correspondence between the actual and the preferred living arrangement. In other words, this indicates the number of people who are in the living arrangement that they want. The analysis will focus on older persons who co-reside with children and the older persons who live alone or live with their spouse. Living arrangement concordance will be analysed separately for co-residence concordance and independent living concordance. Those who live independently and prefer to do so are coded as 1, and discordance or the lack of concordance is coded as 0. In a similar manner, those who co-reside and prefer to do so are coded as 1, otherwise 0. The BKPAI survey collected extensive information on demographic characteristics, socio-economic status, health status, both self-rated health and morbidity of older persons and data on the family and social support systems.

Both bi-variate analysis and multivariate binary logistic regression analysis are employed here to understand the determinants of living arrangement concordance and its linkages to health. What has to be noted here is that the relationship between living arrangement and health need not be unidirectional. The living arrangement pattern can affect the health of the older persons and, at the same time, the health of the older person can also determine their living arrangements. However, in this paper, the impact of health on living arrangements has not been analysed. Two different sets of binary logistic regression are employed: the first for understanding the predictors of living arrangement concordance, and the second to understand the impact of the living arrangement concordance on health. The demographic variables included are age and sex, the socio-economic variables included are place of residence, education, economic dependency and household economic status, and the family-care variables included are marital status and number of living children. Age and sex are two important variables that impact on living arrangements. Previous studies have also established the linkages between living arrangements and the educational status of the older persons and their household economic status (Hu et al, 2019; Bolina et al, 2016). It is therefore important to control the effect of these factors while analysing living arrangement concordance.

Results of the actual and preferred living arrangements of older adults in India

Table 4.1 shows that a majority (70 per cent) of older adults in India co-reside with children, grandchildren and others, while 22 per cent live independently (either living alone or live with their spouse). Although more women in India live alone than men, the proportions for independent living seem to be nearly the same for both men and women. More women living alone could also be due to their state of being abandoned or due to their less resources that can be shared with the other members of the family. When older men have financial resources such as pension or property, they are more likely to receive care from children or relatives, though often in expectation of accrued returns at a later stage. This data also confirms that older men have better financial resources than older women. A higher proportion of older men (18 per cent) than women (7 per cent) receive salaries or wages and 20 per cent of older men and 4 per cent of older women receive a pension from employers. Similarly, asset ownership is also higher for older men (51 per cent) than older women (24 per cent) and rates of household ownership were 80 per cent for older men and 46 per cent for older women. Further, considering the differing life expectancies between males and females, it could also be possible that the women who live alone are mostly widows whereas most men might have had a partner in later life.

Table 4.1: Distribution of older men and women by living arrangement

	Men	Women	Total
Alone	2.0	9.6	6.0
Spouse only	21.1	11.3	16.0
Spouse and/or, children and grandchildren	70.1	70.4	70.3
Others	6.8	8.7	7.7
N	4,672	5,180	9,852

Table 4.2: Distribution of older men and women by living arrangement preferences

	Male	Female	Total
Alone	2.6	6.4	4.6
With spouse only	35.0	23.6	29.0
With sons only	47.3	52.0	49.8
With daughters only	2.1	4.7	3.5
With sons or daughters	5.2	5.7	5.5
Relative and others	7.6	7.2	7.5
In old age home	0.2	0.4	0.3
N	4,672	5,180	9,852

Table 4.2 provides data on living arrangement preferences among older men and women in India. Although the data do not show any sizable difference in preference from a conventional co-residence arrangement, one third of older persons in India expressed a preference for independent living arrangements. This is indicative of a shift in living arrangement preferences in the future. Notably, the proportion of older persons who prefer to live in institution is just 0.3 per cent, which suggests that older adults in India have negative views of old-age care homes.

Although there is certain information on how the socio-economic and demographic factors determine the pattern of actual living arrangement, as of 2022, there is virtually no information in the Indian context on living arrangement preferences. It is therefore of interest to better understand what factors are associated with these preferences. Table 4.3 provides the living arrangement preferences according to various demographic and socio-economic characteristics of older adults. The preference for independent living is strongly associated with the place of residence, economic independence, marital status and the presence of children. The preference for independent living is higher for those older persons

Table 4.3: Socio-economic characteristics and living arrangement preferences

	Preferred living arrangements		
	Independent living (%)	Co-residence (%)	N
Age*			
60–69	34.1	65.7	6239
70–79	33.5	66.1	2601
80+	30.9	68.6	1012
Sex*			
Male	37.6	62.2	4672
Female	29.9	69.7	5180
Residence*			
Rural	36.0	63.8	5138
Urban	26.9	72.8	4714
Marital status*			
Currently married	41.7	58.2	5847
Widowed	20.5	79.1	3768
Others	32.6	65.2	237
Education*			
None	34.7	64.9	4528
1–4 years	26.5	73.3	1263
5–7 years	31.7	68.2	1324
8+ years	36.0	63.8	2682
Economic dependency*			
Not dependent	44.6	55.0	2488
Fully dependent	29.6	70.2	2432
Partially dependent	31.4	68.3	4923
Wealth index*			
Lowest	36.0	63.4	1954
Second	34.9	64.9	1974
Middle	31.5	68.4	1938
Fourth	30.3	69.5	1962
Highest	34.6	65.3	2018
Number of children*			
0	57.7	41.2	133
1	26.9	72.6	1199

(Continued)

Table 4.3: Socio-economic characteristics and living arrangement preferences (continued)

	Preferred living arrangements		
	Independent living (%)	Co-residence (%)	N
2	34.7	65.3	2003
3+	32.7	67.1	6117

Note: * p < .01.

who live in rural areas rather than in urban areas, who are economically independent as compared with those who are partially or fully dependent economically on others, who are currently married versus those who are widowed, divorced or separated and those who do not have children. Overall, living arrangement preferences seem to be largely dependent on the actual living arrangement pattern and the needs and resources of the older persons. With 23 per cent of the older persons living independently in rural areas, against 19 per cent in urban areas (UNFPA, 2012), it is evident that a higher proportion of the rural persons in this study prefer independent living which might be reflecting their actual living arrangement pattern.

A greater proportion of older adults in rural areas live independently compared to those in urban areas because of the large rural to urban migration of younger people. Older people may also be making a rational assessment of the resources available to them in terms of kin availability and financial circumstances before indicating a preference. This is clear from the data on the preference for independent living among older adults who are childless and the preference for co-residence among those who are economically dependent. Hence, preferences on the living arrangements among older persons are largely shaped by their needs and resources.

Living arrangement concordance

There can be several types of living arrangement patterns and preferences existing in any society. In this chapter, the aspects of actual living arrangement and the preferences are grouped into two distinct categories, namely living independently versus co-residence. Living arrangement concordance is classified here into two sets: co-residence concordance and independent living concordance. Co-residence concordance indicates those older persons who co-reside with children, grandchildren and/or others and also have expressed a preference to co-residence. Independent living concordance means that the older persons who either live alone or live with their spouse also prefer to do so.

Figure 4.1: Living arrangement concordance

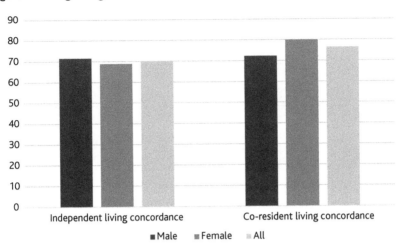

Figure 4.1 shows that independent living concordance is 70 per cent whereas co-residence concordance is 76 per cent. Further, independent living concordance is higher for males while co-residence concordance is higher for females. This implies that nearly a one third (30 per cent) of the older adults who live independently and nearly a quarter (24 per cent) of co-residing older adults were in discordance with their living arrangements.

A binary logistic regression model (shown in Table 4.4) is employed to understand the factors associated with living arrangement concordance. Determinants have been analysed separately for independent living concordance and co-residence concordance. In the first model, the dependent variable – independent living concordance – is 1 if they are in concordance and 0 if they are not in concordance. In the second model, the dependent variable – co-residence concordance – is 1 if they are in concordance and 0 if they are not in concordance. The independent variables are age, place of residence, marital status, education, individual economic dependency, household wealth index and number of children. After controlling all the factors, rural–urban residence, widowhood, years of schooling and household wealth index have been found to be statistically significant in determining the independent living concordance. Older adults living independently in urban areas are less likely to report that their current living arrangements are their preferred living arrangement as compared to the older adults living in rural areas. Similarly, widows also have a lower likelihood of being in concordance than those who are currently married. Education seems to have a negative effect on independent living concordance as higher-educated older persons are more at discordance with their living arrangements. This shows that better educated persons who

Table 4.4: Binary logistic regression analysis on living arrangement concordance

	Model 1: Independent Living Concordance	Model 2: Co-Residence Concordance
	OR (95%CI)	OR (95%CI)
60–69		
70–79	1.13 (0.88–1.45)	**1.21 (1.04–1.36)**
80+	1.17 (0.76–1.79)	1.06 (0.81–1.22)
Male		
Female	0.82 (0.62–1.06)	0.91 (0.78–1.04)
Rural		
Urban	**0.64 (0.51–0.82)**	**1.31 (1.14–1.45)**
Married		
Widowed	**0.62 (0.46–0.82)**	**2.98 (2.52–3.93)**
Others	1.88 (0.67–5.20)	**1.81 (1.15–3.07)**
No education		
1–4 years education	**0.61 (0.43–0.89)**	**2.03 (1.62–2.41)**
5–7 years education	**0.55 (0.38–0.80)**	**1.42 (1.14–1.62)**
8+ years education	**0.31 (0.22–0.44)**	**1.33 (1.11–1.54)**
Not economically dependent		
Partially dependent	0.87 (0.65–1.17)	**1.55 (1.32–1.82)**
Fully dependent	1.15 (0.82–1.67)	**1.81 (1.54–2.09)**
Lowest wealth quintile		
2nd wealth quintile	**1.73 (1.27–2.38)**	**0.72 (0.57–0.86)**
3rd wealth quintile	1.16 (0.82–1.67)	**0.53 (0.44–0.67)**
4th wealth quintile	**1.82 (1.22–2.79)**	**0.52 (0.43–0.65)**
Highest wealth quintile	**3.00 (1.92–4.71)**	**0.46 (0.37–0.58)**
0 children		
1 child	**0.41 (0.22–0.75)**	**2.75 (1.48–4.60)**
2 children	0.63 (0.35–1.14)	**2.55 (1.42–4.32)**
3+ children	0.72 (0.41–1.28)	**2.74 (1.54–4.55)**

Note: Bold figures significant; $p \leq 0.05$.

actually live independently do not prefer to live independently. However, greater household economic status increases the likelihood of independent living concordance. The coefficients for place of residence, marital status, education, economic dependency and household wealth index are significant in determining co-residence concordance but are not in the same direction as independent living concordance. Unlike independent living concordance, the urban residents, highly educated older persons – those who are economically independent or with better household economic status – are more in concordance with their living arrangements.

Living arrangement concordance and health

Ill health and disability are serious concerns during later life in any population (Dean et al, 1992; Brown et al, 2002; Zimmer, 2005). Age-friendly living arrangements are generally associated with better health outcomes for older adults. Studies linking health and living arrangements have mainly addressed two major dimensions, namely the impact of health of the older persons on the living arrangements and the impact of living arrangement on health of the older persons. The studies linking health and living arrangement have looked at ill health and disability as a factor for co-residence (Lee et al, 1995; Brown et al, 2002; Pal, 2004). It is generally agreed that older people with poor health or with disability cannot take care of themselves and hence tolder adults may opt for co-residence (Da Vanzo and Chan, 1994; Hermalin, 1997; Grundy, 2000). Studies conducted in other developed countries assessing the impact of living arrangements on health have shown that older adults living alone have better health than those in co-residence (Palloni, 2001), though living alone in principle might have adverse effects on health due to depression and loneliness (Dean et al, 1992; Grundy, 2001; Reynolds, 2020). Several other studies have shown that parents co-residing with their children have better health because they feel less lonely and are less likely to become depressed (Allen et al, 2000; Grundy, 2001; Hughes and Waite, 2002; Pal, 2004; Liang et al, 2005). In the developing countries too, such mixed results were observed (Vlassoff, 1990; Anh et al, 1997; Knodel and Chayovan, 1997; Hughes and Waite, 2002). Therefore, it is not clear whether ill health promotes co-residence or whether co-residence leads to ill health.

It is also important to look at the health outcomes of older adults, vis-a-vis their preferred living arrangements. Differences in the preferred and actual arrangements could impact on the health of older adults. Studies on this are lacking. Most studies linking health and living arrangements have neglected the importance of preferred living arrangements. This could be due to the fact that, in the Western context, these preferred and actual places of stay always converge. However, this may not be the case with most developing countries, especially India, where there could be a deviation from the preferred and actual living arrangements. In such circumstances, it is of interest to see the impact of living arrangement concordance on the health of the older adults. Two health indicators are used here: the first is self-rated health and the second is the mental health status assessed through General

Table 4.5: Living arrangement concordance and health of older persons

Living arrangement	Concordance	% of older persons in excellent or very good self-rated health	% of older persons with GHQ ≤12
Independent living	Yes	14.4	63.0
	No	12.0	47.4
Co-residence	Yes	13.9	57.0
	No	18.7	50.0

Health Questionnaire 12 (GHQ). The self-rated health is considered as a strong predictor in understanding the health status of people in general, and older adults in particular. The BKPAI survey asked all the older respondents to rate their current health status on a 5-point scale from (i) excellent, (ii) very good, (iii) good, (iv) fair to (v) poor. Here, the excellent and very good categories were compared against the other three. The GHQ is used as an instrument for screening psychological distress. This questionnaire has been extensively used to measure mental health status in different settings and different cultures (Goldberg and Blackwell, 1970). The score ranges from 0 to 36, with higher scores indicating greater psychological distress. The accepted threshold score is 12 or below, reflecting better mental health status, and a score above 12 reflects psychological distress.

Table 4.5 shows the proportions of older persons who rated their health by their living arrangement concordance. It shows that the number of older persons who have reported their health as excellent or very good is slightly higher among those who live independently and also prefer to do so, whereas the opposite is true for those who co-reside and also prefer to do so. However, in both cases, the relationship is not statistically significant. Apart from living arrangement patterns, health status is also influenced by a number of demographic and socio-economic variables. Two different binary logistic regression models were run in order to understand the effect of health on different socio-economic variables, one for those who live independently and another for those who co-reside. In the first model, dependent variables are self-rated health, categorised as excellent or very good versus good, fair or bad. In the second model, dependent variable is GHQ with cut off less than or equal to 12 versus above 12.

Tables 4.6 and 4.7 clearly show that, in the unadjusted model and after controlling for socio-economic and demographic variables, no significant differences in self-rated health are observed among those who are in concordance as against those who are not in concordance for either living arrangement. In other worlds, living arrangement concordance did not appear to be a significant determinant of self-rated health status of the

Table 4.6: Binary logistic regression analysis on self-rated health and GHQ for those who live independently

| | Self-rated health as excellent/ very good | | GHQ (≤12) | |
| | Model 1 | Model 1A | Model 2 | Model 2A |
	OR (95% CI)	OR (95% CI)	OR (95% CI)	OR (95% CI)
Living alone concordance				
No				
Yes	1.27 (0.97–1.67)	1.25 (0.92–1.70)	**0.57 (0.47–0.69)**	**0.62 (0.48–0.78)**
Age				
60–69	-		-	
70–79	-	1.00 (0.74–1.36)	-	0.79 (0.61–1.01)
80+	-	0.71 (0.39–1.28)	-	0.84 (0.55–1.26)
Sex				
Male	-		-	
Female	-	0.90 (0.65–1.26)	-	**1.31 (1.01–1.71)**
Residence				
Rural	-		-	
Urban	-	1.01 (0.75–1.37)	-	1.14 (0.89–1.45)
Marital status				
Currently married	-		-	
Widowed	-	**0.65 (0.43–0.98)**	-	**0.55 (0.41–0.73)**
Others	-	1.15 (0.37–3.59)	-	1.03 (0.41–2.58)
Education				
None	-		-	
1–4 years	-	**1.69 (1.08–2.64)**	-	1.11 (0.78–1.56)
5–7 years	-	0.84 (0.51–1.39)	-	1.19 (0.84–1.69)
8+ years	-	0.93 (0.61–1.42)	-	**1.52 (1.09–2.15)**

(Continued)

Table 4.6: Binary logistic regression analysis on self-rated health and GHQ for those who live independently (continued)

	Self-rated health as excellent/ very good		GHQ (≤12)	
Economic dependency				
Not dependent	-		-	
Partially dependent	-	**0.63** (0.42–0.93)	-	**0.56** (0.42–0.75)
Fully dependent	-	0.74 (0.53–1.04)	-	**0.35** (0.27–0.46)
Wealth index				
Lowest	-		-	
Second	-	**2.18** (1.41–3.39)	-	**2.65** (1.99–3.48)
Middle	-	**2.70** (1.65–4.43)	-	**3.90** (2.73–5.44)
Fourth	-	**4.74** (2.88–7.93)	-	**4.04** (2.68–5.97)
Highest	-	**6.41** (3.75–10.99)	-	**8.25** (5.03–13.20)
Number of children				
0 (R)	-		-	
1	-	0.79 (0.32–1.97)	-	1.27 (0.70–2.33)
2	-	1.27 (0.54–3.00)	-	1.26 (0.71–2.24)
3+	-	1.68 (0.73–3.87)	-	1.27 (0.72–2.21)
Constant	0.000	-2.814	0.554	-0.193
Log likelihood	-733.31387		-1037.346	

Note: Bold figures significant; $p \leq 0.05$.

older persons. However, in case of GHQ, the relationship was significant only in the case of independent living concordance and not in co-residence concordance. In all the models, household economic status was the most significant variable that determined the health status of older persons. Overall, this finding raises several questions on the applicability of the congruence theory of Person–Environment (P–E) Fit in the context of older persons in India. When co-residence is the normative pattern of living arrangement, older adults may strive to maximise their efforts to be

Table 4.7: Binary logistic regression analysis on self-rated health and GHQ for those in co-residence

	Self-rated health as excellent/ very good		GHQ (≤12)	
	Model 1	Model 1A	Model 1	Model 1A
	OR (95% CI)	OR (95% CI)	OR (95% CI)	OR (95% CI)
Co-residence concordance				
No (R)				
Yes	0.75 (0.65–0.85)	0.95 (0.81–1.09)	0.76 (0.68–0.84)	0.96 (0.84–1.07)
Age				
60–69	-		-	
70–79	-	0.95 (0.82–1.11)	-	**0.63 (0.56–0.70)**
80+	-	**0.70 (0.55–0.90)**	-	**0.50 (0.42–0.59)**
Sex				
Male	-		-	
Female	-	1.14 (0.97–1.34)	-	1.02 (0.91–1.15)
Residence				
Rural	-		-	
Urban	-	1.04 (0.91–1.19)	-	**0.86 (0.77–0.95)**
Marital status				
Currently married	-		-	
Widowed	-	**0.63 (0.53–0.74)**	-	0.90 (0.80–1.02)
Others	-	**0.51 (0.27–0.94)**	-	1.01 (0.67–1.54)
Education				
None	-		-	
1–4 years	-	1.18 (0.97–1.45)	-	1.05 (0.90–1.22)
5–7 years	-	1.12 (0.92–1.37)	-	**1.17 (1.00–1.35)**
8+ years	-	**1.23 (1.02–1.48)**	-	**1.56 (1.34–1.81)**

(Continued)

Table 4.7: Binary logistic regression analysis on self-rated health and GHQ for those in co-residence (Continued)

| | Self-rated health as excellent/ very good | | GHQ (≤12) | |
| | Model 1 | Model 1A | Model 1 | Model 1A |
	OR (95% CI)	OR (95% CI)	OR (95% CI)	OR (95% CI)
Economic dependency				
Not dependent	-		-	
Partially dependent	-	**0.43** (0.37–0.52)	-	**0.65** (0.56–0.76)
Fully dependent	-	**0.41** (0.35–0.48)	-	**0.48** (0.41–0.55)
Wealth-index				
Lowest	-		-	
Second	-	1.22 (0.95–1.54)	-	**1.56** (1.32–1.84)
Middle	-	**1.31** (1.02–1.65)	-	**2.33** (1.96–2.76)
Fourth	-	**1.62** (1.26–2.04)	-	**3.66** (3.07–4.36)
Highest	-	**1.61** (1.24–2.06)	-	**4.33** (3.58–5.22)
Number of children				
0 (R)	-		-	
1	-	1.22 (0.54–2.82)	-	**2.11** (1.19–3.74)
2	-	1.60 (0.71–3.63)	-	1.65 (0.94–2.91)
3+	-	1.36 (0.61–3.07)	-	1.68 (0.96–2.93)

Note: Bold figures significant; p ≤0.05.

in co-residence on the belief that such arrangements will be beneficial to them. In such situations, better outcomes (in this case, health) need not be dependent on their preference. In other words, outcomes have little to do with preference or choices in living arrangement. Secondly, the congruence theory also discusses the adaptation of individuals to their environment. Even when there is a discordance, older persons might be trying to adapt to the available situations in an effort to cope up with the demands of the environment. In such situations a positive outcome need not always depend on a perfect fit. Thirdly, when congruence is defined here as the alignment between actual and the preferred living arrangements, whether the older persons are in concordance or discordance depends greatly on the objectivity of preference measurement. In the case of older persons, there is always a scope for rationalisation of their actual living arrangement as their preference. Considering these circumstances, P–E theory as postulated requires certain level of modifications to suit the Indian cultural context.

Discussion

The preference data reveal that approximately one third of older adults in India state a preference for independent living. These figures are slightly higher than the proportion who actually live independently which suggests that this form of living arrangement might become more prevalent in the future. However, contrary to concerns about the demise of the extended family, the majority of older adults in India express a preference to live with their adult children, with the greatest proportion (50 per cent) wishing to live with their sons. This fits with the cultural norms in which sons are responsible for parental care, although the actual caregiving role is most often handled by their wives, the daughters-in-law of the older adult (Ugargol and Bailey, 2018, 2021). These findings further support the argument by James and Kumar (Chapter 3) that independent living among older adults in India is most likely accidental rather than intentional and that, contrary to second demographic transition theories (Lesthaeghe, 2010), individualism due to structural changes in society are not manifest among older adults in India. Nonetheless, there are some interesting gender differences that are worth reflecting upon: a larger proportion of men (one third) than women (one quarter) want to live with their spouse. It is possible that this difference reflects gender differences in the value of spousal relationships for men (who tend to gain) and women (who tend to lose) (Coombs, 1991). Further research could explore whether older women generally want to live with their sons (and daughters-in-law) where they are more likely to receive support/care or live with their husbands they are more likely to become caregivers. Certainly some of the accounts provided by older adults in Chapter 6 show the benefits of co-residing with sons and daughters-in-law. However, they also highlight the potential for negative and/or abusive situations where sons fail to properly care for their older parents. Thus, future research would benefit from exploring the extent to which older adults' preferences for living with sons is based on an idealised cultural norm or the direct experience of others who have these living arrangements.

The results of the analyses on the factors associated with living arrangement concordance reveal some interesting patterns. Foremost among these factors is the role that education plays. The results clearly show an inverse gradient of living arrangement concordance among those who live independently, that is, those who are more highly educated and live independently are less likely to want to live independently. The reason for this result is not immediately clear and would benefit from further research. However, taken together with the findings from Chapter 3, that it is those in the lowest socio-economic groups who are least likely to co-reside with their children (due to the migration of adult children for work), it is possible that those with lower education who live independently are less likely to express a preference for co-residence with their children as that would mean their children would not have access to work. However, such a conclusion does not fit well with the results that wealth is positively associated with independent living concordance. In contrast, wealth appears to be negatively associated with co-residence concordance in India. This somewhat contradicts findings of a study of living arrangement concordance among older adults in China (Sereny, 2011) which found that economic status had no association with co-residence concordance. Clearly, there is still much work to be done to explore the inter-relationships between different measures of socio-economic status and living arrangement concordance in India.

Finally, the positive association between independent living concordance and better mental health offers some tacit support for the P–E model. However, the lack of any statistically significant results of the impact of either form of living arrangement concordance on self-rated general health or for the impact of co-residence concordance on mental health raises some questions about the wider applicability of the P–E model in this context. As noted, this could be due to the ability of older adults to develop coping mechanisms. This is definitely a topic worthy of future investigation. Indeed, in the aforementioned study in China, once the analyses was controlled for 'positive outlook' among older adults, the relationship between living arrangement discordance and self-rated health was also not statistically significant. Interestingly, however, although co-residence concordance was not significantly related to self-rated health in China (with or without controlling for positive outlook), it was associated with having more functional limitations (Sereny, 2011). Future research in India could benefit from exploring a wider range of health and well-being outcomes.

Conclusion

The study of living arrangement concordance among older adults in India is relatively new. This is one of the first studies to carry out such an analysis using the unique BKPAI data. The analysis clearly indicates the need to contextualise the living arrangement concordance in line with the cultural norms and gender-role behaviours expected of older adults and their linked family members. Such contextualisation is also needed to delineate the culturalist explanation of care and caregiving dynamics within the household and the individual aspirations and choice of living arrangement. The analysis in this chapter and the qualitative examples presented later in this book highlight the need to unpack the agency of older adults in adapting to the environment they live in. The gender component also indicates that, compared to older men, older women face greater precarity while living alone. A deeper and meaningful engagement between older adults (including their families) and public and private care and housing agencies is essential to improve the fit with the living environment.

References

Allen, S. M., Ciambrone, D. and Welch, L. C. (2000) 'Stage of life course and social support as a mediator of mood state among persons with disability', *Journal of Ageing and Health*, 12(3): 318–41.

Anh, T. S., Goodkind, D. and Knodel, J. (1997) 'Living arrangements, patrilineality and sources of support among elderly Vietnamese', *Asia Pacific Population Journal*, 12(4): 69–88.

Asis, M. M. B., Domingo, L., Knodel, J. and Mehta, K. (1995) 'Living arrangements in four Asian countries: a comparative perspective', *Journal of Cross-Cultural Gerontology*, 10(1–2): 145–62.

Bolina, A. F. and Tavares, D. M. (2016) 'Living arrangements of the elderly and the sociodemographic and health determinants: a longitudinal study', *Latin American Journal of Nursing*, 24, https://doi.org/10.1590/1518-8345.0668.2737

Bongaarts, J. and Zimmer, Z. (2002) 'Living arrangements of older adults in the developing world: an analysis of demographic and health survey household surveys', *Journal of Gerontology, Series B. Psychological Science and Social Sciences*, 57(3): S145–57.

Brown, J. W., Liang, J., Krause, N., Akiyama, H., Sugisawa, H. and Fukaya, T. (2002) 'Transitions in living arrangements among elders in Japan', *The Journal of Gerontology Series B: Psychological Sciences and Social Science*, 57: S209–S220.

Browne-Yung, K., Walker, R. B. and Luszcz, M. A. (2017) 'An examination of resilience and coping in the oldest old using life narrative method', *The Gerontologist*, 57(2): 282–91.

Burr, J. and Mutchler, J. (1992) 'The living arrangement of unmarried Hispanic females', *Demography*, 29: 93–112.

Carp, F. M. and Carp, A. (1984) 'A complementary/congruence model of well-being or mental health for the community elderly', *Human Behaviour and Environment: Advances in Theory and Research*, 7: 279–336.

Chan, A. and Davanzo, J. (1996) 'Ethnic differences in parent's co-residence with adult children in peninsular Malaysia', *Journal of Cross-Cultural Gerontology*, 11(1): 29–59.

Coombs, R. H. (1991) 'Marital status and personal well-being: a literature review', *Family Relations*, 40(1): 97–102.

Da Vanzo, J. and Chan, A. (1994) 'Living arrangements of older Malaysians: who co-resides with their adult children?', *Demography*, 31(1): 95–113.

Dean, A., Kolody, B., Wood, P. and Matt, G. E. (1992) 'The influence of living alone on depression in elderly persons', *Journal of Aging and Health*, 4(1): 3–18.

Domingo, L. J. and Asis, M. M. B. (1995) 'Living arrangements and the flow of support between generations in the Philippines', *Journal of Cross-Cultural Gerontology*, 10(1–2): 21–51.

Edwards, J. R. (1991) 'Person-job fit: a conceptual integration, literature review and methodological critique', *International Review of Industrial and Organizational Psychology*, 6: 283–357.

Elman, C. and Uhlenberg, P. (1995) 'Co residence in the early 20th century: elderly women in the United States and their children', *Population Studies*, 49: 501–17.

Festinger, L. (1957) *A Theory of Cognitive Dissonance*, Stanford, CA: Stanford University Press.

Goldberg, D. P. and Blackwell, B. (1970) 'Psychiatric illness in general practice: a detailed study using a new method of case identification', *British Medical Journal*, 1: 439–43.

Goldsheider, F. K. and Goldscheider, C. (1989) 'The new family economy: residential and economic relationship among the generations', in F. K. Goldscheider and C. Goldscheider (eds) *Ethnicity and the New Family Economy: Living Arrangements and Intergenerational Financial Flows*, Boulder, CO: Westview, pp 1–14.

Grundy, E. (2000) 'Co residence of mid-life children with their elderly parents in England and Wales: changes between 1981 and 1991', *Population Studies*, 54: 193–206.

Grundy, E. (2001) 'Living arrangements and the health of older persons in developed countries', *Population Bulletin of the United Nations*, 42/43: 311–29.

Hermalin, A. I. (1997) 'Drawing policy lessons for Asia from research on ageing', *Asia Pacific Population Journal*, 12(4): 89–102.

Hermalin, A. and Yang, L. S. (2004) 'Levels of support from children in Taiwan: expectations versus reality, 1965–99', *Population and development Review*, 30(3): 417–48.

Hu, Y., Leinonen, T., van Hedel, K., Myrskylä, M. and Martikainen, P. (2019) 'The relationship between living arrangements and higher use of hospital care at middle and older ages: to what extent do observed and unobserved individual characteristics explain this association?', *BMC Public Health*, 19(1011).

Hughes, M. E. and Waite, L. J. (2002) 'Health in household context: living arrangements and health in late middle age', *Journal of Health and Social Behaviour*, 43: 1–21.

Kahana, E. (1975) 'A congruence model of person–environment interaction', in P. G. Windley, T. Byerts and E. G. Ernst (eds) *Theoretical Development in Environments and Aging*, Washington, DC: Gerontological Society, pp 181–214.

Kahana, E. (1982) 'A congruence model of person–environment interactions', in M. P. Lawton, P. G. Windley, T. O. Byerts (eds) *Aging and the Environment: Theoretical Approaches*, Berlin: Springer, pp 97–120.

Kahana, E., Liang, J., and Felton, B. J. (1980) 'Alternative models of person–environment fit: prediction of morale in three homes for the aged', *Journal of Gerontology*, 35(4): 584–95.

Kim, C. S. and Rhee K. O. (1997) 'Variations in preferred living arrangements among Korean elderly parents', *Journal of Cross-Cultural Gerontology*, 12(2): 189–202.

Knodel, J. and Chayovan, N. (1997) 'Family support and living arrangements of Thai elderly: an overview', *Asia Pacific Population Journal*, 12(4): 51–68.

Kristof, A. L. (1996) 'Person-organization-fit: an integrative review of its conceptualization, measurement and its implications', *Personal Psychology*, 49(1): 1–49.

Lai, D. W., Tsang, K. T., Chappell, N., Lai, D. C. Y. and Chau, S. B. Y. (2007) 'Relationships between culture and health status: a multi-site study of the older Chinese in Canada', *Canadian Journal on Aging*, 26: 171–84.

Lawton, M. P. and Nahemow, L. (1973) 'Ecology and the aging process', in C. Eisdorfer and M. P. Lawton (eds) *The Psychology of Adult Development and Aging*, Washington, DC: American Psychological Association, pp 619–74.

Lawton, M. M. and Simon, B. (1968) 'The ecology of social relationships in housing for the elderly', *The Gerontologist*, 8: 108–15.

Lee, M. L. Lin, H. S. and Chang, M. C. (1995) 'Living arrangements of the elderly in Taiwan: qualitative evidence', *Journal of Cross-Cultural Gerontology*, 10(1–2): 53–78.

Lesthaeghe, R. (2010) 'The unfolding story of the second demographic transition', *Population and Development Review*, 36(2): 55–81.

Lewin, K. (1935) *A Dynamic Theory of Personality: Selected Papers*, trans. D. K. Adams and K. E. Zener, New York: McGraw Hill.

Lewin, K. (1951) *Field Theory in Social Science*, New York: Harper.

Liang, J., Brown, J. W., Krause, N. M., Ofstedal, M. B. and Bennett, J. (2005) 'Health and living arrangements among older Americans: does marriage matter?', *Journal of Aging and Health*, 17(3): 305–35.

Logan, J. R. and Bian, F. (1999) 'Family values and co-residence with married children in urban China', *Social Forces*, 77(4): 1253–82.

Murray, H. A. (1938) *Explorations in Personality*, New York: Oxford University Press.

Pal, S. (2004) 'Do children act as security in rural India? Evidence from an analysis of elderly living arrangements', Cardiff: Cardiff Business School, http://ideas.repec.org/e/ppa99.html

Palloni, A. (2001) 'Living arrangements of older persons', *Population Bulletin of the United Nations*, 42/43: 54–110.

Phillips, D. R., Cheng, K. H. C., Yeh, A. G. O. and Siu, O. L. (2010) 'Person-environment (PE) fit models and psychological well-being among older persons in Hong Kong', *Environment and Behaviour*, 42(2): 221–42.

Reynolds, R. M., Meng, J. and Dorrance Hall, E. (2020) 'Multi-layered social dynamics and depression among older adults: a 10-year cross-lagged analysis', *Psychology and Aging*, 35(7): 948–62.

Rudkin, L. (1993) 'Gender difference in economic well-being among the elderly of Java', *Demography*, 30(2): 209–26.

Sereny, M. (2011) 'Living arrangements of older adults in China: the interplay among preferences, realities, and health', *Research on Aging*, 33(2): 172–204.

Shah, N. M., Yount, K. M., Shah, M. A. and Menon, I. (2002) 'Living arrangements of older women and men in Kuwait', *Journal of Cross-Cultural Gerontology*, 17(4): 337–55.

Thomas, K. and Wister, A. (1984) 'Living arrangements of older women: the Ethnic Dimension', *Journal of Marriage and the Family*, 46: 301–11.

Ugargol, A. P. and Bailey, A. (2018) 'Family caregiving for older adults: gendered roles and caregiver burden in emigrant households of Kerala, India', *Asian Population Studies*, 14(2): 194–210.

Ugargol, A. P. and Bailey, A. (2021) 'Reciprocity between older adults and their caregivers in emigrant households of Kerala, India', *Ageing and Society*, 41(8): 1699–725.

UNFPA (2012) Report of the Status of the Elderly in Selected States of India, 2011. New Delhi: United Nationals Population Fund.

van Vianen, A. E. M. (2018) 'Person-environment fit: a review of its basic tenets', *Annual Review of Organizational Psychology and Organisational Behaviour*, 5: 75–101.

Vlassoff, C. (1990) 'The value of sons in an Indian village: how widows see it', *Population Studies*, 44: 5–20.

Wahl, H. and Gerstorf, D. (2020) Person–environment resources for aging well: environmental docility and life space as conceptual pillars for future contextual gerontology', *The Gerontologist*, 60: 368–75.

Zhang, Z., Gu, D. and Luo, Y. (2014) 'Co-residence with elderly parents in contemporary China: the role of filial piety, reciprocity, socioeconomic resources, and parental needs', *Journal of Cross-cultural Gerontology*, 29(3): 259–76.

Zimmer, Z. (2005) 'Health and living arrangement transitions among China's oldest-old', *Research on Aging*, 27(5): 526–55.

Zimmer, Z. and Kim, S. K. (2001) 'Living arrangements and socio-demographic conditions of older adults in Cambodia', *Journal of Cross-Cultural Gerontology*, 16(4): 353–81.

5

Family size and living arrangements among older adults in Kerala: panel data analysis, 2004–19

S. Irudaya Rajan and S. Sunitha

Introduction

The onset of disability is a natural part of the ageing process. However, this can often lead to the need for care. In India, it has been a traditional practice that older adults obtain socio-economic support and health care from a family caregiver, usually from their children, spouse or immediate family members (Ugargol et al, 2016). Hence, the household living arrangements of older people in India are seen as important for the availability of family support. Kerala is one of the states in India that has undergone rapid demographic transition (Liebig and Rajan, 2003; Guilmoto and Rajan, 2005). Due to the decrease in infant mortality rates and increases in average life expectancy, both of which are comparable to some developed nations, Kerala is reported to have the highest proportion of older adults in its population in India (Bhat and Rajan, 1990; Rajan, 1989; Rajan, Mishra and Sarma, 1999; Rajan and Sunitha, 2018). According to the 2011 Census, 12.6 per cent of the population were aged 60 and over and this proportion is increasing at a rate of 2.3 per cent per year (Rajan and Mishra, 2014). By 2026, the state will have 6.8 million older adults, up from 5.9 million in 2021, which will constitute approximately 16 per cent of the total population (Rajan and Mishra, 2020). In addition, Kerala has also experienced large internal and international migration (about 10 per cent of the population) of younger age groups which led many households to be without an adult member of 'working age'. It is assumed that this will have serious implications for care and living arrangements among older people in Kerala.

Living arrangements of older adults in India

The 2011 Census revealed that the average household size in India was 4.5 and the average number of older adults in a household was 2.4. This reflects the traditional image of the Indian family that has two older individuals who are looked after in the home. Also, it was found that the number of single-person older households increased during the inter-census period 2001–11 (Rajan and Sunitha, 2019). Figures from the Longitudinal Ageing Survey in India (LASI) in 2017–18 show that 5.1 per cent of older adults are living alone. Shrinking family size and the decreasing number of children from whom the parents can draw support in their later age are a consequence of the demographic transition in Kerala (Rajan et al, 1995; Rajan and Mishra, 1997a, 1997b; Rajan and Zachariah, 1998). It is assumed that this change in family size will affect the living arrangements of older adults which, in turn, is assumed to have a major effect on their health. Theoretically, living arrangements have a substantial impact on the health of older adults (Rajan et al, 2000; Pollen, 2001). Household-based social ties (marital, intergenerational and siblings) can provide both economic and emotional support enhancing health in later life. The idea of co-residence is based on the flow of support to both directions in a way that children take care of their parents and provide health care and daily needs while parents provide childcare for young grandchildren (Sudha et al, 2004, 2006; Rajan et al, 2008; Rajan and Prasad, 2008; Agarwal 2012). Living arrangements for older adults can play a vital role in empowering the older persons by giving them dignity. Previous research in India shows that older adults experienced greater life satisfaction and dignity when they are living with their family (Rajan and Sunitha, 2018). However, living alone and living only with a spouse has been on the increase in India. This may partially be explained by improvements in the financial ability to live independently (Tohme et al, 2011, Ugargol et al, 2016), but other factors such as family conflict, not having children or children living elsewhere due to migration and marriage might force older people to live alone (Rajan, 2013). Ill health and disability also affect the level of dependence and living arrangements for older adults (Bloom et al, 2010). In this chapter we will explore how the living arrangements have changed among older adults in Kerala, examine how the change in family size influences the living arrangements of older adults and study whether this change in living arrangements or household size is associated with the changes in the health and survival status of older adults.

Panel analysis in ageing research

Many studies use panel data for analysing the trends in intergenerational relations, such as co-residence and the intergenerational flow of resources and services (Albertini et al, 2007), verticalisation of the kinship structure (relations between generations rather than between siblings) and extended duration of generational roles (both children and parents experience a process of co-aging as they spend many years during which both are in later life) (Saraceno, 2008). To examine changes over time in living arrangements for older adults in Kerala we have used panel data from the Kerala Ageing Surveys (KAS). This is the first longitudinal survey of ageing in Kerala.

Kerala emerged as an ageing society in the 1980s and is going through its last stage of demographic transition experiencing low or nearly equal birth and death rates (Rajan and Sunitha, 2015, 2017, 2018). In this context the KAS started its first panel in 2004, based on the observation that there was a change in the household structure such that households with at least one older person had increased. The sample was drawn from the Kerala Migration Survey 2003 (Zachariah and Rajan, 2004, 2007, 2009; Rajan, 2004), which covered 47,830 individuals from 10,000 households across Kerala. It was decided to incorporate all those aged 60 and over from those 10,000 households to form the KAS in 2004. Thus, a total of 4,940 older persons were recruited, which comprised 2,272 males and 2,668 females (Rajan and Mishra, 2020). The survey has been repeated every three years across a span of 15 years. Among the surveyed older adults in 2004, 11.6 per cent had died by 2007. Among those surveyed in 2007, 16.5 per cent had died by 2010. Between 2010 and 2013 10.7 per cent of the sample had died. Between 2013 and 2016 a further 14.8 per cent of the sample had died. Finally, between 2016 and 2019 about 16.2 per cent of the sample had died. A total of 38.6 per cent were untraceable (Rajan and Balagopal, 2017; Rajan et al, 2017). The study was funded by Canadian Institutes of Health Research (CIHR) and Indian Council of Social Science Research – Indo Dutch Programme on Alternatives in Development (ICSSR-IDPAD) (Zachariah and Rajan, 2004).

Data

The study has used data from 2004, treated as baseline, and 2019, treated as follow-up. Table 5.1 shows the retention and attrition of the sample in each wave.

Analytical approach

Initial descriptive statistics were performed to understand the changes in family size among older persons in Kerala. Chi square tests were employed to identify group differences in proportions. Following this Kaplan–Meier analysis was carried out to examine the survival rate and mean survival time in years for older adults living in households of different sizes at baseline. Difference was tested for statistical significance using log rank test. Finally, survival analysis of older persons in different household (HH) sizes was

Table 5.1: Sample retention and attrition of the Kerala Ageing Study, 2004–19

	Total	Alive	Died	Untraced	Response Rate
2004	4940	–	–	–	–
2007	–	3697	575	668	86.5
2010	–	3008	609	80	97.8
2013	–	2030	322	656	78.2
2016	–	1441	301	288	85.8
2019	–	992	234	215	85.1

performed using Cox regression analysis. Cox regression analysis was used to generate the survival curves based on the HH size and hazard ratios adjusted for functional limitations (measured using the activities of daily living, for example difficulty bathing oneself, difficulty shopping for groceries, and so on) and self-rated health.

Characteristics of the sample

Of the 4,940 respondents to KAS 2004, 992 individuals had survived to 2019 and 2,041 were deceased. The baseline characteristics of those who had survived and those who had deceased are described in Table 5.2. Interestingly, there does not appear to be any major difference in the likelihood of dying based on living arrangements or household size in 2004. Those who had survived until 2019 were slightly more likely to have been in either a two- or three/four-person household than those who died. However, around equal proportions of those who survived (2.4 per cent) and those who died (2.7 per cent) were living alone/in one-person households in 2004. Conversely, among those who died, a slightly higher proportion (66 per cent) had been living in households of 5+ in 2004, compared to those who were still alive (59.4 per cent).

Aside from living arrangements, age, gender, marital status, education and health were all related to the likelihood of death between 2004 and 2019. Those who had died were more likely to be older, male, not married, less educated, in poorer health, have greater limitations in activities of daily living and had a chronic disease at baseline.

Change in the household size in 15 years

Figure 5.1 shows that compared to the household size in 2004, the proportion of one-person and two-person households had increased by 2019, while the proportion of households with more than five members has decreased over the period of the study.

Table 5.2: Baseline characteristics of KAS participants who survived to 2019 and those who died between 2004 and 2019

Indicators	Alive	Died	Indicators	Alive	Died
Sex			Age		
Male	39.6	54.0	60–69	75.1	36.2
Female	60.4	46.0	70–79	21.8	40.5
Marital status			80+	3.0	23.3
Single	2.5	2.4	Health perception		
Married	71.9	59.9	Good/excellent	27.7	17.4
Widowed	24.6	36.1	Fair	34.4	25.6
Divorced/separated	1.0	1.6	Poor/poorer	37.9	57.0
Education			ADL score		
Illiterate	13.9	23.6	No disability	96.4	82.0
Less than primary	20.9	27.3	Have disability	3.6	18.0
Primary up to upper primary	39.5	34.8	Living arrangements		
High school and above	25.7	14.3	Living alone	2.4	2.7
Household size			Living with spouse only	7.3	6.0
1	2.4	2.7	All older adults living together	0.7	0.9
2	11.7	9.8	Living with children or others	89.6	90.4
3–4	26.5	21.5	Chronic diseases		
5 or more	59.4	66.0	No	40.5	31.0
			Yes	59.5	69.0

Source: Compiled from Kerala Ageing Surveys, 2004 and 2019

Figure 5.2 shows that there are gender differences in living arrangements. In both 2004 and 2019 older women were more likely than men to live alone. They were also more likely than men to live in households of 5 or more people. Conversely, men were more likely to live in households of two or three/four people. In general, these patterns remain quite stable (although the levels change) between 2004 and 2019. The exception is the drop in the proportion of men living in three/four-person households (by 2019 women were now more likely to live in these types of households). This drop has been accompanied by a rather significant jump in the proportion of men living in two-person households. In 2004 14.2 per cent of men lived with one other person. By 2019 this had increased to 22.9 per cent and was on a par with the proportion who lived in three/ four-person households.

Figure 5.1: Percentage of older adults living in households of different sizes in 2004 and 2019

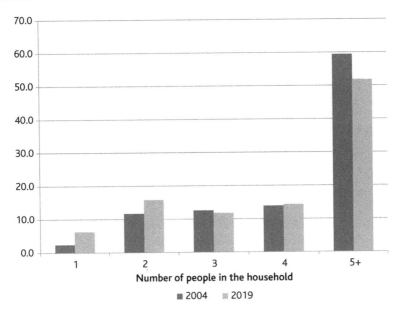

Figure 5.2: Distribution of household size by sex among older persons in 2004 and 2019

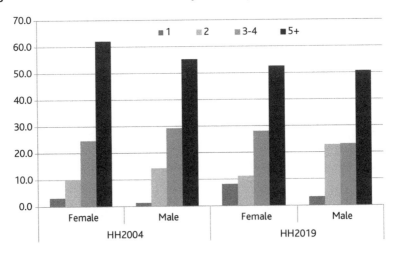

Table 5.3 shows the percentage of older adults who experienced a change in the size of their household between 2004 and 2019 based on their household size in 2019. For example, the first row shows that 42 per cent of those who lived in a one-person household in 2019 had lived in a household with more than one person in 2004, that is, they have experienced a decrease in the

Table 5.3: Change in the proportion of household size over the period 2004–19

Relative change in HH size during 2004–19	Decrease	No Change	Increase
1 person household	41.7	58.3	0.0
2 person household	37.9	46.6	15.5
3–4 person household	48.7	16.0	35.4
5+ person household	18.0	28.7	53.3
Total	29.0	28.1	42.8

number of people in their household. Conversely 53 per cent of those who lived in a household of five or more people in 2019 had lived in a household with fewer than five people in 2004, that is, they had experienced an increase in the number of people in their household. For the sample as a whole 43 per cent of older adults had experienced an increase the number of people in their household, while 29 per cent experienced a decrease and there was no change for the remaining 28 per cent. However, the patterns are quite different for the different types of household. We can see that a significant proportion of those living in one-, two- and three/four-person households experienced a shrinking of their household size over this period. However, we also see evidence of a significant proportion people from one- or two-person households moving in with wider family. Conversely, relatively few people moved from a one-person household to a two-person household. The majority of people in one- or two-person households (notably in one-person households), had been so since 2004.

Table 5.4 shows the health status of older adults by household size. The figures for self-rated health show that older adults living in households with three/four people or five or more people are about twice as likely to say that there health was poor compared to older adults living alone or in a two-person household. Older adults living in two-person households were also the least likely to report any disability, while those in three/four-person households were most likely. However, the figures are quite similar across the households, especially for those in one-person households and those with five or more inhabitants. Similarly, there is no clear pattern of chronic illness by household size. Those living alone are somewhat less likely to have any chronic illness, while those in two-person households are somewhat more likely, though overall the distributions look quite similar for each of the household types.

However, we must be cautious in interpreting these results as showing that household size impacts on the health of older adults. It is highly likely that following bereavement older adults with poorer health will either move

Table 5.4: Household size and health characteristics of older persons in 2019 (%)

	1	2	3–4	5+	Total
Self-rated health					
Good/Excellent	45.8	55.2	41.1	46.9	46.3
Fair	41.7	34.5	38.0	34.8	35.8
Poor/poorer	12.5	10.3	20.9	18.3	17.9
ADL score					
No disability	29.2	35.3	20.5	27.8	26.8
Have disability	70.8	64.7	79.5	72.2	73.2
Chronic disease					
No disease	4.2	1.7	2.3	3.4	2.9
One	12.5	5.2	7.6	9.5	8.6
Two	8.3	6.0	12.5	13.2	12.1
Three or more	75.0	87.1	77.6	73.9	76.4

in with their children or their children will move in with them to care for them. Hence, some of those living in two-person households may have become widowed and their son or daughter has moved in to care for them (Vlassof, 1990). A good example of this is presented in Chapter 6 where a daughter (Sophie) moved in to care for her mother after she sustained an injury to her hand that meant she was less able to look after herself. Likewise, the higher rates of disability for older adults living in 3three/four-person households could be due to adult children who themselves have children moving back in with their parents to care for them or, alternatively, bringing their parents to live with them in their home. Again, such a case can be seen in Chapter 6 where a daughter (Agatha) moved home from Dubai with her children to live with her mother (Josephine) after she had been widowed and suffered a paralytic stroke that required intensive care and rehabilitation.

Effect of household size on older persons' survival

The mean survival rates with 95 per cent confidence interval (CI) were calculated and compared for each group to test for statistically significant difference. Figure 5.3 shows the average number of years from 2004 to death for men and women separately. Older men had an overall average of nine years' (95 per cent CI: 9.14–9.63) survival and women had an average of 10.6 years (95 per cent CI: 10.327–10.800). If we look at the

Figure 5.3: Mean number of years and 95% confidence intervals until death for men and women by household size in 2004 (N = 3033)

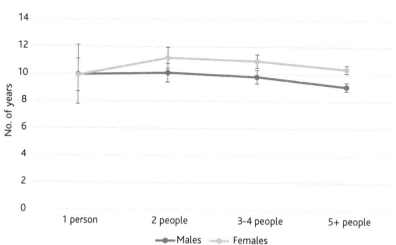

pattern by household size, we can see that, for women, those in two- and three/four-person households had a slightly higher average length of survival compared to those in one-person households or those with five or more inhabitants. However, the differences are not huge; for example, women in one-person households lived for a further 9.9 years on average, while those in two-person households lived for an average of a further 11.2 years. For men the pattern is even flatter, with hardly any difference in the survival rates between those in one-, two- or 3three/ four-person households and only a slight drop for those in households of five or more inhabitants.

Figures 5.4 and 5.5 show the Kaplan–Meier survival curves based on the HH size for older men and women. Although all curves decreased throughout the course of the follow-up years, the reduction was greater in the households with more than five members. The reduction times are ordered from the smallest to the largest with the censored data.

In order to control for the various covariates, Cox proportional hazard regression analyses were performed. It is assumed that the ratio of hazard rates is constant across study period and is the same for each time interval. Hence, the hazard ratio represents the risk of event (death in survival analysis) in the treatment group compared to control group at any time during the study period. Here, Cox regression analysis was performed to find the effect of household size after adjusting for the ADL score, health perception, sex and age. The results in Table 5.5 show that after adjusting for these factors, the older people in two-person and three/four-person households have a significantly lower risk of death compared to the older

Figure 5.4: Kaplan–Meier survival curves for men based on household size in 2004

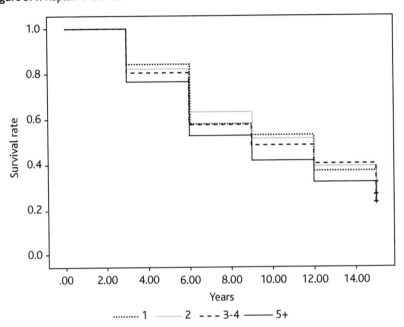

persons living with five or more family members. There was no statistically significant difference in the risk of dying for those living alone compared to those living in households with five or more people. Hence, living alone was not a risk factor for mortality.

Discussion

This chapter examined the association between survival status and risk of mortality on the basis of changes in household size. We found that the health of older persons improved as the years progressed (see Table 5.4) which is contrary to the assumption that self-rated health would decline with age. In terms of living arrangements, the data showed that the majority of older persons live with more than five family members in Kerala. The study found that older persons who live with one other person had a lower chance of dying, while those who lived with five or more household members had an increased risk of mortality. This finding remained even after adjusting for daily living activities score, health perception, sex and age.

Households in Kerala underwent a process of shrinking household size due to the decreasing birth rates and a decline in the availability of younger adults as a result of migration. The impact of migration has reduced population growth, and sex ratio favourable to females (Rajan and Sivakumar, 2018; Rajan and Sunitha, 2021). There has been a decrease in potential care

Figure 5.5: Kaplan–Meier survival curves for women based on household size in 2004

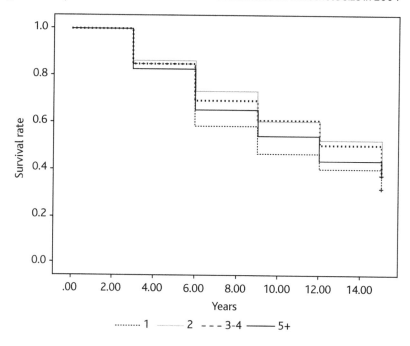

Table 5.5: The Cox regression analysis for older persons based on their household size, Kerala Ageing Survey, 2004–19

	Hazard ratio (95% CI)
1-person household	0.94 (0.72–1.23)
2-person household	**0.86 (0.74–0.99)**
3–4-person household	**0.87 (0.78–0.97)**
5+ person household (reference)	
No limitations in activities of daily living	**0.49 (0.44–0.55)**
Limitations in activities of daily living (reference)	
Good/Excellent health	**0.69 (0.61–0.78)**
Fair health	**0.73 (0.66–0.81)**
Poor or very poor health (reference)	
Male	**1.42 (1.30–1.55)**
Female (reference)	
60–69	**0.34 (0.30–0.39)**
70–79	**0.65 (0.58–0.73)**
80+ (reference)	

Note: Figures in **bold** are significant at the p<0.5 level.

and support for the older people of these households. The number of older persons living alone or living with their spouse only is increasing. Health and financial status determine in part who can live alone (Burr and Mutchler, 1992). Hence, the increase in the proportion of older adults living independently could be a product of improvements in their health and health behaviours. Indeed, the evidence suggests that older adults tend move to households with more members following a decline in their health (Korinek, Zimmer and Gu, 2011). Zimmer and Korinek (2010) have shown that older adults who have died (an outcome positively correlated with widowhood and relatively poor functional health) are more likely to have shifted their co-residence situation during the survey interval than those who had survived. In deciding where to live, older people often view their existing home or community as having the advantages of maintaining a sense of connection, security and familiarity, and as being related to their sense of identity and autonomy (Brooker, 2015). Nevertheless, a change in living arrangements can have an impact on their environment, since it may force them to remain in their current residence or to relocate to a more supportive environment (Greenblat, 2012). Rogers (1996) found that the risk of mortality influences the living arrangements of older persons. The results from the analysis in the current chapter, examining the the risk of mortality among older adults who lived in larger households, lends support to this argument. Another study found that older people who live with other household members for health reasons may curtail their activities and therefore remain dependent and socially isolated (Mindel and Wright, 1982). The distress associated with illness can aggravate disease and increase the risk of death (Antonucci, 1990). However, it must also be noted that mortality risks also depend on the relationship between the carer and the older person (Wang et al, 2015). Hence, future research should also incorporate measures of the quality of the interpersonal, and any caregiving, relationships in the household.

The socio-economic condition of the household helps older persons by providing care and financial support. According to Rajan and Kumar (2003), care and support given to older persons are essential for their well-being. They found that support can be provided through financial assistance, such as pension and social security, and care can be provided via emotional support from family members or by those persons with whom the older persons live (Rajan et al, 2020). Several studies in China explained the association of living arrangements and health of older adults. The researchers found that those living with family members had a more than three times higher risk of disability than those living alone (Chen et al, 2015; Chen, 2017). There is a significant association between care, dependency and household size.

As in most countries, women in India live longer than men and the proportion of women, especially widows, has increased over the years.

Older men usually receive care from their spouse, but the majority of older women may not receive care from that source. Upon widowhood, older women undergo a shift in their living arrangements from living with spouse to either living alone or living with adult children, while a few older men face the same situation. In a study by Chaudhuri and Kakoli (2009) it was observed that older women are more likely to live alone than older men, irrespective of their socio-economic and demographic characteristics, health status and economic independence.

Conclusion

In India, it is traditionally the duty of children to provide support for parents as they age. The common assumption is that this is done through co-residence (Jadhav et al, 2013). However, migration of children in search of employment from their birthplace has impacted on the family structure in India. In the absence of children for support, spouses act as caregivers when needed and seek help from their children and other immediate relatives only in case of emergencies (Rajan and Sunitha, 2019). This is thought to be a particular issue in Kerala as it has the highest rates of out-migration of any state in India, as well as experiencing rates of population ageing that are comparable to countries in the developed world.

However, as the figures presented in this chapter show, a high proportion of the population aged 60 and over in Kerala still live with their family members. Indeed, from 2004 to 2019 many of the sample members moved into households with three/four or even five or more people. This strongly suggests that opportunities for co-residence are still very much available in Kerala. Moreover, there does not appear to be clear evidence that older adults who live alone have worse health or have greater care needs than adults who live in households with greater numbers of inhabitants. This could be because older adults with better health are better able to live independently or because once older adults acquire some form of disability or impairment, they move in with other family members or the family members move in with them.

These results are interesting and raise some crucial questions about the assumptions around the impact of demographic change on older adults in Kerala and India more widely. There is still much research that needs to be done to gain a fully comprehensive picture of the changing nature of living arrangements and care for older adults in Kerala. It would be desirable if future research could explore whether older adults who become widowed move in with their families and whether this leads to a change in health and/or whether the likelihood of moving in with family is mediated by their health. More work could be done to look at whether specific limitations in activities of daily living are associated with changing living arrangements, for example, whether some limitations are easier to manage at home, while others require support from children/relatives.

References

Agarwal, S. (2012) 'Effect of living arrangement on the health status of elderly in India', *Asian Population Studies*, 8(1): 87–101.

Albertini, M., Kohli, M. and Vogel, C. (2007) 'Intergenerational transfers of time and money in European families: common patterns-different regimes?', *Journal of European Social Policy*, 17(4): 319–34.

Antonucci, T. (1990) 'Social supports and social relationships', in R. H. Binstock and L. K. George (eds) *Handbook of Aging and the Social Sciences*, 3rd edn, New York: Academic Press, Inc., pp 205–6.

Bhat, P. N. M. and Rajan, I. S. (1990) 'Demographic transition in Kerala revisited', *Economic and Political Weekly*, 25(35/36): 1957–980.

Bloom, D. E., Mahal, A., Rosenberg, L and Sevilla, J. (2010) 'Economic security arrangements in the context of population ageing in India', *International Social Security Review*, 63(3–4): 59–89.

Brooker, D. (2015) *Person-Centred Dementia Care: Making Services Better* (2nd edn), London: Jessica Kingsley Publishers.

Burr, J. A. and Mutchler, J. E. (1992) 'The living arrangements of unmarried elderly Hispanic females', *Demography*, 29: 93–112.

Chaudhuri, A. and Kakoli, R. (2009) 'Gender differences in living arrangements among older persons in India', *Journal of Asian and African Studies*, 44(3): 259–77.

Chen, X. (2017) 'Old age pension and intergenerational living arrangements: a regression discontinuity design', *Review of Economics of the Household*, 15(2): 455–76.

Chen, W., Fang, Y., Maom, F., Hao, S., Chen, J., Yuan, M., Han, Y. and Hong, Y. A. (2015) 'Assessment of disability among the elderly in Xiamen of China: a representative sample survey of 14,292 older adults', *PLoS One*, 10(6): e0131014.

Greenblat, C. (2012) *Love, Loss and Laughter: Seeing Alzheimer's Differently*, Guildford, CT: Lyons Press.

Guilmoto, C. Z. and Rajan, I. S. (eds) (2005) *Fertility Transition in South India*, New Delhi: Sage.

Jadhavapoorva, K. M., Sathyanarayana, S. K. and James, K. S. (2013) 'Living arrangements of the elderly in India: who lives alone and what are the patterns of familial support?', Presented in Session 301: Living arrangement and its effect on older people in ageing societies, IUSSP, Busan, Korea.

Korinek, K., Zimmer, Z. and Gu, D. (2011) 'Transitions in marital status and functional health and patterns of intergenerational coresidence among China's elderly population', *Journals of Gerontology: Social Science*, 66B (2): 260–70.

Liebig, P. S. and Rajan, S. I. (2003) 'An aging India: perspectives, prospects and policies', *Journal of Aging and Social Policy*, 15(2–3): 1–9.

Mindel, C. H. and Wright, Jr., R. (1982) 'Satisfaction in multigenerational house-holds', *Journals of Gerontology*, 37: 483–9.

Pollen, A. (2001) 'Living arrangements of older persons', *Living Arrangements of Older Persons: Critical Issues and Policy Responses*, 42, 54–110.

Rajan, S. I. (1989) 'Aging in Kerala: one more population problem?', *Asia-Pacific Population Journal*, 4(2): 19–48.

Rajan, S. I. (2004) 'From Kerala to the Gulf: Impacts of labour migration', *Asia Pacific Migration Journal*, 13(4): 497–510.

Rajan, S. I. (ed) (2013) *India Migration Report 2013: Social Costs of Migration*, New Delhi: Routledge.

Rajan, S. I., Mishra, U. S. and Sarma, P. S. (1995) 'Living arrangements among the Indian elderly', *Hong Kong Journal of Gerontology*, 9(2): 20–8.

Rajan, S. I. and Mishra, U. S. (1997a) 'Kerala: restructuring welfare programmes – emerging trends', *Economic and Political Weekly*, 32(6): 261–3.

Rajan, S. I. and Mishra, U. S. (1997b) 'Population aging: causes and consequences', in K. C. Zachariah and S. I. Rajan (eds) *Kerala's Demographic Transition: Determinants and Consequences*, New Delhi: Sage, pp 44–57.

Rajan, S. I. and Zachariah K. C. (1998) 'Long term implications of low fertility in Kerala', *Asia Pacific Population Journal*, 13(3): 41–66.

Rajan, S. I., Mishra, U. S. and Sarma, P. S. (1999) *India's Elderly: Burden or Challenge?*, New Delhi: Sage.

Rajan, S. I., Mishra, U. S. and Sarma, P. S. (2000) 'Aging in India: retrospect and prospect', *Indian Social Science Review*, 2(1): 1–47.

Rajan, S. I. and Kumar, S. (2003) 'Living arrangements among Indian elderly: new evidence from national family health survey', *Economic and Political Weekly*, 38(1): 75–80.

Rajan, S. I., Risseeuw, C. and Perera, M. (2008) *Institutional Provisions and Care for the Aged: Perspectives from Asia and Europe*, New Delhi: Anthem Press.

Rajan S. I. and Prasad, S. (2008) 'Pensions and social security in India', in S. I. Rajan, C. Risseeuw and M. Perera (eds) (2008) *Institutional Provisions and Care for the Aged: Perspectives from Asia and Europe*, New Delhi: Anthem Press.

Rajan, S. I. and Mishra, U. S. (2014) Situation of Elderly in Kerala: Evidence from Kerala Ageing Survey, 2013. Report submitted to the Government of Kerala.

Rajan, S. I. and Sunitha, S. (2015) 'Demography of ageing in India— 2011–2101', *HelpAge India Research and Development Journal*, 21(2): 13–22.

Rajan, S. I. and Balagopal, G. (2017) 'Caring India: an introduction', in S. I. Rajan and G. Balagopal (eds) *Elderly Care in India—Societal and State Response*, Singapore: Springer Nature.

Rajan S. I., Sunitha, S. and Arya, U. R. (2017) 'Elder care and living arrangement in Kerala', in S. I. Rajan and G. Balagopal (eds) *Elderly Care in India: Societal and State Responses*, Singapore: Springer.

Rajan S. I. and Sunitha, S. (2017) 'Life satisfaction among the elderly in Kerala – a longitudinal analysis', in S. I. Rajan and U. S. Mishra (ed) *India's Aged: Needs and Vulnerabilities*, Hyderabad: Orient Blackswan.

Rajan S.I. and P. Sivakumar (2018) *Youth Migration in Emerging India: Trends, Challenges and Opportunities*, New Delhi: Orient BlackSwan.

Rajan, S. I. and Sunitha, S. (2018) 'Demographic changes in Kerala', in B. A. Prakash and J. Alwin (eds) *Kerala's Economy Since 2000: Emerging Issues*, New Delhi: Sage.

Rajan, S. I. and Sunitha, S. (2018) 'Empowering the elderly by giving dignity, geriatrics health hülyaçakmur', IntechOpen, https://www.intechopen. com/books/geriatrics-health/empowering-the-elderly-by-giving-dignity

Rajan S. I. and Sunitha, S. (2019) 'Living arrangements among the elderly', *Geography and You*, 19(19–20): 26–31.

Rajan, S. I. and Mishra, U. S. (2020) *Senior Citizens of India: Emerging Challenges and Concerns*, Singapore: Springer.

Rajan, S. I., Shajan, A. and Sunitha, S. (2020) 'Ageing and elderly care in Kerala', *China Report*, 56(3): 354–73.

Rajan, S. I. and Sunitha, S. (2021) 'Demographic dimensions and gerontological issues in India', in M. K. Shankardass (ed) *Gerontological Concerns and Responses in India*, Berlin: Springer, pp 57–64.

Rogers, R. G. (1996). 'The effects of family composition, health, and social support linkages on mortality', *Journal of Health and Social Behavior*, 37(4): 326–38.

Saraceno, C. (2008) 'Patterns of family living in the enlarged EU', in J. Alber, T. Fahey and C. Saqraceno (eds) *Handbook of Quality of Life in the Enlarged European Union*, London and New York: Routledge, pp 47–72.

Sudha, S., Rajan, S. I. and Sarma, P. S. (2004) 'Intergenerational family support for older men and women in South India', *Indian Journal of Gerontology*, 18 (3–4): 449–65.

Sudha, S., Suchindran, C., Mutran, E. J. Rajan, S. I. and Sarma, P. S. (2006) 'Marital status, family ties, and self-rated health among elders in South India', *Journal of Cross-Cultural Gerontology*, 21(3–4): 103–20.

Tohme, R., Yount, K., Yassine, S., Shideed, O. and Sibai, A. (2011) 'Socioeconomic resources and living arrangements of older adults in Lebanon: who chooses to live alone?', *Ageing and Society*, 31(1): 1.

Ugargol, A. P., Hutter, I., James, K. S. and Bailey, A. (2016) 'Care needs and caregivers: associations and effects of living arrangements on caregiving to older adults in India', *Ageing International*, 41: 193–213.

Vlassof, C. (1990) 'The value of sons in an Indian village: how widows see it', *Population Studies*, 44(1): 5–20.

Wang, X., Robinson, K. M. and Hardin, H. K. (2015) 'The impact of caregiving on caregivers' medication adherence and appointment keeping', *Western Journal of Nursing Research*, 37(12): 1548–62.

Zachariah, K. C. and Rajan, S. I. (2004) Gulf Revisited: Economic Consequences of Emigration from Kerala: Emigration and Unemployment. Centre for Development Studies (Thiruvananthapuram) Working Paper No.363.

Zachariah, K. C. and Rajan, S. I. (2007) Economic and Social Dynamics of Migration in Kerala, 1999–2004: Analysis of Panel Data. Centre for Development Studies (Thiruvananthapuram) Working Paper No.384.

Zachariah, K. C. and Rajan, S. I. (2009) *Migration and Development: The Kerala Experience*, New Delhi: Daanish Publishers.

Zimmer, Z. and Korinek, K. (2010) 'Shifting coresidence near the end of life: comparing decedents and survivors of a follow-up study in China', *Demography*, 47: 537–54.

6

Care arrangements for older adults: exploring the intergenerational contract in emigrant households of Goa, India

Allen P. Ugargol, Ajay Bailey, Inge Hutter and K. S. James

Introduction

Demographic ageing and the associated changes in population health are necessitating a complex reorientation of health systems, public spending, social security and living arrangements of older adults in developing countries (Bloom et al, 2015; Goodman and Harper, 2013; Lamb, 2013). In countries such as India, the consequences of ageing are far more severe because insufficient social security systems make families the main providers of support to older adults (Bloom et al, 2010). Changing demographic circumstances, such as the increased mobility of adult children, fewer siblings and increased longevity of parents, are influencing care arrangements in Indian households (Croll, 2006; Dhillon et al, 2016). The BKPAI (2011) study on the elderly in India reports that 6.2 per cent of older adults live alone, 14.9 per cent live exclusively with their spouse and 78.9 per cent of them live with children and other family members respectively, and importantly, the proportion of older adult women who live alone is nearly four times in comparison to older adult men (Ugargol et al, 2016). The traditional Indian family is in transition and the *modified extended family* where parents, children and other relatives do not necessarily live under one roof or share a hearth is now becoming common (Rajan and Kumar, 2003; Medora, 2007). Simultaneously, a cultural norm exists in India that older adults will continue to live with and receive their care from family members (Bongaarts and Zimmer, 2002; Ruggles and Heggeness, 2008) and living alone or in old age homes is interpreted as a sign of breakdown of traditional Indian values in public discourses (Medora, 2007; Lamb, 2013).

Though migration of adult children is considered one of the most effective poverty reduction strategies for families in the developing world (Stark and Lucas, 1988; Clemens, 2011) and increased incomes from migration can provide support for parents left behind, often the physical presence of a caregiver is the most desired but missing element (Bohme et al, 2015; Dobrina et al, 2015). Miltiades (2002) found from her study of left-behind Indian older parents that migration of adult children changes household dynamics and leaves families, mainly older adults, in disarray. Migration, whether in-country or overseas, tends to create nuclear family units and more often the older family members are left behind (Miltiades, 2002; Varghese and Patel, 2004; Ugargol et al, 2016; Ugargol and Bailey, 2020). In lower- and middle-income countries such as India, the care needs of older adults are invariably managed by family members in the absence of state-supported services (Brinda et al, 2014; Ugargol et al, 2016) (see Chapter 11 for a list of programmes for older adults in India). When adult children move away for employment or post marriage to set up a separate household, older couples who are left behind often reside independently for longer periods until the loss of spouse leads to the widowed parent either living alone or being incorporated into one of the adult child's family (Croll, 2006; Ha and Ingersoll-Dayton, 2008). It is, however, interesting to note that adult children and their older parents, though living in separate households, make efforts to live in close proximity to each other so that care and support exchanges are easy to provide and receive (Croll, 2006; Mulder and van der Meer, 2009) under the intergenerational contract. On the other hand, Kochar (2002) and Azariadis and Lambertini (2003) have argued that despite the inability to commit to the intergenerational contract through co-residence, exchanges are clearly visible and continue through the life cycle between generations.

The goal of this chapter is to explore the evolving nature of care frameworks for older adults in the Indian context through examining the changing household living arrangements and complexities that exist in identifying caregiving motives and primary caregivers to older adults, especially in an emigration context where older adults are left behind. With this motive, we focus on Goa, a known emigration pocket in India and try to understand how migration affects family caregiving patterns and the dynamics that influence care arrangements for older adults in emigrant households. The findings from this study contribute to theory on co-residence, acknowledge reciprocity in the caregiving process and reflect on the cultural influences that guide adaptive intergenerational care arrangements (Johar et al, 2015; Isherwood et al, 2016), especially in an emigration context. The accounts of caregivers and older adults are 'situated' according to the status of the interactants and are standardised within the cultural context; hence reflecting routinely expected behaviours (Scott and Lyman, 1968) while capitalising and treating the relationship as a reciprocal one (Sykes and Matza, 2002; Ugargol and Bailey, 2021).

Evidence indicates that care and support from children is obtained in return for intergenerational transfers and exchanges from the older adult. Older adults offer their material wealth as an incentive in order to earn reciprocation through co-residence or receive support through intergenerational care arrangements (Johar et al, 2015; Isherwood et al, 2016). However, co-residence with adult children might not always be beneficial for older adults even after they have carefully selected one among their children to live with. There are also instances of older adults being neglected by adult children who received their property and intergenerational wealth but failed to provide care and support in return (Skirbekk and James, 2014). To address such issues of neglect and abuse, the Maintenance and Welfare of Parents and Senior Citizens Act (Government of India, 2007) provides for legislative and legal support to older parents and senior citizens in India. Not only can the older parent now claim maintenance from the children to whom he had given the property by way of gift or otherwise but can also reclaim his property from the transferee in case of neglect and abuse. Though parents do not have much choice in determining who will receive a share in the property in cases of ancestral property, it was however observed that parents *gifted* their share of land to their sons, who are culturally expected to care for their parents, in order to circumvent the law (Deininger et al, 2013). Daughters were often compensated for this disinheritance through alternative transfers in the form of either higher dowries or more education (Roy, 2015).

Care for older adults is understood to be shared by a complex but cooperative array of caretakers (Brijnath, 2012) as individual family members are finding it difficult to provide care individually owing to increasing mobility, urbanisation and development of nuclear households (Dhillon et al, 2016). Apart from co-residence and close-proximity residence, even separate nuclear households in which older and younger family members reside separated by geographical distance are enmeshed in complex webs of intergenerational exchanges, and are termed *embedded* households (Whyte, 2003; Croll, 2006). Attempts by older adults and their adult children to retain traditional kinship ties and functional reciprocal exchanges in the backdrop of modernisation are visible through the formation of adaptive intergenerational living arrangements (Smith and Whitlock, 2004; Croll, 2006). We term these adaptive living arrangements as *intergenerational care arrangements* that encompass all forms of negotiated support arrangements for older adults either through co-residence or various forms of non-co-resident care arrangements such as close-proximity residence and distant but 'embedded' households – the ultimate aim being to enable and sustain intergenerational resource flows between children and their older parents.

In this chapter we examine how the contract of intergenerational reciprocity is maintained between older adults and their adult children through the formation of adaptive intergenerational care arrangements.

We qualitatively explore how older adults and their caregivers recognise, negotiate and interpret reciprocal support motives that influence and result in adaptive reciprocal intergenerational care arrangements and caregiving decisions relying on in-depth interviews of older adults and their family caregivers from emigrant households of Goa.

Background and concepts

Intergenerational care arrangements

Though the intergenerational filial contract is clearly visible even today, there seems to be a reinterpretation and renegotiation of the intergenerational living arrangement (Croll, 2006; Brijnath, 2012). What hitherto resulted chiefly in co-residence is now increasingly depicted through other newer forms of adaptive living and care arrangements. Firstly, when we look at co-residence as a type of intergenerational care arrangement, there are two ways in which this can be established. Either the younger generation continues to reside with older parents after marriage or alternatively the younger generation establishes a separate household at the time of marriage, birth of children or when there is a household division into which widowed parents are later incorporated. The second possibility is that even when adult children do not co-reside with their parents, they try to remain in close proximity so that there is in essence no real breakdown in intergenerational resource flows. Thirdly, even when generations live in separate households geographically dispersed due to occupational mobility or migration, they rely on the greater ease of communication and transport that facilitate intergenerational resource flows across the distance through what are called 'embedded' or 'enmeshed' households (Whyte, 2003; Croll, 2006). We, therefore, build on the work of Croll (2006), Brijnath (2012) and Whyte (2003) and consider *intergenerational care arrangements* as all forms of care arrangements that enable continued intergenerational resource flows between children and older parents irrespective of whether they co-reside, reside nearby (proximate residence) or are geographically dispersed (distant).

Reciprocal motives in the formation of intergenerational care arrangements

Reciprocity has been recognised as an abiding norm that directs support exchanges between parents and their children across the life course and is a central tenet of both equity and social exchange theory (Silverstein et al, 2002; Lowenstein et al, 2007; Leopold and Raab, 2013; Ugargol and Bailey, 2021). Though co-residence can be regarded as a form of reciprocation for parental investment (Croll, 2006; Johar et al, 2015; Isherwood et al,

2016), the motives to co-reside, reside close to the older parents or to remain connected through embedded households are driven by reciprocal calculations. These filial notions of obligation are embedded within a context of indebtedness due to parents in return for early care during childhood (Croll, 2006; Sharma and Kemp, 2012) and children who have received greater investments from their parents in terms of time, money and affection are more likely than other siblings to similarly reciprocate when the parent experiences challenges in later life such as widowhood or health concerns (Silverstein et al, 2006b; Johar et al, 2015; Ugargol and Bailey, 2021) through co-residence and giving time (Johar et al, 2015; Isherwood et al, 2016).

With adult child migration, mobility and other factors, care and support exchange for older parents through non-co-residence is also increasingly visible in the Indian context (Vera-Sanso, 1999; Desai and Banerji, 2008). Living apart from children does not necessary preclude exchanges of support between generations just as co-residence does not automatically guarantee support for the older adult (Antonucci et al, 2011). Since provision of care needs personal contact, greater direct costs as well as opportunity costs of caregiving rise for those who live far from the parental home (Pillemer and Suitor, 2014; Ugargol and Bailey, 2021) and children who live in closer proximity are more likely to become caregivers for their parents (Mulder and van der Meer, 2009). Adult children who live abroad contribute remittances to their older parents in exchange for the custodial care of grandchildren and maintaining the family property (Antonucci et al, 1990; Silverstein et al, 2006a; Roff et al, 2007; Singh et al, 2010; Ugargol and Bailey, 2021) and provide emotional support exchanges through regular communication (Ingersoll-Dayton et al, 2001). While poor health, disability and loss of spouse are key triggers which motivate adaptive intergenerational care arrangements between older parents and adult children (Sengupta and Agree, 2002; Medora, 2007; Li et al, 2009), on the other hand, adult children could also be motivated to seek co-residence with parents when they need assistance from their parents, including financial support, childcare and as a mechanism to offset the rising costs of housing (Forrest Zhang, 2004; Croll, 2006; Goodman and Harper, 2013).

Culture, gender and intergenerational care arrangements

Though traditional multi-generational joint family households are decreasing in India together with a rise in the number of nuclear households (Croll, 2006; Dhillon et al, 2016), there is still a substantially high rate of intergenerational co-residence (see Chapters 3, 4 and 5 for the changing nature of co-residence) compared to the developed world (Croll, 2006; Bawdekar and Ladusingh, 2012). However, a paradox exists between traditional expectations for assisting parents and actual support available when it comes to older parent–adult child relationships. Gender assumes significance in intergenerational care arrangements as greater numbers of women are widowed compared to men (Sengupta and Agree, 2002; Ugargol et al, 2016) and culturally older women seek support and co-residence with their son/sons in exchange for property and assets (Medora, 2007; Brijnath, 2012; Ugargol and Bailey, 2021). Co-residence seems to help integrate widowed older women into the sociocultural nucleus of the family (Wells and Kendig, 1997; Knodel and Saengtienchai, 1999; Lamb, 2013), provides them a sense of belonging and purpose (Van Willigan and Chaddha, 1999) and is associated with improved health outcomes (Sengupta and Agree, 2002). After the death of the spouse when the headship of the household is transferred to the oldest son (Sengupta and Agree, 2002), older women find protection in co-residing with their sons and it is assumed that the property and assets will transfer to the oldest son (Brijnath, 2012; Ugargol and Bailey, 2021).

In India where sons are culturally responsible for parent care, the actual caregiving role is most often handled by their wives, that is, daughters-in-law of the older adult (Jamuna and Ramamurti, 1999; Kadoya and Khan, 2015; Ugargol and Bailey, 2018, 2021) and the relationship between the parent-in-law and the daughter-in-law often dictates the course and type of intergenerational care arrangement (Jamuna and Ramamurti, 1999; Vera-Sanso, 1999; Allendorf, 2015; Ugargol and Bailey, 2018, 2021). The preference to co-reside with sons rather than daughters becomes clearer when we understand the context of Indian marriage customs and kinship system in which daughters are considered as lost into the natal family after marriage (Medora, 2007). Older women have strong ties with daughters; however, there is also equal antipathy towards co-residing with daughters (Bhat and Dhruvarajan, 2001; Kalavar and Jamuna, 2011). In the physical absence of the emigrant son, however, the responsibility of care provision is perceived by older adults to be shared among the other children, including the daughters (Dharmalingam, 1994; Miltiades, 2002; Ugargol and Bailey, 2018).

Therefore, intergenerational care arrangements for older adults in India assume special significance since support and care mechanisms are mutually negotiated between adult children and parents given the reliance on the family and not on the state to care for older adults (Medora, 2007; Brijnath, 2012; Ugargol et al, 2016). The intergenerational care contract between older parents and their adult children (Croll, 2006) continues to be the framework for filial and familial obligations albeit with changing needs and circumstances. In order to support more balanced and symmetrical resource flows, intergenerational living arrangements are being continuously adapted and adjusted to accommodate changes in parental needs as well as to suit the availability, familiarity, motivation and preference of family caregivers. These accounts of older adults and their caregivers in reflecting on their care exchange relationships are situated in the cultural context and rely on the status of the interactants (Scott and Lyman, 1968). Through analysis of in-depth interviews of older adults and their family caregivers from emigrant households in Goa, we qualitatively explore how different forms of intergenerational care arrangements emerge as negotiated reciprocal contracts between adult children and their older adults to enable reciprocal support exchanges.

Ageing and migration in Goa: the context

Goa is the smallest state in India with an area of 3,702 km² and measures 105 km from north to south and 62 km from east to west. Goa has one of the best health and development indices among other Indian states (Patel and Prince, 2001; Mukherjee et al, 2016). The primary language in Goa is Konkani, though Marathi, Hindi and English are also commonly spoken (Newman, 1988). Sporadic migration from Goa, voluntary and forced, has been witnessed for centuries. Goa was a Portuguese colony for over four centuries until 1961 when it was liberated by the Indian army and became a Union Territory of India along with Daman and Diu. Goa eventually attained complete statehood in 1987 in the Indian Union (da Silva Gracias, 2000). Consequent to the formation of the new state of Goa, it was divided into two districts, North Goa and South Goa, with their headquarters at Panaji and Margao respectively.

Goans, have been migrating for centuries: before, during and after the colonial period. In the first phase that covers the sixteenth and seventeenth centuries, Goans migrated primarily to the neighbouring kingdoms of India. During the colonial times, when India was ruled by the British, Goans predominantly migrated to British India and Africa. In the last phase of migration, that is, the postcolonial phase, Goans migrated to the Gulf, the West (Europe, Canada, USA and Brazil) as well as to Australia and New Zealand. Since the oil-boom, Goans have been migrating to the Gulf, where conditions arising from the discovery of oil provided good job opportunities (da Silva Gracias, 2001). In recent years, many Goans have reclaimed their Portuguese nationality so that they can migrate to Europe, giving them an opportunity to work and settle across Europe. Portuguese nationality is available to any individual who can prove s/he was born in or has/had a parent or grandparent born in Portuguese India prior to 1961 and this has resulted in a new migration industry in Goa (da Silva Gracias, 2001).

Among Indian states, the proportion of older adults in Goa at 11.2 per cent of the total population is second only to the state of Kerala with a proportion of 12.6 per cent and considerably higher than the Indian average of 8.6 per cent (General, I.R., 2011). The mean size of Goan households based on the 2011 census is 4.52 (Nayak and Behera, 2014) and parents usually live with their sons, son's wife and grandchildren. Migration and seafaring have been a traditional and historically documented occurrence in Goa, is male-dominated and women and children are notably left behind (Sampson, 2005; Government of India, 2008; Tumbe, 2012). In emigrant households of Goa, 31 per cent of older adults lived with their spouses exclusively, while 46 per cent of them lived with either married sons or married daughters (Government of India, 2008). Emigration from Goa is predominantly seen among the Christian population (42 emigrants per 100 households) although they make up only a fourth of the state's population (Frenz, 2008; Government of India, 2008). While South Goa had a higher emigration rate of 22.8 emigrants per 100 households compared to 10.7 emigrants for North Goa, the Salcete taluk municipality (in South Goa) had the highest emigration index of 40.4 emigrants per 100 households (Government of India, 2008).

Prior research on intergenerational support exchanges from Goa's emigration context is scarce and reciprocal motivations to caregiving and care arrangements between emigrant/non-emigrant children and their parents have not been explored. The formation of adaptive intergenerational care arrangements that make it conducive for support exchanges between parents and adult children to exist and continue is also underexplored. Goa, being one of the most developed states in India, presents a compelling setting for examining the intergenerational care contract under the influence of modernisation and emigration of adult children.

Methods
Setting and participant profile

The study was conducted in Salcete taluk, a district of South Goa, which boasts of the highest emigration index among all taluks in the state of Goa. The field site for this study included the adjoining towns of Chinchinim, Navelim, Verna, Varca and Benaulin in Salcete taluk. Given the safety concerns and vulnerability of older adults, it was felt inappropriate to randomly knock on people's doors to ask about the composition of the family. Moreover, since there were no available lists that we could access which described the household composition, a snowball technique was employed to recruit the participants. The first group of participants were recruited during an interactive workshop organised for older adults by Caritas-Goa, a charitable society organization under the Archdiocese of Goa, at Panaji. The researcher used this opportunity to briefly introduce his proposed research to the participants. Thereon, the researcher made contact with older adults and sought their consent to participate in the study. Using a snowball technique where each participant helped identify another left-behind older adult in the neighbourhood, 22 older adults, aged above 60 years, and their corresponding primary caregivers were approached and recruited for the study.

Table 6.1 describes the sample. Primary caregivers were identified by the older adults themselves. Caregivers were required to be primarily co-residing with the older adult. Criteria for older adults required that they had to be aged 60 years and above and have at least one emigrant adult child. Of the 22 caregivers, nine were daughters-in-law, five were female spousal caregivers (wives), there was one male spousal caregiver (husband), five daughter-caregivers and two sons as caregivers. Caregivers ranged from 35 to 78 years old, while older adults ranged in age from 60 to 102. Nine of the older adults were currently married while 13 were widowed. All participants were native to the region and spoke Konkani as well as English. The researcher employed the services of a local interpreter for the interviews that were carried out in Konkani. Twenty-three interviews were conducted in Konkani and 21 interviews in English based on the participants' preferences. Households that participated in the study represented the middle to lower socio-economic class of society and all families identified themselves as Catholic Christians. Many of the households reflected Portuguese cultural influence and many of these families had ties with family members who had chosen to move to Portugal. It is important to note that seafaring children would return home once or twice a year and spend a few months at home, while those working abroad on oil rigs, for example, would return home more frequently.

Ethics

The study was submitted for ethical approval and was approved by the Institutional Ethics Review Board of the University of Groningen, the Netherlands. Participants were informed about the study objectives and explained the interview process. After obtaining written informed consent to conduct the interviews and to audio-record the conversations, interviews were conducted at the convenience of the participants. Privacy and anonymity were observed. Pseudonyms have been used to provide context but not to link the participant.

Data collection

Between October 2014 and March 2015, 44 in-depth interviews that involved 22 older adults and 22 caregivers were conducted in Salcete taluk, South Goa. Semi-structured in-depth interview guides were employed. The first author conducted

Table 6.1: Description of older adults and their caregivers: Goa

| Primary caregiver details | | | | Details of older adult | | | | Details of children | | Co-resides with |
Co-resident caregiver	Name	Age	Work history	Name	Marital status	Age	Gender	Emigrant children	Non-emigrant children	
Daughter-in-law	Andrea	55	Homemaker	Magdalene	Widowed	78	F	2 sons, both seafarers	Both daughters of older adult live in Goa	Elder daughter-in-law and grandchildren
	Monica	41	Homemaker	Elizabeth	Married	73	F	2 sons, both seafarers	Daughter lives in Goa	Spouse, elder daughter-in-law and grandchildren
	Rachel	45	Homemaker; had been employed	Mary	Widowed	84	F	1 son, worked in Dubai initially, now a seafarer	2 daughters live in Goa, 1 in Mumbai	Daughter-in-law and grandchildren
	Archangel	37	Homemaker; had worked earlier	Isabel	Married	75	F	1 son, seafarer	2 daughters live in Goa	Spouse, daughter-in-law and grandchildren
	Natalia	39	Homemaker; had been employed	Jennifer	Widowed	70	F	1 son, seafarer	2 daughters live in Goa	Daughter-in-law and grandchildren
	Ana	52	Homemaker; had been employed as a teacher	Peter	Widowed	102	M	2 sons, both seafarers	4 daughters live in Goa, 1 son lives in Mumbai	Wife of youngest son (daughter-in-law) and grandchildren

(continued)

Table 6.1: Description of older adults and their caregivers: Goa (continued)

Primary caregiver details				Details of older adult				Details of children		Co-resides with
Co-resident caregiver	Name	Age	Work history	Name	Marital status	Age	Gender	Emigrant children	Non-emigrant children	
	Lorna	45	Homemaker; gave up her nursing career	Patricia	Widowed	75	F	1 son, worked in Dubai initially, now a seafarer	2 sons and 3 daughters live in Goa	Wife of younger son (daughter-in-law) and grandchildren
	Rita	35	Homemaker	Joana	Widowed	72	M	1 son, seafarer	None	Daughter-in-law and grandchild
	Sabina	30	Currently homemaker; doctor by profession	Louisa	Widowed	88	F	3 sons, one each in USA, Australia and Canada; 1 daughter, works in USA.	1 son and 1 daughter live in Goa	Youngest son, daughter-in-law and grandchild
Wife	Lucy	60	Homemaker; had worked abroad	Rosario	Married	67	M	2 sons, both seafarers	Daughter lives in Goa	Spouse
	Rose	65	Homemaker	Anton	Married	75	M	1 son, seafarer	3 daughters live in Goa	Spouse, daughter-in-law and grandchildren
	Martha	61	Currently employed; had worked as nanny in Kuwait	Laurence	Married	60	M	Both sons, seafarers; daughter, working in Kuwait	None	Spouse

(continued)

Table 6.1: Description of older adults and their caregivers: Goa (continued)

Primary caregiver details				Details of older adult				Details of children		
Co-resident caregiver	Name	Age	Work history	Name	Marital status	Age	Gender	Emigrant children	Non-emigrant children	Co-resides with
Co-resident caregiver	Agnes	68	Homemaker; had worked in fields	Paul	Married	81	M	1 daughter, working in United Kingdom	Son lives in Goa	Spouse, son, daughter-in-law and grandchildren
	Marianne	52	Homemaker; entrepreneur	Vincent	Married	68	M	1 daughter, works in USA as physiotherapist	1 daughter works in Mumbai, India	Spouse
Husband	Sebastian	78	Retired	Perpetua	Married	72	F	1 son, seafarer; 1 daughter, works in Muscat	1 son lives in Goa	Spouse
Daughter	Catherine	53	Homemaker; had worked abroad in Muscat	Margaret	Widowed	80	F	1 son, was a seafarer initially, now works in the Netherlands	2 sons and 3 daughters live in Goa	Youngest daughter and grandchild
	Sophie	51	Homemaker	Veronica	Widowed	82	F	1 son, seafarer; 1 daughter, works in Kuwait	2 daughters and 1 son live in Goa, 2 daughters live in Mumbai	Fourth daughter and grandchildren
	Teresa	35	Fisherwoman	Crescentia	Widowed	60	F	1 daughter, lives in United Kingdom	1 son and 1 daughter live in Goa	Son and daughter-in-law; although spent much the day time with daughter and son-in-law

(continued)

Table 6.1: Description of older adults and their caregivers: Goa (continued)

Primary caregiver details			Details of older adult				Details of children		
Co-resident caregiver	Name	Age	Work history	Name	Marital status	Age	Gender	Emigrant children	Non-emigrant children	Co-resides with
	Agatha	44	Homemaker; had worked in Dubai, returned to care for mother	Josephine	Widowed	80	F	1 daughter, works in Dubai	4 daughters are in India; 2 in Goa and 2 in Mumbai	Youngest daughter and grandchildren
	Lourdes	51	Fisherwoman	Hyacintha	Widowed	72	F	1 son and grandson, seafarers	1 son and 1 daughter live in Goa	Daughter and grandchildren
Son	Basil	38	Emigrant son; works in an oil rig abroad	Jacinta	Married	69	F	1 son, works in Africa	3 daughters live in Goa	Spouse, son, daughter-in-law and grandchild
	Leander	39	Entrepreneur; had worked abroad	Madeleine	Widowed	73	F	1 son and 1 daughter, both work in United Kingdom	1 son and 3 daughters live in Goa	Son, daughter-in-law and grandchildren

Note: All potential identifiers have been removed from the data. Pseudonyms have been used.

all interviews in the participants' homes at their convenience. Interviews ranged in duration from 45 minutes to 2 hours. Co-resident participants were interviewed separately based on their convenience. Interviews had to be rescheduled at times to provision for privacy. Confidentiality was maintained and answers provided by one were not shared with the other family member.

Older adults were asked to reflect on their care needs, the caregiving relationship, impact of emigration on the household, evaluation of care options, linked lives with their family members, cultural beliefs and expectations, perceived reciprocity in the care exchange process and caregiving contributions from children, children-in-law and other family members. Caregivers were asked to speak about their caregiving relationship, understanding of the needs of the older adult, motivation to providing care, perceived reciprocity in the care exchange process, support received from other family members and caregiving contributions of siblings or children-in-law. Interviews were conducted up to the point of data saturation.

Data analysis

Qualitative data used for analytical purposes were derived from both interview transcriptions and the researcher's field notes. All interviews were typed and transcribed verbatim. Interviews carried out in Konkani were transcribed into Konkani and then translated into English for textual analysis. The text was coded using Atlas.Ti Version 7.5.10 computer software. Specifically, we have followed these steps in data analysis: transcribing raw data verbatim, translating from Konkani to English, immersion in the data, importing data into Atlas.Ti, open coding, detailed line-by-line coding, identify concepts, axial coding, reassembling open codes into subcategories, selective coding and integrating theories and literature (social exchange). Refined codes and categories came up after multiple readings and re-examination of coded transcripts. From the primary codes that emerged we developed secondary codes such as 'expectations of care', 'care received from family', 'care options', 'caregiver perceptions', 'reciprocity', 'linked lives', 'perceptions of older adults' and 'gender'.

Intergenerational care arrangements: findings

The following themes emerged from analysis of in-depth interviews of caregivers and older adults and reflect how intergenerational co-residence and intergenerational care arrangements across households evolved as negotiated contracts and how reciprocity was effected through cultural norms, sharing of resources, recognising parental needs, care and support exchanges, sharing of caregiving responsibilities and practical negotiation of family obligations between older adults and their younger family members.

The themes that emerged are: (A) transition events and reciprocity in the formation of intergenerational co-residence; (B) exchange of care through intergenerational co-residence; (C) exchange of intergenerational care in close proximity households; and (D) exchange of intergenerational care through 'embedded' or 'enmeshed' separate nuclear households.

Transition events and reciprocity in the formation of intergenerational co-residence

Transition events such as widowhood, birth of a grandchild, increased parental care needs and emigration are known to direct adult children and older adults into incorporating either one into their household to co-reside. The reciprocal support exchanges that guide these patterns of co-residence and support and the ensuing resource flows come forth in this theme.

Perpetua lives with her husband Sebastian in a large house. Since Perpetua has been diagnosed with a type of cancer and is undergoing chemotherapy for it, she depends on her husband for care and support. Perpetua is quite relieved to note that she is able to co-reside with her husband until now and feels co-residing with her non-emigrant son would have meant tolerating the daughter-in-law with whom she did not share a particularly good relationship:

> 'younger fellow (son) also, he's a captain on the ship (paused) he has a flat in Bombay (paused) he stays in Bombay (*paused*) like that you know, he will (paused) I feel having such a big house (paused) built this house before they got married (paused) of course daughter was married, but then one way I feel, I'm thankful that God has not kept them here (paused) because that daughter-in-law, they come once in a while (smiles), where they do all the mischief (fights), (*paused*) they come sometime and they go.' (Perpetua, older adult, 72 years, Chinchinim)

Transition events such as the emigration of children often led older couples or widowed parents to co-reside with one of their adult children (often the daughter-in-law when the adult child had emigrated) either by being incorporated into their child's household or by incorporating the adult child into their household. Hyacintha, a widowed older adult, narrates how she moved into her daughter's household after the loss of her spouse and due to her health needs:

> 'at first I used to stay at my husband's place with my 3 children (*paused*), after he died (*paused*) then I fell sick and then my daughter brought

me here, before that I used to stay at my sister's place (*paused*), she got (suffered) a heart attack and expired.' (Hyacintha, older female, 72 years, Varca)

Lorna is the wife of Patricia's youngest son. Lorna currently co-resides with her mother-in-law, Patricia, and looks after her. Lorna's husband contributed his earnings (remittances) to demolish and restore the house and hence it was mutually understood that the house would be bequeathed to her husband:

> 'from the time I got married, I was here and this was her (mother-in-law's) house so I was brought here (*paused*) this was the old house (*paused*) so they (sisters-in-law) went separately (*paused*), my husband did not go because she did not want him to go. He was a mother's boy (*paused*) so she wanted him always to be with her (paused) first we use to stay in the old house. We demolished that and built this new one. Since we are staying here. I take care of all in the house. I take care of my mother-in-law.' (Lorna, daughter-in-law caregiver, 51 years, Verna)

This theme informs us how spouses tend to depend on each other as long as they are able to co-reside and manage on their own until events such as widowhood, emigration of an adult child or increased care needs necessitate them to either incorporate their children or children-in-law into their households or lead them to move into their children's households for care and security. Older adults who perceived that their care needs had increased often invited adult children, especially daughters, who were residing in close proximity, to move into their residence. This was often mutually beneficial as children who did not own a home found recourse to the parental home and the older adult benefitted from co-residence through care provision and security from the adult child. In other instances, adult children who had remained with their parents even after marriage and had contributed to the older adult's household through financial support, often remittances (if emigrant) and were on course to inherit the assets of the older adult in reciprocation.

Intergenerational care through co-residence

The motives and expectations that guided co-residence patterns between older parents and their adult children are described under this theme. The sub-themes below provide insights into how adults' decisions to co-reside with their sons, daughters-in-law or daughters were indicative of the reciprocal support exchanges perceived in their care relationships and the mutual aim to adapt and accommodate to the changing needs and circumstances in order to keep mutual resource flows going.

Older adults co-residing with adult sons

Many older adults who were co-residing with their adult sons were actually living in their own home which the adult son had not left even after his marriage. Expectations of support from children, realisation of support received and the role of daughters-in-law in this reciprocal arrangement who often continued to co-reside with the older adult even after their husbands emigrated is explained in this section.

Madeleine was widowed several years ago and continued to stay in her house alone. Her youngest son, Leander, decided to return from abroad to co-reside with her, along with his wife and children. Madeleine's eldest son and the eldest daughter have emigrated to the United Kingdom, while her other three daughters are married and live in Goa.

> 'Sometimes, those who are in Goa (*daughters*), they come and visit me. The one in Neura, she come every Saturday for mass, comes here for coffee, she is also a teacher, the other one also comes. I live here with Leander, his wife and his 2 sons and the servant. He has a factory there and all the people of the factory also stay here. My thinking is like that (*paused*), we have to put in your children's mind to do all those things when they are young to look after the elderly people.' (Madeleine, older female, 73 years, Benaulin)

Co-residence with an adult son, however, was not always mutually reciprocal or beneficial as there were instances where parents perceived neglect and felt disconnected in the co-residential relationship. Crescentia's daughter had emigrated and although she co-resided with her son and daughter-in-law in her own home, she perceived no care and support from her son although the house belonged to her. She felt neglected and would end up at her daughter's doorstep (who lived nearby) every day for care and support:

> 'he is not supporting me like how a son should be with his mother (*paused*), my son only has to do this (care for me) now because my daughters have got married and he is at home. He is not looking after me that's why I am coming here (daughter's house).' (Crescentia, older female, 60 years, Navelim)

Basil works on an oil rig offshore in Africa and returns home every second month for a few days. His mother Jacinta is 69 years old and lives with her husband, daughter-in-law (Basil's wife) and grandchild. Jacinta identified Basil as her primary caregiver and his temporary absence from the household does not seem to affect the caregiving role that she identifies with Basil.

Basil felt caregiving was an extension of his relationship with the co-residing mother:

> 'Ya, as I said, it is not one person (not only me) who looks after her. I have an old dad also, basically she needs some extra care that is the only thing, otherwise duties are the same.' (Basil, emigrant son, 38 years, Verna)

In co-residing with their adult sons, older adults would select one among their children for the role and expected to receive care and support from their children and daughters-in-law in return for bequeathing ownership to the house and property. This pattern of co-residence is interesting to note since one among the many children is selected into this role and he or she continues to live with the parent while other children emigrate or move away to setup their families. Even when these adult sons emigrate, they leave behind their spouses to continue the reciprocal relationships in their absence. However, not all older parents who decided to co-reside with their sons realised their expectations and a few of them perceived neglect and felt constrained in the relationship forcing them to reach out to other children who lived nearby hence relying on care arrangements beyond co-residence.

Older adults co-residing with daughter-in-law

This sub-theme brings forth the reciprocal motives and circumstances that lead older adults to co-reside with their daughters-in-law. Usually what starts as co-residence with the adult son ends up being co-residence with the daughter-in-law and grandchildren when the son emigrates leaving behind his family.

Joana, a widowed older adult, had been co-residing with her only son in her own home. Even after the son became a seafarer, Joana continued to live with her daughter-in-law, Rita, and her grandchild in the same home. Since her support came from her son through her daughter-in-law, she was appreciate of the care she was receiving and recognized the mutual support exchange with her daughter-in-law:

> 'this girl (daughter-in-law) has my responsibility (*paused*) she only does (*paused*) everything is on her, and sister-in law and brother also ... yes more, responsibility is on her (*paused*) I am free with her (*paused*) because she is there at home all the time (*paused*) ya she is at home with me.' (Joana, older female, 72 years, Benaulin)

Lorna is Patricia's daughter-in-law and co-resides with her. Lorna narrates how Patricia feels free and independent in her own house. Patricia had decided to co-reside with her and daughter-in-law, Lorna, as she felt comfortable with them as compared to her other children:

> 'Because it is her house, so she can do anything, she can jump, she can shout, she can yell, she can (*paused*) means she feels very comfortable. After all its her house no she means (*paused*) earlier when she was okay (in better health), whatever used to happen she used to tell me … she used to go there (children's homes). She will do everything (help the other children) but she will never stay there, only sometimes in emergency (when her help was required) she used to stay there, otherwise she always used to come back to stay here.' (Lorna, daughter-in-law caregiver, 51 years, Verna)

Older parents who co-resided with their daughters-in-law usually owned the house and the now emigrant son had continued to live with his parents even after marriage. Thus, older parents and their daughters-in-law shared a relationship that is marked by a joint internalizationon of the emigrant event with both longing for the same individual. Married older spouses tended to provide care for the partner and counted on the daughter-in-law only when the primary caregiver had to go out of the household for certain errands. Widowed older parents who were co-residing with the adult son even before he emigrated continued to co-reside with the daughter-in-law. The emigrant son and his left-behind wife were naturally selected not only to co-reside and provide care but would benefit from intergenerational transfers in time to come.

Older adults co-residing with daughters

Though daughters were not expected or obliged to care for the parents after they get married when they assume caregiving duties in their husband's household, a few older adults did obtain care from their daughters through co-residence. This theme describes how daughters responded to the needs of the older parent, usually widowhood or increased care needs, and had decided to co-reside to provide care to the parent.

Agatha's mother Josephine was living alone after the loss of her spouse. Soon afterwards, since she suffered a paralytic stroke that required intensive care and rehabilitation, her youngest daughter Agatha returned home from Dubai along with her children to co-reside with her while her spouse continued to work in Dubai:

> 'I am staying here, I think it is 3 years became since I have come down. After my dad's death, there was nobody in the house, so I had to come back. I had to leave my job. I was working in Dubai actually,

so I had to leave my job and come here.' (Agatha, daughter caregiver, 44 years, Chinchinim)

Sophie was the fourth daughter to her widowed mother, Veronica. She lived in her mother's home along with her grandchildren even though her husband was away in the adjacent town. While some of her siblings chose to emigrate and the rest lived in Goa, she could not see her mother living alone, especially after an injury to her hand, and decided to come in and co-reside with her mother:

'See, I am her daughter and she is my mother. As she was alone, it was my responsibility to take her care. Somebody has to take care of her.' (Sophie, daughter caregiver, 51 years, Varca)

Daughters had responded to the increased care needs of the older adult, the absence of other siblings around and some had even sacrificed their careers to return back home in order to provide care to their parent. It is quite rare to imagine in an Indian context that daughters return back to their parental home to provide care and this indicates to us how caregiver selection happens. Relationships between siblings and the older parent, motives of obtaining intergenerational transfers through provision of care along and parental selection seem to direct daughters to take up primary roles of caregiving through co-residence. Thus, while older adults can benefit through investing in their children and building up beneficence, the younger generation is recognising their parents as more of a resource rather than a burden and hence filial obligations through co-residence continue in word and deed.

Intergenerational care through close-proximity households

This theme describes exchange of care between older parents and their children or children-in-law through living in close proximity, for example, within the same city, village, sometimes sharing the same courtyard such that there is ease of contact and support between adult children and their parents. This arrangement also facilitated sharing of filial roles between non-emigrant adult children and also between non-emigrant and emigrant siblings.

Margaret lived in her own house along with her daughter Catherine, who was widowed. Margaret had lost her spouse many years ago and had been living alone after the loss of her spouse. Margaret had planned and divided the property among all the sons in such a way that she expected the sons to live in the same courtyard in separate units even after they got married:

'I have got three sons, so I constructed these units separately, for all the sons it is separate, this portion is actually for the son, Alistair (who emigrated to Netherlands).' (Margaret, older female, 80 years, Varca)

Catherine, Margaret's daughter, considers it a blessing for her mother that the non-emigrant sons are living in the same courtyard, which is allowing for the pooling of support, assistance and reciprocal care within the family:

'For her, it is very nice because she has got all of her sons close by and they are married and they staying all together. So, in terms of somebody looking after her when it is required, all of them are here. That is a big blessing because nowadays, it doesn't happen that way (*paused*), her children I think are her assets. Children are the main thing for her at this stage. That she has she got all her grandchildren there.' (Catherine, co-residing daughter caregiver, 53 years, Varca)

Madeleine is 73 years old and lives with her son Leander and his family. She received frequent visits and support exchanges from her two daughters who live nearby in Goa and also from her other daughter who lives in Bengaluru, India. Madeleine had told this daughter to stay back with her as the house was large enough and the assets could be shared between her and Leander, her co-resident son:

'Sometimes, those who are in Goa, they come and visit me. The one in Neura (a village in Goa), she comes every Saturday for mass (church), after mass she comes here for coffee, she is also a teacher, the other one also comes (*paused*), the son (who emigrated to United Kingdom) comes once in a year for Christmas (*paused*), but he calls often. Even my daughters, they are like my sisters now. One is in Bengaluru, two are in Goa. Even the Bangalore one used to come here. When I was sick, she came here. This one (Leander) was on the ship, so she came down and then I told her not to go (*paused*) , we have enough (assets and house to share) here, that is what I said to her.' (Madeleine, older female, 73 years, Benaulin)

There were also instances where siblings were competing for assets and wealth of the older adult and hence a lot of mistrust and disconnect existed between them. In this case, cooperation and sharing of caregiving duties and support exchanges among siblings is absent and the daughter-in-law who co-resided with the older adult felt pained by the experience.

'I wanted their (sisters-in-law) help otherwise I had never asked with them I always manage it because they I know what is their this like, and it is no point in telling them forcing them but only when I was pregnant and bed ridden means bed rest (*paused*) so that time my husband requested them to take her (mother-in-law); now that government pension that my mother-in-law gets, the elder one (daughter), she comes to take the pension, because she (Jennifer) has already done the signatures on the cheques.' (Natalia, daughter-in-law caregiver, 39 years, Chinchinim)

Through this theme, perspectives of how older adults and their adult children negotiated care needs, careers, likes and dislikes for each other, widowhood, emigration and relations with and between children-in-law and among siblings to form close proximity nuclear residence with support exchanges and transfer of material and non-material exchanges between households are visible. We see instances where older parents invested in keeping adult children in close proximity through providing them residences within the same courtyard, done usually through partitioning the existing large property. This provided an opportunity for closer, regular and almost routine exchange of material and non-material transfers between these households usually directed through the co-residing primary caregiving child and aided siblings to share and cooperate together in care provision. In other instances we see how children living in close proximity would visit, enquire and share their concern and provide care to the older adult although difficulties arose when daughters-in-law had to now cooperate and share caregiving roles with other sisters-in-law who were competing for the assets and wealth of the older adult.

Intergenerational care through 'embedded' or 'enmeshed' separate nuclear households

This theme reflects an attempt to adapt and retain traditional kinship ties through functional support exchanges even though older parents and their adult children lived in separate nuclear households. These households were closely connected, spatially or remotely, through a complex web of intergenerational exchanges. These were characteristic of adult children living in separate nuclear households but where resource flows were not constrained by physical boundaries of separate households or on account of being away from the older adult and there was significant cooperation among the households.

Children living abroad were connected and available to interact with their parents and siblings making use of technology that helped overcome the distance. Margaret, who co-resides with her daughter Catherine, describes how she is able to maintain regular communication with her other children apart from those who live in the same courtyard with her:

'My elder son has Skype, so we watch him on Skype, and he calls regularly every Sunday. He sends money also. All the time he asks, "you have got money, right?" Don't stop going to the doctor because of money, like that, he is concerned. Even other sons are also the same, but since I am getting pension, so I told them, if I need money, I will ask them. Even the other two also, they send me some money. I tell them, see I don't need money at the moment; I can manage with my own. If I need, I will ask.' (Margaret, older female, 80 years, Varca)

Louisa is 88 years old and lives with her youngest son, daughter-in-law and grandchild in Goa. Three of her sons and one of her daughters have emigrated while one of her daughters lives nearby in Goa. Louisa describes how all her children, though living in separate nuclear households, are closely connected and resource flows go back and forth between these households. Louisa also describes how her children keep in touch over the phone or through the internet and check on her everyday:

'All the children share the responsibility; when they come down they all sit and discuss the needs I have. They phone my daughter-in-law and ask her, they order and directly send (things) to me. They talk to my doctors. All the children do the work (*paused*) I prefer to read newspaper on my iPad; I get my serials on my iPad. I read messages on my iPad. All my children contact me every day on my iPad. Even now just before you came my son from America was talking to me. He said he will phone tomorrow again. My daughter phones me every day.' (Louisa, older adult, 88 years, Navelim)

This section on embedded families illustrates how geographic distance did not play a role in the continuance and robustness of the inter-household caregiving process. We see that adult children who lived farther away from their parents as well as those who lived abroad attempted to keep in constant touch, use newer modes of communication and regularly enquire and provide care and attention. This highlights the spatially or remotely extended family which continues to provide mutual help and cooperation albeit between separate nuclear households. This form of reciprocal support exchange also brings into focus the nuclear-extended family which emphasises the relations, exchanges and connections between separate but close kin-related nuclear households. Thus, reciprocal resource flows which are usually associated with co-residence are not constrained by the physical boundaries of separate households, and that living farther away as opposed to living with children, does not necessarily mean that there are fewer reciprocal resource flows between the generations.

Discussion

The importance of studying family response to emigration and exploring the reciprocal intentions and motivations that guide the formation of adaptive intergenerational care arrangements are highlighted in this paper. In order that mutually supportive exchanges between older parents and their adult children continue, the efforts, assumptions and actions of co-resident and non-co-resident adult children and their older parents within the context of emigration has been explored here. This chapter serves to initiate dialogue on the negotiated intergenerational contract (Croll, 2006) that seems to have evolved in the background of changing family situations and modernisation, however, serves to still makes possible reciprocal support exchanges between older adults and their adult children. Findings from our study indicate that adult children from emigrant households are responsive to parental needs of support and finds way to effect supportive exchanges as found across intergenerational reciprocity literature (Grundy, 2005; Quashie and Zimmer, 2013). Although adult children subscribe to the notion of repayment or reciprocity for past care, there were few indications of feeling indebted but more motivations of mutual need, mutual interdependence and mutual support for two-way exchanges of support and care. This growing emphasis on mutual care, reciprocal exchanges and interdependence seems to have somewhat broken down hierarchical intra-family relations too (Ugargol and Bailey, 2021). Older adults are increasingly being viewed as important in passing on family values to grandchildren and their non-monetary time-related support through childcare is being increasing recognised and sought (Silverstein et al, 2006a; Yamada, 2006) either through co-residence, close proximity residence or by retaining contact through remote but 'embedded' households.

Adult children (both emigrant and non-emigrant), their spouses and older adults have positioned themselves and their behaviour as driven by certain motives while they attempt to construct new identities as caregivers and care receivers (Mills, 1940; Scott and Lyman, 1968). The motive to provide care can hinge on reciprocal expectations and the possibility of intergenerational transfers (Johar et al, 2015; Isherwood et al, 2016). The way in which these participants talked about their transition to caregiver and care receiver roles tell us about how people account for taking on a new identity. The findings also inform us how care arrangements evolve between the family members and how each one relates to an identity in action. Researchers who have been working in the Asian context tend to agree that unless mutual need, reciprocal interests and inter-dependence are perceived by older parents and their younger family members, there would have been no need for both generations to adapt, adjust and mutually accommodate changing needs and circumstances (Sokolovsky, 2000; Croll, 2006; Ugargol and Bailey,

2021) through intergenerational care arrangements. India's National Policy for Senior Citizens (Government of India, 2011), for example, encourages filial obligation, continuing and renewed investment in the intergenerational relationship as the primary source of mutual care, support and services. While many researchers had predicted the downfall of filial norms with the simultaneous decrease in rates of co-residence in most Asian societies, we are actually witnessing the resilience of a renewed intergenerational contract with simultaneous and shorter cyclical resource flows that is enabling older parents and adult children to reinvent ways to support each other through adaptive forms of co-residence, proximate residence and distant but 'connected' residences.

Our results corroborate evidence from Asia that points that emigrant children support their older parents financially and emotionally – financially through remittances and emotionally by maintaining frequent contact via telephone or return visits (Silverstein et al, 2006a; Singh et al, 2010). Even households in which older parents lived separately or co-resided with one of their children with few or none proximate adult children households (Zimmer and Korinek, 2008) and maybe one or more distant adult children (who live far away due to occupational mobility or emigration) were all found to be enmeshed in complex grids of intergenerational exchanges, a family form which researchers have referred to as an 'embedded family' (Croll, 2006), a 'networked family' (Whyte, 2003), an 'aggregate family' (Croll, 2006) or a 'spatially extended family' (Dube, 1997). It is pertinent to note that many of the seafaring adult children from these households in Goa would visit their homes at least once a year and spend a few months while those working on oil rigs would visit more often, indicating more frequent interaction and less perception of them being permanently away. These terms illustrate the strong linkages and exchanges that characterise these related nuclear households. The threads that emerge reflect the strong linkage between ageing, social expectations and family norms that facilitate care provision for the elderly and are significant in contributing to ageing research in India. We are also now able to visualise the modified extended family which provides emotional and communication support, as evidenced by the frequency of social interaction either through telephone calls, visits or newer forms of technology such using computers and the internet between older adults and their children abroad.

These intergenerational care arrangements reflect the emigration event-led adaptation of family and household structure to retain traditional familial ties and enable mutually supportive exchanges between adult children and their parents. These findings have significant implications for those interested in the role of families in caregiving to older adults, for researchers who have been exploring reciprocal motivations to care and for policy makers concerned about the provision and availability of family support for older adults in a rapidly evolving society such as India (Dey, 2017). It is very unlikely that governments in developing countries will offer any alternatives to family-based intergenerational care in the near future and will indirectly encourage and support families to care for older adults either through incentivising caregivers, penalising adult children who evade responsibility or merely taking moral stands (Medora, 2007; Brijnath, 2012). Given that older adults are more likely to be dependent, fragile and less equipped to reciprocate for care received from their children or other family members, non-family-based care provision needs to be explored in the Indian context (Ugargol et al, 2016; Datta, 2017). It is clear that re-emphasising existing legislative provision and encouraging intergenerational care practices is unlikely to lead to reciprocal intergenerational care arrangements unless these arrangements evolve based on reciprocal motives and interdependence between older parents and their children.

Acknowledgments

The authors would like to thank the older adults and their caregivers who contributed their time and personal experiences towards this study. This chapter is a token of appreciation to older adults and their family caregivers who continue to find reciprocity in their care relationships after emigration events changed their lives and households altogether. We thank Caritas-Goa, Piedade Institute, Panaji, Goa, who helped us obtain access to the households and facilitated the research.

Statement of funding

This work was supported by the Indian-European Research Networking Grant: Ageing and Well-Being in a Globalising World, funded by NWO-ESRC-ICSSR (Project Number: 465–11–009). The participating institutions include the Institute for Social and Economic Change, Bangalore, India; Center for Development Studies, Trivandrum, India; Population Research Centre, University of Groningen, the Netherlands and the University of Southampton, United Kingdom.

References

Allendorf, K. (2015) 'Like her own ideals and experiences of the mother-in-law/daughter-in-law relationship', *Journal of Family Issues*, 38(15): 2102–27.

Antonucci, T. C., Fuhrer, R. and Jackson, J. S. (1990) 'Social support and reciprocity: a cross-ethnic and cross-national perspective', *Journal of Social and Personal Relationships*, 7(4): 519–30.

Antonucci, T. C., Birditt, K. S., Sherman, C. W. and Trinh, S. (2011) 'Stability and change in the intergenerational family: a convoy approach', *Ageing and Society*, 31(7): 1084–106.

Azariadis, C. and Lambertini, L. (2003) 'Endogenous debt constraints in lifecycle economies', *The Review of Economic Studies*, 70(3): 461–87.

Bawdekar, M. and Ladusingh, L. (2012) 'Intergenerational time and monetary support among urban Indian families', *Asian Population Studies*, 8(2): 187–205.

Bhat, A. K. and Dhruvarajan, R. (2001) 'Ageing in India: drifting intergenerational relations, challenges and options', *Ageing and Society*, 21(5): 621–40.

Bloom, D. E., Mahal, A., Rosenberg, L. and Sevilla, J. (2010) 'Economic security arrangements in the context of population ageing in India', *International Social Security Review*, 63(3–4): 59–89.

Bloom, D. E., Chatterji, S., Kowal, P., Lloyd-Sherlock, P., McKee, M., Rechel, B. and Smith, J. P. (2015) 'Macroeconomic implications of population ageing and selected policy responses', *The Lancet*, 385(9968): 649–57.

Böhme, M. H., Persian, R. and Stöhr, T. (2015) 'Alone but better off? Adult child migration and health of elderly parents in Moldova', *Journal of Health Economics*, 39: 211–27.

Bongaarts, J. and Zimmer, Z. (2002) 'Living arrangements of older adults in the developing world an analysis of demographic and health survey household surveys', *The Journals of Gerontology Series B: Psychological Sciences and Social Sciences*, 57(3): S145–S157.

Brijnath, B. (2012) 'Why does institutionalised care not appeal to Indian families? Legislative and social answers from urban India', *Ageing and Society*, 32(4): 697–717.

Brinda, E. M., Rajkumar, A. P., Enemark, U., Attermann, J. and Jacob, K. S. (2014) 'Cost and burden of informal caregiving of dependent older people in a rural Indian community', *BMC Health Services Research*, 14(1): 207. https://doi.org/10.1186/1472-6963-14-207.

Building Knowledge Base on Population Ageing in India (BKPAI) Survey Data. (2011) http:// www.isec.ac.in/prc-AginginIndia-Data-Release.html.

Clemens, M. A. (2011) 'Economics and emigration: trillion-dollar bills on the sidewalk?', *The Journal of Economic Perspectives*, 25(3): 83–106.

Croll, E. J. (2006) 'The intergenerational contract in the changing Asian family', *Oxford Development Studies*, 34(4): 473–91.

da Silva Gracias, F. (2000) *Beyond the Self: Santa Casa da Misericórdia de Goa*, Panjim: Surya Publications.

da Silva Gracias, F. (2001) 'Goans away from Goa: migration to the Middle East', *Lusophonies asiatiques, Asiatiques en lusophonies*, 7: 423–32.

Datta, A. (2017) 'Old age homes in India: sharing the burden of elderly care with the family', in S. I. Rajan (ed) *Elderly Care in India*, Singapore: Springer, pp 77–93.

Deininger, K., Goyal, A. and Nagarajan, H. (2013) 'Women's inheritance rights and intergenerational transmission of resources in India', *Journal of Human Resources*, 48(1): 114–41.

Desai, S. and Banerji, M. (2008) 'Negotiated identities: male migration and left-behind wives in India', *Journal of Population Research*, 25(3): 337–55.

Dey, D. (2017) '"Fragile body and failing memory": the construction of care for the elderly by the laws and policies in India', in S. I. Rajan (ed) *Elderly Care in India*, Singapore: Springer, pp 53–68.

Dharmalingam, A. (1994) 'Old age support: expectations and experiences in a south Indian village', *Population Studies*, 48(1): 5–19.

Dhillon, P., Ladusingh, L. and Agrawal, G. (2016) 'Ageing and changing patterns in familial structure for older persons in India: a decomposition analysis', *Quality in Ageing and Older Adults*, 17(2): 83–96.

Dobrina, R., Vianello, C., Tenze, M. and Palese, A. (2015) 'Mutual needs and wishes of cancer patients and their family caregivers during the last week of life a descriptive phenomenological study', *Journal of Holistic Nursing*, 34(1): 24–34.

Dube, L. (1997) *Women and Kinship: Comparative Perspectives on Gender in South and South-East Asia*, Tokyo: UNU Press, 1997.

Forrest Zhang, Q. (2004) 'Economic transition and new patterns of parent–adult child co-residence in urban China', *Journal of Marriage and Family*, 66(5): 1231–45.

Frenz, M. (2008) 'Global Goans. migration movements and identity in a historical perspective', *Lusotopie*, 15(1): 183–202.

General, I. R. (2011) 'Census Commissioner, Census of India, 2011'. Provisional Population Totals Paper, 1.

Goodman, R. and Harper, S. (2013) *Ageing in Asia: Asia's Position in the New Global Demography*, London: Routledge.

Government of India (2007) Maintenance and Welfare of Parents and Senior Citizens Act, Ministry of Social Justice. http://socialjustice.nic. in/writereaddata/UploadFile/Annexure-X635996104030434742.pdf.

Government of India (2008) 'Goa Migration Study. Available: http://cds. edu/wp-content/uploads/2012/09/3_Goa-Migration-Study-2008.pdf.

Government of India (2011) 'National Policy for Senior Citizens (2011) 'Available: http://socialjustice.nic.in/writereaddata/UploadFile/dnpsc.pdf.

Grundy, E. (2005) 'Reciprocity in relationships: socio–economic and health influences on intergenerational exchanges between third age parents and their adult children in Great Britain', *The British Journal of Sociology*, 56(2): 233–55.

Ha, J. H. and Ingersoll-Dayton, B. (2008) 'The effect of widowhood on intergenerational ambivalence', *The Journals of Gerontology Series B: Psychological Sciences and Social Sciences*, 63(1): S49–S58.

Ingersoll-Dayton, B., Neal, M. B. and Hammer, L. B. (2001) 'Aging parents helping adult children: the experience of the sandwiched generation', *Family Relations*, 50(3): 262–71.

Isherwood, L. M., Luszcz, M. A. and King, D. S. (2016) 'Reciprocity in material and time support within parent–child relationships during late-life widowhood', *Ageing and Society*, 36(8): 1668–89.

Jamuna, D. and Ramamurti, P. V. (1999) 'Contributants to good caregiving: an analysis of dyadic relationships', *Social Change*, 29(1–2): 138–44.

Johar, M., Maruyama, S. and Nakamura, S. (2015) 'Reciprocity in the formation of intergenerational co-residence', *Journal of Family and Economic Issues*, 36(2): 192–209.

Kadoya, Y. and Khan, M. (2015) 'The role of gender in long-term care for older parents: evidence from India', *Economic Research Center Discussion Paper: E-Series*, E14–15.

Kalavar, J. M. and Jamuna, D. (2011) 'Aging of Indian women in India: the experience of older women in formal care homes', *Journal of Women and Aging*, 23(3): 203–15.

Knodel, J. and Saengtienchai, C. (1999) 'Studying living arrangements of the elderly: lessons from a quasi-qualitative case study approach in Thailand', *Journal of Cross-Cultural Gerontology*, 14(3): 197–220.

Kochar, A. (2002) *Inter-generational Income Sharing and Schooling Investments* [Paper presentation]. April, Microeconomics Workshop on Labor and Population, Stanford University, CA.

Lamb, S. (2013) 'In/dependence, intergenerational uncertainty, and the ambivalent state: perceptions of old age security in India', *South Asia: Journal of South Asian Studies*, 36(1): 65–78.

Leopold, T. and Raab, M. (2013) 'The temporal structure of intergenerational exchange: a within-family analysis of parent–child reciprocity', *Journal of Aging Studies*, 27(3): 252–63.

Li, L. W., Zhang, J. and Liang, J. (2009) 'Health among the oldest-old in China: which living arrangements make a difference?', *Social Science and Medicine*, 68(2): 220–7.

Lowenstein, A., Katz, R. and Gur-Yaish, N. (2007) 'Reciprocity in parent–child exchange and life satisfaction among the elderly: a cross-national perspective', *Journal of Social Issues*, 63(4): 865–83.

Medora, N. P. (2007) 'Strengths and challenges in the Indian family', *Marriage and Family Review*, 41(1–2): 165–93.

Mills, C. W. (1940) 'Situated actions and vocabularies of motive', *American Sociological Review*, 5(6): 904–13.

Miltiades, H. B. (2002) 'The social and psychological effect of an adult child's emigration on non-immigrant Asian Indian elderly parents', *Journal of Cross-Cultural Gerontology*, 17(1): 33–55.

Mukherjee, S., Chakraborty, D. and Sikdar, S. (2016) 'Three decades of human development across Indian states: inclusive growth or perpetual disparity?', *Prajnan-Journal of Social and Management Sciences*, 45(2): 97–122.

Mulder, C. H. and van der Meer, M. J. (2009) 'Geographical distances and support from family members', *Population, Space and Place*, 15(4): 381–99.

Nayak, D. K. and Behera, N. B. (2014) 'Changing household size in India: an inter-state comparison', *Transactions. India: Institute of Indian Geographers*, 36(1): 1–18.

Newman, R. S. (1988) 'Konkani Mai ascends the throne: the cultural basis of Goan statehood', *South Asia: Journal of South Asian Studies*, 11(1): 1–24.

Patel, V. and Prince, M. (2001) 'Ageing and mental health in a developing country: who cares? Qualitative studies from Goa, India', *Psychological Medicine*, 31(1): 29–38.

Pillemer, K. and Suitor, J. J. (2014) 'Who provides care? A prospective study of caregiving among adult siblings', *The Gerontologist*, 54(4): 589–98.

Quashie, N. and Zimmer, Z. (2013) 'Residential proximity of nearest child and older adults' receipts of informal support transfers in Barbados', *Ageing and Society*, 33(2): 320–41.

Rajan, S. I. and Kumar, S. (2003) 'Living arrangements among Indian elderly: new evidence from national family health survey', *Economic and Political Weekly*, 38(1): 75–80.

Roff, L. L., Martin, S. S., Jennings, L. K., Parker, M. W. and Harmon, D. K. (2007) 'Long-distance parental caregivers' experiences with siblings: a qualitative study', *Qualitative Social Work*, 6(3): 315–34.

Roy, S. (2015) 'Empowering women? Inheritance rights, female education and dowry payments in India', *Journal of Development Economics*, 114: 233–51.

Ruggles, S. and Heggeness, M. (2008) 'Intergenerational coresidence in developing countries', *Population and development review*, 34(2): 253–81.

Sampson, H. (2005) 'Left high and dry? The lives of women married to seafarers in Goa and Mumbai', *Ethnography*, 6(1): 61–85.

Scott, M. B. and Lyman, S. M. (1968) 'Accounts', *American Sociological Review*, 33(1): 46–62.

Sengupta, M. and Agree, E. M. (2002) 'Gender and disability among older adults in North and South India: differences associated with co-residence and marriage', *Journal of Cross-Cultural Gerontology*, 17(4): 313–36.

Sharma, K. and Kemp, C. L. (2012) ' "One should follow the wind": individualized filial piety and support exchanges in Indian immigrant families in the United States', *Journal of Aging Studies*, 26(2): 129–39.

Silverstein, M., Conroy, S. J., Wang, H., Giarrusso, R. and Bengtson, V. L. (2002) 'Reciprocity in parent–child relations over the adult life course', *The Journals of Gerontology Series B: Psychological Sciences and Social Sciences*, 57(1): S3–S13.

Silverstein, M., Cong, Z. and Li, S. (2006a) 'Intergenerational transfers and living arrangements of older people in rural China: consequences for psychological well-being', *The Journals of Gerontology Series B: Psychological Sciences and Social Sciences*, 61(5): S256–S266.

Silverstein, M., Gans, D. and Yang, F. M. (2006b) 'Intergenerational support to aging parents: the role of norms and needs', *Journal of Family Issues*, 27(8): 1068–84.

Singh, S., Cabraal, A. and Robertson, S. (2010) 'Remittances as a currency of care: a focus on "twice migrants" among the Indian diaspora in Australia', *Journal of Comparative Family Studies*, 41(2): 245–63.

Skirbekk, V. and James, K. S. (2014) 'Abuse against elderly in India: the role of education', *BMC Public Health*, 14(1): 336.

Smith, T. and Whitlock, S. (2004) 'Community care and informal carers in Japan and England', in Y. Maya (ed) *Health and Welfare: Security of the Earth and Mankind in the 21st Century*, Tokyo: Nihon University, pp 85–101.

Sokolovsky, J. (2000) 'Living arrangements of older persons and family support in less developed countries', *Population Bulletin of the United Nations*, 42/53, 162–92.

Stark, O. and Lucas, R. E. (1988) 'Migration, remittances, and the family', *Economic Development and Cultural Change*, 36(3): 465–81.

Sykes, G. M. and Matza, D. (2002) 'Techniques of neutralization', in S. Cote (ed) *Criminological Theories: Bridging the Past to the Future*, New Delhi: SAGE Publications.

Tumbe, C. (2012) 'Migration persistence across twentieth-century India', *Migration and Development*, 1(1): 87–112.

Ugargol, A. P. and Bailey, A. (2018) 'Family caregiving for older adults: gendered roles and caregiver burden in emigrant households of Kerala, India', *Asian Population Studies*, 14(2): 194–210.

Ugargol, A. P. and Bailey, A. (2021) 'Reciprocity between older adults and their caregivers in emigrant households of Kerala, India', *Ageing and Society*, 41(8): 1–27.

Ugargol, A. P., Hutter, I., James, K. S. and Bailey, A. (2016) 'Care needs and caregivers: associations and effects of living arrangements on caregiving to older adults in India', *Ageing International*, 41(2): 193–213.

Van Willigan, J. and Chadha, N. K. (1999) *Social Aging in a Delhi Neighborhood*, Westport, CT: Bergin and Garvey.

Varghese, M. and Patel, V. (2004) 'The graying of India', in S. Agarwal, D. Goel, R. Salhan, R. Ichhpujani and S. Shrivastava (eds) *Mental Health: An Indian Perspective 1946–2000*, New Delhi: Elsevier, pp 240–8.

Vera-Sanso, P. (1999) 'Dominant daughters-in-law and submissive mothers-in-law? Cooperation and conflict in South India', *Journal of the Royal Anthropological Institute*, 5(4): 577–93.

Wells, Y. D. and Kendig, H. L. (1997) 'Health and well-being of spouse caregivers and the widowed', *The Gerontologist*, 37(5): 666–74.

Whyte, M. K. (2003) 'The persistence of family obligations in Baoding', in M. K. Whyte (ed) *China's Revolutions and Intergenerational Relations*, Ann Arbor: University of Michigan Center for Chinese Studies, pp 85–120.

Yamada, K. (2006) 'Intra-family transfers in Japan: intergenerational co-residence, distance, and contact', *Applied Economics*, 38(16): 1839–61.

Zimmer, Z. and Korinek, K. (2008) 'Does family size predict whether an older adult lives with or proximate to an adult child in the Asia-Pacific region?', *Asian Population Studies*, 4(2): 135–59.

7

All my responsibilities towards my children are over! Linked lives and life course obligations among older adults with migrant children in India

Ajay Bailey, K. S. James and Jyoti S. Hallad

Introduction

This chapter investigates how life course obligations, expectations and practices are linked to older adults' sense of well-being. Linked lives, which is one of core dimensions of the life course approach, recognises that life trajectories of individuals are socially embedded and closely linked to the transitions of the significant others (Elder, 1975, 1985; Dannefer, 2003; Moen and Hernandez, 2009). The studies that have examined linked lives in the context of migration (Bailey et al, 2004; Cooke, 2008) tend to focus on western countries or on internal migration (Mulder and Hooimeijer, 1999; Thomas et al, 2017). However there are some new studies emerging on international migration (Kõu et al, 2015, 2017; Statham, 2020). Some strands of work in Asia focus on transnational families (Yeoh et al, 2005), aging in diasporas (Lamb, 2002, 2009; Fluit et al, 2019) and marriage migration (Charsley, 2005; Gallo, 2006; Shaw and Charsley, 2006; Gardner, 2009; Le Bail, 2017). In non-Western multi-generational co-residential families the determinants of well-being need to be evaluated in relation to the reciprocity and support exchanged between older adults and other family members (Ugargol and Bailey, 2020). In our study the concept of linked lives is translocal and broadened to include older adults in migrant households, their adult children (co-residing or migrant children), grandchildren, caregivers and non-kin social networks. The focus in this chapter is on how the broader well-being of the older adult is linked to the life course obligations of older adults towards their families. This chapter also discusses how we can better contextualise life course decisions and trajectories in non-Western settings.

Living arrangements, migration and care

The population aged 60 years and older in India constitutes over 7 per cent of the total population (1.21 billion) and is projected to triple in the next four decades, from 92 million to 316 million (James, 2011). In the past, the family has been the major source of support in later life. However, increased mobility may challenge the continued reliance on family in the future. Jamuna (2000) finds that in the Indian ethos elder care was generally seen as a duty of the adult children, which meant the primary caregiver was usually the daughter-in-law. The lowering of fertility in certain states in India (for example, Kerala, Karnataka and Tamilnadu) and among middle classes has led to nuclear families where adult children and the older spouse are the principal caregivers (Bhat and Dhruvarajan, 2002). Bloom et al (2010) observe that increased longevity has meant taking care of older adults has become more expensive due to increasing prevalence of chronic health conditions and due to reduced child-bearing the intergenerational care network has further reduced. With the migration of adult children the tasks of care giving are left to the aged spouse or to hired non-kin caregivers. The UNFPA-Building Knowledge Base on Population Ageing in India (BKPAI) data (2012) show that nearly 25 per cent of the older adults in India live in households without their children, with almost 10 per cent of older women living alone compared to 2 per cent men living alone. The recent Longitudinal Ageing Study in India (IIPS, 2020) shows that about 6 per cent of adults aged 60 years and above are living alone – the main reasons being not having children or children living in other cities. In a comparison of 43 developing countries Bongaarts and Zimmer (2002) find that older women were more likely to live alone compared to men, and in Asia older adults were more likely to co-reside with adult children. Studies carried out by the OECD (2011), as well as by Rajan (2012), show increasing trends in migration in recent years. Internal migration to large urban centres is linked to rapid industrialisation and an increase in service industries. This has led to smaller towns acting as escalator spaces (people move to these towns for education but have no plans to settle) for education and retirement spaces for older adults. Internationally, the Indian diaspora constitutes nearly 25 million people worldwide. This diaspora plays an active role in engaging with the country of origin and with their families who have remained in India. Indeed, India is now one of the largest receivers of economic remittances in the world (Mallick, 2012; Ratha and Mohapatra, 2013) and received US$83 billion in international remittances in 2019 alone (World Bank, 2020). The sending of remittances can be seen as a form of care provision where the hired caregiver is seen to fill the gap created by migration.

Life course from a non-Western perspective

The life course framework largely focuses on Western societies and life course events that are more attuned to Western, individualised life goals. There is a pressing need to examine the life course framework and life events as played out in in a non-Western context, embedding it within local ideologies, religious beliefs and cultural norms. In this study we examine the life stage conceptualization as presented within Hinduism as a worldview rather than as a religion (Saraswathi et al, 2011), as much of this conceptualisation permeates or crosses over into other religious groups such as Indian Muslims, Buddhists and Christians. The life stage conceptualisation underpins many of the behaviours and ideas employed by people to motivate their actions in relation to their own life course decisions and those of their significant others. The key difference here is that the life course framework considers family as a nuclear household whereas the life stage conceptualisation considers family as a multi-generational household.

According to the life stage conceptualisation in Hinduism, there are four main stages which are called as *ashramas*. The stages include Brahmacharya (stage of student), Grihasta (stage of a householder), Vanaprastha (stage of retirement) and Sanyasa (stage of disengagement). In these stages, in addition to age, it is the stage-specific roles, obligations and tasks which add to the personhood of being a Hindu both for men and women (van Willigen et al, 1995; Majumdar, 2005). Hence life satisfaction needs to be situated within this cultural prism and the ability of older adults to successfully transition to each stage. These stage-specific roles and obligations include acquiring a good education, marriage, procreation, educating children, arranging marriage of children and giving care during childbirth. Previous studies have shown in the South Asian context older adults who complete some or all of these obligations are able to then hand over their householder duties to the next generation (Nagalingam, 2007; Shrestha and Zarit, 2012). Completion of the duties need not be equal to retirement as these are cultural roles and responsibilities and not solely connected to work or occupation.

With higher levels of education among younger cohorts, as well as internal and international migration, many of these tasks and roles cannot be completed by older adults. Recent literature shows that the younger generation in India make different life course choices with regard to marriage (Fuller and Narasimhan, 2008; Banerji and Deshpande, 2020) and child-bearing (Pande and Malhotra, 2012; Das and Žumbytė, 2017), which has an impact on the roles of the older adults. In the Asian context, studies have shown that grandparental caregiving was integral to life satisfaction and well-being experienced by the older adults (Ang and O, 2012; Xu et al, 2012; Gray et al, 2019). In this chapter we argue that older adults who are able to carry out these life course obligations have a greater sense of life satisfaction. This sense of life satisfaction is not only related one's own life course but the duties and obligations the older adults have towards their children.

Data and methods

The study was conducted in Dharwad city, in the southern state of Karnataka. Dharwad is part of the twin cities of Huballi-Dharawad. As per the last census in 2011 the population was 943,857. Dharwad city attracts many students from other cities and surrounding rural areas. The city hosts four universities, three medical colleges and many technical schools and has had a long history as an educational centre. There are very few jobs due to lack of industries and manufacturing companies, which prompts both internal and onward migration. Due to its temperate climate and access to tertiary health care facilities, many older adults prefer to stay in the city and many have returned to the city in retirement to live in close proximity to extended family members. In this study we use a mixed methodology approach; the qualitative study (37 in-depth interviews) was followed by the individual survey interviews of older adults (N=477). The data gathered from in-depth interviews and support network mapping fed into the formulation of the survey instrument. In this chapter we focus on the qualitative component as we aim to explore the lived experiences of older adults on their life course obligations, linked lives and their sense of well-being.

Selection of the participants

The city of Hublli-Dharwad has many higher education institutions but not many industries; therefore, those who are more highly educated tend to move to the nearest big cities in Karnataka, such as Bengaluru or outside the state to Pune or Mumbai. We observed that many of the international migrants had either lived part of the time in other cities in India before migrating to other countries. We had two criteria for selection: one was that the household must have at least one adult child who had migrated abroad or to a different city in India, and the other involved the living arrangement of the older adults (co-residing with other children/kin, living with spouse or living alone). Eligible households in the study area were listed and then approached for in-depth interviews. We used a snowball technique for identifying participants. We included different nodes in the snowball technique to avoid recruiting participants from the same social circle. Most of what we report in this chapter draws on middle-class Indians who have relatively high education levels (both the older adults and their children). The areas we chose are also places inscribed with middle-class aspirations such as owning a house, areas populated by retirees with good access to health care and the ability to pay for care and who have children living abroad or in other cities. Therefore, the discussion in this chapter does not necessarily apply to those from lower socio-economic groups where their immediate concerns may be more about meeting day-to-day needs.

In-depth interviews

Participants were asked about what meaning they give to the situation of living away from their children and how this shapes their experience of ageing. The interviews ranged from 30 to 90 minutes and explored the various domains where older adults perceive the absence of their children. They were conducted in Kannada, the main language spoken in Karnataka, by trained interviewers. Each household was visited by one male and one female interviewer. Where households had more than one person, the interviews with the different household members were held at the same time in separate rooms where possible. If this was not possible the interviewer made appointments to interview household members on separate days. The main sections in the interview guide included: daily neighbourhood activities, economic situation, living arrangements, information on migrant children and their family, marriage of children, caregiving during childbirth, provision of care for older adults, perceptions on the impact of their children's migration, autonomy and decision-making, health problems and treatment and comparison with older adults having different living arrangements. The interviews also focused on the manner in which older adults manage caregiving and -receiving from both kin and non-kin members, through the exchange of both material and non-material resources. We conducted 37 in-depth interviews with couples, widows and widowers. Participants in this study include both older adults co-residing with kin and older adults residing on their own.

Ethical considerations

The interviewers were trained to ask for consent. To gain trust of the participants each interviewer was given a badge and letter of reference about the study. Before the interview could start, the interviewer explained the nature of the project, that the information would remain anonymous and asked consent to digitally record the information. During the interview, if the older adults were observed experiencing any physical discomfort or if they became emotional, the interviewer halted the recording and offered to complete the interview at a later point in time. The interviews were transcribed and translated by the project staff. All identifying information was taken out of the transcripts. Each transcript was assigned a code and linked personal information was stored safely with the principal investigators.

Analysis of qualitative data

The analysis followed the principles of grounded theory and derived a range of codes, categories and themes (Hennink et al, 2020). The interview transcripts were analysed using qualitative data software Atlas-Ti™. The first cycle of coding involved identifying both inductive and deductive codes and in the second cycle the codes were grouped together in code families. The main code families include life course obligations, caregiving, marriage of children, family relationships and plans for future. We report the findings below as related to these code families.

Findings and discussion: 'children responsibilities'

Many older adults felt a sense of contentment that they had completed their 'children responsibilities'. These responsibilities include life course obligations: providing education, arranging marriage, inculcating cultural values and caregiving during critical transitions such as pregnancy and childbirth. The successful migration, work and career of their children were seen as positive outcome of these life course obligations. Many of the older adults had invested their life savings to carry out these life course obligations; this was especially the case for the education and marriages of their children.

Education

Providing the right kind of education for their children was perceived to be one of the main responsibilities. In the study area, most of the older adults, especially men, were university educated and had been in working in the formal sector. Education and more specifically professional education such as medicine and engineering were seen to be the way of moving up in the social hierarchy. Older adults had saved and spent considerable resources in educating their children in private schools and colleges. In India education is a key cultural capital that would help the household to move into the higher brackets of middle-class lifestyles (Krishnan and Hatekar, 2017).

P: '… my opinion is different because half of our life will go in providing them good education and settling their life and if there are 2 children then we should give good education whether it may be boy or a girl then our responsibility will be over and we will be free.' (Older adult male)

For some of the older adults, adhering to these norms meant they had to move from rural areas to Dharwad to secure a better education. Due to smaller family sizes compared to previous generations, older adults could afford to send their children for higher professional education. Migration to urban areas and the setting up of the household meant that older adults could also host the children of the extended family members who were pursuing their education. Hence life course obligations in relation to education was not restricted to their own children but also extended as an opportunity for other members of the wider household. This illustrates the argument that obligations towards education are shared and the larger multi-generational household is responsible for the caring and development of younger members of the household.

P: 'Yes our relatives were also staying here for education as we are a joint family and most of the peoples are illiterate so I was asking my relatives that let they complete their high school education in Sindagi and after that I was asking them to come here for further study and it was unavoidable for us. I have given education to 4 children and one is in New Zealand, one has completed Library Science and now he is in Bijapur working as Librarian, and one has done Diploma in Pharmacy and has opened Pharmacy and last one has done MBA and he did not go for higher job as he was willing to stay in Sindagi, so he has opened medical shop over there. What education I have to give to my children similarly I have given education to my brother's children as well. I have 5 brothers and some of our brothers' children got good education and job and some brother children did not get any education or job, so it nobody can be held responsible because if the children do not study well then who are responsible? So what I have done is I have given ₹50000/ – to all three children to purchase some land and get settled.' (Older adult male)

P: 'My mother was there, three children and we a total 5 members, later my sisters daughter was staying here, she was homeopathy doctor, after she completed her education she worked as a lecturer in Homeopathy colleges, also my younger sister daughter also was there, she was in the same class of my last child, as there were no good schools in Bijapur, so she stayed here for 2 years, after that only elder sister's daughter came for study and stayed for 7–8 years.' (Older adult female)

The successful transition of children from education to work, and in some cases to international migration, was seen by the older adults as an accomplishment of their goal of providing education.

'When my son was going to Qatar we did not have even 10,000 rupees also. He had made loan, with the loan amount he had gone there and after working there continuously he had paid the entire amount. He says, if I stay here means I will also (in comparison to his lower educated brothers) not progress in life.' (Older adult female)

Economic independence of adult children also ensured that the older adults could save the resources for their retirement. Among families who did not have a pension but depended on the adult children for their financial well-being, the successful transition to paid employment meant security for the older adults as well. Among families where adult children could not transition successfully into paid employment, older adults often faced feelings of anxiety and fear for the future as the older adults worried that their adult children would be continuously dependent on them economically.

P: 'Even if they are here (in Dharwad) they should be good position if they don't do job again it is burden only right? They should be educated and should be involved in some job either in Belgaum, Dharwad or in Bangalore. They should be educated and work till their retirement age. They should not be dependent of the parents and they should depend on parents only till they pursue education and job after that they should be independent.' (Older adult male)

In some of the families that we studied, siblings of the more successful children who migrated took on the role of caregivers for the older adults. There was less pressure to conform to successful transitions to work on the younger siblings. Often these siblings who were not able to find work were self-employed or worked on a part-time basis in a family business or venture. In the case below, the elder son is unmarried and is living with the parents. This family has three sons and two daughters. All the children except the eldest son are married, have children and have migrated to other cities. The elder son is the primary caregiver and his siblings and parents supported him financially to set up a medical shop. This goes further to show that in families with greater numbers of children the expectations were not equally enforced, though educational opportunities were offered to all the children.

I: 'You said that your eldest son is here (co-residing)?'
P: 'Yes he is with us. He is running medical shop means he had done D.Pharma, diploma. He is has his own medical shop since 20 years. He is not married. We also feel sad for some time, if at least one daughter-in-law is with us means it could be better. Its their wish, we cannot force them. By seeing others family he might have been

disappointed. He tells no for it so we have not asked him. When he told no we did not force him.' (Older adult female)

The negotiation of who stays behind to provide care for the older adults is not often very explicit. The siblings who are not able to migrate or do not have the right skill set to find jobs often remain with the parents.

Building a house

Building a house for the family was seen as one of the key life events which the older adults aspired to achieve. The buying of land and construction of the house were seen as essential elements in the role of the Grihasta (householder). Men earlier in their career had taken loans or saved enough money to build houses for their families. Older men who were employed by a state-run organisation could secure loans at low interest rates and paid these loans back until their retirement. The building of a house was linked to the life course obligations on provision of shelter for the family. The house provided a sense of security for the older adults but was also a means of intergenerational transmission of wealth. The promise of transfer of the house to the next generation also came with the implicit understanding that reciprocal care was expected by the older adults. In some of the households older adults had used up all their savings and retirement benefits to build or buy a house/apartment for the family.

P: 'When I was working in Hubli I took a site with help of my brother who was working in P&T, in housing society, so I built a house there. For education of my children Dharwad Hubli is good so I did that.' (Older adult male)

P: 'Large expenditure means, at present I do not have any. All the responsibilities have got over, daughter got married, son is working and I have my own house, so no problem. So now as large expenditure I do not have any thing.' (Older adult male)

The owning of property and building of a home was also meant that they could establish roots there and make a place for their children. However, in the neighbourhoods we studied, the higher-educated children had left the parental home. Migration to other cities and countries meant that adult children had set up new households and bought homes in these cities. Older adults often travelled to these cities or countries as a way to reconnect with their children. In the course of the interviews, participants who were either living on their own or were living close to a daughter were asked if they would like to migrate to live with their children. Most of the participants said they would prefer to live in Dharwad as long as they are able to care for themselves and their spouses. They would agree to move only if there was a health care emergency or the death of a spouse.

P: 'Ours is a retired life, so we only have to go [to Bangalore] if we need to go for treatment. Nowadays it is not possible for them to come here and stay with us for a month or fifteen days, it would be problematic. Besides which, we can't inconvenience them. Till now that type of situation has not happened, but if it comes then we can explain the problem and pain: if I am sick I would need 15 days treatment, which means I can go to Bangalore for that and stay with them … [That way] they can take care of me without missing any work. It is difficult for them to come here and take care of us, so …' (Male, 60 years, living with spouse)

With regard to international migration, the parents preferred to live in Dharwad and to visit their children once a year. They found they could not adjust to the cold climate, different cultural settings and the fact that they had to depend on their children for most things.

P: 'No, there (in USA) they don't care for us in the hospital, [the insurance] only allows treatment of his wife and children; they don't have that facility. Anyway, we can only stay for six months, and they don't check us nor even give tablets, so we are afraid to go there. Also, if he were to call us now [and ask us to], we wouldn't be ready to go because it would be problematic for him. My sugar level fluctuates [dramatically], so I will not go. Sir (husband) went once, but I will not go.' (Female, 65 years, living with spouse)

Living in their own house and close to friends and relatives was perceived to be the ideal choice. They thought that they had more time with their children when the children came to visit them than when they went to visit the children. The shorter visits to their children were something that the older adults also looked forward to. This gave them an opportunity to spend time with their grandchildren.

In living arrangements where at least one adult male child was living with them, the maintenance of the house was passed on to the son. We present here two cases where older adults have divided the property to maintain social ties and connections with adult children and their families. In these cases, older adults had divided the land and built houses for their children (see Chapter 6, which describes how house building can also be a way to secure proximity of care provision). In the first case, an older adult, from relatively low economic group, had built three houses on the small piece of land and had divided them among his sons. He had built these houses from the funds he received on retirement from a private company. He had invested all his earnings and resources into creating separate houses for his children. The only drawback was that he had not created a household or a living unit for himself and his wife. This led to the older adult and his wife moving into the house of the migrant son and were also economically dependent on him. In situations where there was a family conflict between the siblings or between the parent and the siblings, the living situation of the older adults became more precarious. Such precarious situations where older adults are exposed to abuse and neglect has been observed in other parts of India as well (see Chapters 8 and 10 for further examples; see also Jahangir et al, 2018; Pazhoothundathil and Bailey, 2020).

In the second case, the older adult had extended his house and built two apartments around it. This he rented out to his daughters. With patrilocal residence, his daughters could not stay or be part of his household where sons-in-law would move into the household of the older adult. By creating two separate homes/apartments, the older adult still manages to retain independence for himself and his wife and when needed could still call on his daughters and their families for support. In the second case, the older adult was formally working in an educational institution and had greater financial literacy for planning his retirement and for distributing his resources between his daughters. Given that he does not have a son who will inherit his property, this was his approach to divide his wealth between his daughters (see also Chapters 6, 8 and 9 on inheritance and care dynamics). In both cases the older adults were satisfied that their children and grandchildren were living close by. This improved their interpersonal relations and produced a feeling of security that support was available to them.

Marriage

The key life course decisions, such as arranging a marriage, were in most cases jointly taken by the parents and their children. In some cases we observed that in addition to the immediate family members the close kin or relatives also played a role in the process of match-making and the final marriage. The older adults believed that it was their duty to find a suitable bride or groom. The adult children were also involved in the decision making and often took the final decision. In addition to religion and caste, older adults also searched for professionally qualified spouses for their children. In some cases caste boundaries were overlooked if the girl or the boy was professionally educated and was living abroad. In such cases the social and cultural capital of being highly educated and living abroad was perceived as being of higher value than caste boundaries. A deeper reading of such practices also reveals the slackening of caste rules and regulations on the one hand, and on the other hand neo-local residence (living abroad) meant that couples did not have to face caste-based prejudice or everyday discrimination in their hometown. The 'arranging' of the marriages also involved agreements on sharing of costs by the parents and the location of the wedding. Many of the older adults had saved money over the years or taken loans to pay off the expenses of their daughter's marriage.

I: 'Did your children tell you anything while searching for their partners?'

P: 'Nothing, what Elders (hireyaru) people will do is final, they used to tell "my parents are not separate from us they will select whoever is suitable for us" like this they had put responsibilities on us so according to that we did that. We felt that this is good and suitable for our children and they also told ok for it, so we arranged the marriage.' (Older adult female)

P: 'Right from the beginning I started accumulating money in the form of Recurring Deport (RD), and plus I use to get money from exam duty and book publication and with that I arranged the marriage. During those days ₹20000/- ($ 275) was enough to do one marriage and if it is our daughter marriage then maximum of ₹80000/- ($ 1100) was required to do the marriage. I did not take any loan and within what I have I have managed.' (Older adult male)

The marriage of adult children was seen as an important life course obligation which led to the creation of a separate household, and for the older adults this meant that they were then passing on their householder tasks to the children. For the older adults who had not yet completed this life course obligation it was one of the main stressors and one of their main goals. This was more so in families with only daughters. They were concerned that their other relatives or close kin would not take on the responsibility of finding a suitable groom and arranging the marriage of their daughter. The example below shows the relational nature of life course and ageing. The successful transition of the offspring is linked to the accomplishment of goals of the older adult.

P: 'I will decide everything and inform each person what things have to be done by him or her, no one should quarrel after my death, I will prepare a will and die, still I have responsibility of my younger daughter marriage. I have to do that and I will.' (Older adult female)

We also found instances where the sons/daughters have found spouses by themselves or through online match-making services and then had involved the parents to create the semblance that it was a family decision.

P: 'First son we have only selected (the bride). She is of our community but last two sons are love marriage. Our son said that he is in love with a girl and even she also informed their parents about her love and later they came to see our house, both the parties liked each other because both the families were good so we all said yes and they married. I used to tell them and it was routine daily at Tiffin time and it had become a slogan that as you all are going to college it is normal thing you get attracted towards opposite sex, so it is a natural thing but you all keep in mind that girl should be of a good family she should may not be a Brahmin at least Hindu I don't like Muslim and Christian girls because they will not know our culture.' (Older adult female)

In situations where the parents were not involved in the decision making or the choice of the spouse, this created animosity between the parents and the adult children. We found one such instance where the son was no longer in contact with his family due to the family conflict surrounding his marriage.

Care at critical transitions

Caregiving and -receiving are some of the main binders of interpersonal relationships. The care cycle is not limited to the children but also extended to grandchildren. Participants in this study provided care during pregnancy and childbirth. This was seen as one of the life course responsibilities of the parents of the daughter. In another study from Karnataka, Bailey (2017) discusses how the exchange of food made specially for post-natal recuperation is exchanged between transnational households to create a sense of co-presence and to ensure that care is circulated between the households. In our study older couples with children living abroad had travelled to the countries to provide care. Where this could not be arranged this task was carried out by the parents-in-law. In other situations, the daughters had returned to the place that they were brought up to be cared for by their family. Depending on the availability of care facilities, in some of the cases the daughters-in law had preferred to stay with the parents-in-law for the birth of the child and subsequent care.

I: 'Where did your daughter deliver?'
P: 'Here in Dharwad, first delivery has to be in mother's place, so we did it here. All care for the mother and the child was done here in our home. Care after delivery (banantana) everything was here. Five months, four months completed and in fifth month her in-laws came and she went with them.'
I: 'Daughter-in-law's delivery?'

P: 'Daughter-in-law's delivery happened in their own maternal home. (...) It was in Dharwad hospital so we used to visit regularly until they went to hospital, I think for 10 to 12 days. Afterwards she went to her mother's place for delivery care (banantana). Elder daughter-in-law's delivery was conducted in America. I did not go. Her mother had gone.' (Older adult female)

Some of the participants who were not able to provide care themselves had hired domestic helpers to prepare food and to take care of the newborn. In the following case the care was still provided in the house as the older adults were working at the time of the childbirth. The older adult female had hired a woman to take care of the young mother and the child. As families become smaller there are fewer people to provide care, hence additional people are hired. This service is emerging as a niche market of female caregivers who live in with the families for a period of 40 days to provide post-natal care.

P: 'I had a vacation during that time (birth of grandson) and even my mother also came at that time and helped us and even my daughter in law was also with us and she also helped me. 10 days we faced problems in hospital and after coming house I used to prepare food for all and we hired a woman (live-in caregiver) who used to prepare food for the lactating mother. She (daughter) stayed here for 4 and ½ months and after that she went home.' (Older adult female)

Grandparenting was seen both as the continuation of care cycle but also as a way to maintain intergenerational personal relations. The latter was more difficult when children were living abroad. Intergenerational care relations were instrumental for the older adults to continue this idea of 'family' across national and international boundaries and contributed to their sense of being embedded in these transnational relations (see Gray et al, 2019; Ho and Chiu, 2020; see also Chapter 6 in this volume). For some older adults it was difficult to care for grandchildren due to their own health situation. In the following case the grandchild was born in the USA but was later brought back to India and was cared for by the maternal grandparents as the paternal grandparents were not able to do so.

P: 'No, now we cannot take any responsibility as such because of that only we have kept our grandson in Bijapur. So openly we have said everybody.'
I: 'He can come here and stay?'

P:	'No we cannot manage him at this stage and so we have told everybody that we cannot take that responsibility.'

I:	'Do you miss you grandchildren?'

P:	'Yes some time we feel but taking him to hospital or school is all done by my daughter-in-law parents and we cannot do as we have grow old but they are comparatively younger to us.' (Older adult male)

Life post-responsibilities

Participants also reflected on their lives after these life course obligations. Among those who had retired there was a sense of satisfaction that they had completed all their life course obligations. As a result, the availability of time on their hands gave the older adults the freedom to think about their own lives and things they had not been able to acconmplish when they were working and caring for their children. Activities such as social work, cultural activities and travel figured in the discussions.

P:	'I am happy because in my childhood stage we have faced many problems and somebody have held our hand and we reached this stage without giving any money to anybody and with the grace of god I got good job without anybody's recommendation and I have struggled to come to this stage and have done my responsibility in a good manner and now I am leading happy retired life.' (Older adult male)

Both older men and women were involved in religious and cultural activities. The range of religious activities included participating in religious discourses, visiting temples, organising special worship events, observing the rituals of the holy months and group pilgrimages to shrines and temples. In the excerpt below we see the combination of travel and cultural activities that this older adult took part in post-retirement. The respondent refers also to other women who are in the same situation as her and that the completion of their responsibilities has given them more free time to pursue their hobbies and dreams. For older adults who had completed their life course obligations, the spare time provided them the opportunities to re-engage with the society. Some older women who were living alone or with a spouse formed groups and organised day trips or longer travels to pilgrimage sites. Dhal (2017) observes that among Indian middle-class retirees, women were more successful in combining multiple activities with caregiving, compared to men.

P:	'Yes, we are three to four ladies of same age, all finished children's responsibilities. Recently, I went to Dubai. I have also been to

America when my son called me there. At that time I was still working. I did not have enough leave that time so I went only for 3 months. Now again he is calling to see his children and his house which he bought there, but first I want to go to Kashi tour. Next month there is an Author's Conference and Poetics Conference. (...) For that also I am member from the past 5 to 6 years. They usually only hold annual functions. They do all cultural activities. There will be seminars during the poetry conference. I participate in all the seminars.' (Older adult female)

Some older men were still working or were economically dependent on their children, therefore, they did not have the leisure time to pursue cultural and religious activities. Older women in low-income households had to continue their caregiving activities often across generations. Many older women cared for their spouses who were ill, other older adults in the same household and for grandchildren. Among older adults who had moved to the urban area, very few of them had local contacts or social capital to ask for help. Older adults who had returned to Dharwad from other cities post retirement often rented or bought homes close to siblings or extended family members. Pandya (2016) notes that among higher-educated and retired women, caregiving still took more than half of their daily time. Economic independence, lessened caregiving tasks and independent living had a larger role to play in a sense of well-being and satisfaction among the older adults.

Discussion and conclusions

This chapter explored how the well-being of older adults is linked to their life course obligations towards their families. Through in-depth qualitative research we have shown that different stages and transitions that are part of the life courses of older adults and their family members. The empirical material clearly shows the need to embed the life course framework and life events within local ideologies, religious beliefs and cultural norms. In this study we examine the life stage conceptualisation as presented within Hinduism as a worldview. Life stages and expectations of successful transition from one stage to the next was perceived as crucial for both the older adults and their offspring. Hence successful ageing was intricately connected to the lives of family members. In line with Lamb (2000, 2002) and Brijnath (2012), we emphasise the need to take a cultural lens in understanding family reciprocities and care within and across generations. In relation to criticisms by Hagestad and Dannefer (2001) on the 'microfication' of life course approaches, we take a broader view to go beyond the nuclear family and examine the asymmetrical care and power relations within the families (Kõu and Bailey, 2014; Bailey, 2017).

This chapter clearly shows the need to better contextualise life course decisions and trajectories in non-Western settings and to specifically move the discussion beyond the culturalist discussion on 'filial piety'. The theoretical concept of linked lives (Elder, 1985) aids in getting an interactional approach to situate the actions of the individual towards his/her own well-being and that of his/her linked significant others. This is one of few studies in India (Lamb, 2000, 2002; Bomhoff, 2011; Brijnath, 2012; Bailey, James and Hallad, 2017; Ahlin, and Sen, 2020; Ugargol and Bailey, 2020), which has investigated the family lives and care reciprocities of older adults from an in-depth qualitative perspective. Such rich qualitative descriptions provide us with a deeper insight into older adults and how they make sense of their lives with the migration of their children. The embedding of the life course obligation into the cultural meaning system of *ashramas* provides us space to further explain the motivational schemas associated with life course obligations. The successful completion of these life course obligations was perceived to lead to better well-being. What emerges from other narratives as well is a process of individualisation wherein the older adults are focusing once more on their own lives and how to lead them and make plans independently of the lives of their children. The experience of this individualisation was, however, dependent on their caregiving roles and the economic situation of the household. One of the limitations of this chapter is that it focuses on middle-class households who have the resources to realise their life course goals; this may not be possible for older adults from lower socio-economic groups. Economic security, social support, health and better living conditions aid in realising the life course obligations and contribute towards the overall well-being of the older adults.

Acknowledgements

This chapter was written within the Indian-European research networking grant: Ageing and Well-being in a Globalising World (NWO 465–11–009), funded by NWO-ESRC-ICSSR. The participating institutions include Institute for Social and Economic Change, Bangalore; Centre for Development Studies, Trivandrum; Population Research Centre, University of Groningen, the Netherlands and the University of Southampton, United Kingdom. The data collection for this study was funded by the UNFPA-India and ISEC programme on Building Knowledge Base on Ageing in India. We acknowledge the support of H. R. Channakki, B. I. Pundappanavar, S. R. Vatavati, R. K. Itagi, Megha and Sulochana in the qualitative and quantitative data collection. This chapter was presented at the 8th International Conference on Cultural Gerontology in Galway, Ireland, 10–12 April 2014.

References

Ahlin, T. and Sen, K. (2020) 'Shifting duties: becoming "good daughters" through elder care practices in transnational families from Kerala, India', *Gender, Place and Culture*, 27(10): 1395–414.

Ang, R. P. and O, J. (2012) 'Association between caregiving, meaning in life, and life satisfaction beyond 50 in an Asian sample: age as a moderator', *Social Indicators Research*, 108(3): 525–34. doi:10.1007/s11205-011-9891-9.

Bailey, A. (2017) 'The migrant suitcase: food, belonging and commensality among Indian migrants in the Netherlands', *Appetite*, 110, 51–60.

Bailey, A. J., Blake, M. K. and Cooke, T. J. (2004) 'Migration, care, and the linked lives of dual-earner households', *Environment and Planning A*, 36(9): 1617–32.

Bailey, A., Hallad, J. and James, K. S. (2018) 'They had to go': Indian older adults' experiences of rationalizing and compensating the absence of migrant children'. *Sustainability*, 10(6): 1946.

Banerji, M. and Deshpande, A. S. (2020) 'Does "love"make a difference? Marriage choice and post-marriage decision-making power in India', *Asian Population Studies*, 17(2): 201–20.

Bhat, A. K. and Dhruvarajan, R. (2002) 'Ageing in India: drifting intergenerational relations, challenges and options', *Ageing and Society*, 21(5): 621–40. doi:10.1017/S0144686X0100842X.

Bloom, D. E., Mahal, A., Rosenberg, L. and Sevilla, J. (2010) 'Economic security arrangements in the context of population ageing in India', *International Social Security Review*, 63(3–4): 59–89.

Bomhoff, M. (2011) 'Long-lived sociality: a cultural analysis of middle-class older persons' social lives in Kerala, India', Doctoral dissertation, Leiden University.

Bongaarts, J. and Zimmer, Z. (2002) 'Living arrangements of older adults in the developing world: an analysis of demographic and health survey household surveys', *The Journals of Gerontology Series B: Psychological Sciences and Social Sciences*, 57(3): S145–S157.

Brijnath, B. (2012) 'Why does institutionalised care not appeal to Indian families? Legislative and social answers from urban India', *Ageing and Society*, 32(4): 697–717.

Charsley, K. (2005) 'Unhappy husbands: masculinity and migration in transnational Pakistani marriages', *The Journal of the Royal Anthropological Institute*, 11(1): 85–105.

Cooke, T. J. (2008) 'Migration in a family way', *Population, Space and Place*, 14, 255–65.

Dannefer, D. (2003) 'Toward a global geography of the life course: challenges of late modernity for life course theory', in J. T. Mortimer and M. J. Shanahan (eds) *Handbook of the Life Course*, New York: Kluwer Academic/ Plenum Publishers, pp 647–59.

Das, M. B. and Žumbytė, I. (2017) 'The motherhood penalty and female employment in urban India', World Bank Policy Research Working Paper 8004. Washington DC: World Bank.

Dhal, G. K. (2017) 'Middle class retirement in India: a qualitative study of active ageing, health, family relationships and quality of life' (Doctoral dissertation, University of Surrey).

Elder, G. H., Jr. (1975) 'Age differentiation and life course', *Annual Review of Sociology*, 1: 165–90.

Elder, G. H., Jr. (1985) 'Perspectives on the life course', in G. H. Elder Jr. (ed) *Life Course Dynamics: Trajectories and Transitions, 1968–1980*, . Ithaca, NY: Cornell University Press, pp 23–49.

Fluit, M., Bailey, A. and Bouwman, R. (2019) 'Diasporic ageing and home-making practices of hindustani surinamese older adults in the Netherlands', in I. Rajan (ed) *India Migration Report 2019: Diasporas in Europe*, Abingdon: Routledge, pp 213–33.

Fuller, C. J. and Narasimhan, H. (2008) 'Companionate marriage in India: the changing marriage system in a middle-class Brahman subcaste', *Journal of the Royal Anthropological Institute*, 14(4): 736–54.

Gallo, E. (2006) 'Italy is not a good place for men: narratives of places, marriage and masculinity among Malayali migrants', *Global Networks*, 6(4): 357–72.

Gardner, K. (2009) 'Lives in motion: the life-course, movement and migration in Bangladesh', *Journal of South Asian Development*, 4(2): 229–51.

Gray, P. B., Longkumer, W., Panda, S. and Rangaswamy, M. (2019) 'Grandparenting in urban Bangalore, India: support and involvement from the standpoint of young adult university students. *Sage Open*, 9(3): 2158244019871070.

Hagestad, G. O. and Dannefer, D. (2001) 'Concepts and theories of aging: beyond microfication in social science approaches', *Handbook of Aging and the Social Sciences*, 5: 3–21.

Hennink, M., Hutter, I. and Bailey, A. (2020) *Qualitative Research Methods*, 2nd ed. London: SAGE Publications Ltd.

Ho, E. L. E. and Chiu, T. Y. (2020) 'Transnational ageing and "care technologies": Chinese grandparenting migrants in Singapore and Sydney', *Population, Space and Place*, 26(7): e2365.

IIPS (International Institute for Population Sciences) (2020) *Longitudinal Ageing Study in India (LASI) Wave 1, 2017–18, India Report*, International Institute for Population Sciences: Mumbai.

Jahangir, S., Nikhil, P. N. N., Bailey, A. and Datta, A. (2018) 'Contextualizing elder abuse and neglect in institutional and home settings: case studies from India', in M. K. Shankardass and S. Irudaya Rajan (eds) *Abuse and Neglect of the Elderly in India*, Singapore: Springer, pp 175–88, https://doi.org/10.1007/978-981-10-6116-5_11

James, K. S. (2011) 'India's demographic change: opportunities and challenges', *Science*, 333(6042): 576–80.

Jamuna, D. (2000) 'Ageing in India: some key issues', *Ageing International*, 25(4): 16–31

Kõu, A. and Bailey, A. (2014) 'Movement is a constant feature in my life: contextualising migration processes of highly skilled Indians', *Geoforum*, 52: 113–22.

Kõu, A., van Wissen, L., van Dijk, J. and Bailey, A. (2015) 'A life course approach to high-skilled migration: lived experiences of Indians in the Netherlands', *Journal of Ethnic and Migration Studies*, 41(10): 1644–63.

Kõu, A., Mulder, C. H. and Bailey, A. (2017) ' "For the sake of the family and future": the linked lives of highly skilled Indian migrants', *Journal of Ethnic and Migration Studies*, 43(16): 2788–805.

Krishnan, S. and Hatekar, N. (2017) 'Rise of the new middle class in India and its changing structure', *Economic and Political Weekly*, 52(22): 40–8.

Lamb, S. (2000) *White Saris and Sweet Mangoes: Aging, Gender, and Body in North India*, Berkeley: University of California Press.

Lamb, S. (2002) 'Intimacy in a transnational era: the remaking of aging among Indian Americans', *Diaspora: A Journal of Transnational Studies*, 11(3): 299–330.

Lamb, S. (2009) *Aging and the Indian Diaspora: Cosmopolitan Families in India and Abroad*, Bloomington: Indiana University Press.

Le Bail, H. (2017) 'Cross-border marriages as a side door for paid and unpaid migrant workers: the case of marriage migration between China and Japan', *Critical Asian Studies*, 49(2): 226–43.

Majumdar, S. (2005) 'Home in the context of religion for elderly Hindus in India', in G. D. Rowles and H. Chaudhury (eds) *Home and Identity in Late Life: International Perspectives*, New York: Springer, pp 81–110.

Mallick, H. (2012) 'Inflow of remittances and private investment in India', *Singapore Economic Review*, 57(1): 1–22.

Moen, P. and Hernandez, E. (2009) 'Social convoys: studying linked lives in time, context, and motion', in G.H. Elder, Jr. and J. Z. Giele (eds) *The Craft of Life Course Research*, New York and London: The Guilford Press, pp 258–79.

Mulder, C. H. and Hooimeijer, P. (1999) 'Residential relocations in the life course', in L. J. G. van Wissen and P. A. Dykstra (eds) *Population Issues: An Interdisciplinary Focus*, New York: Kluwer Academic/Plenum Publishers, pp 159–86.

Nagalingam, J. (2007) 'Understanding successful aging: a study of older Indian adults in Singapore. *Care Management Journals*, 8(1): 18–25.

OECD (2011) *International Migration Outlook 2011. International Migration*, France: OECD Press.

Pande, R. and Malhotra, A. (2012) 'Fertility decline and changes in women's lives and gender equality in Tamil Nadu, India', *International Center for Research on Women Fertility and Empowerment Working Paper Series*, 007–2012.

Pandya, S. P. (2016) 'What do highly qualified professionally achieving women do after retirement in India? Exploring time use, leisure, and volunteering', *Journal of Women and Aging*, 28(5): 431–43.

Pazhoothundathil, N. and Bailey, A. (2020) 'Cherished possessions, home-making practices and aging in care homes in Kerala, India', *Emotion, Space and Society*, 36. https://doi.org/10.1016/j.emospa.2020.100706.

Rajan, S. I. (2012) *India Migration Report 2011: Migration, Identity and Conflict*, New Delhi: Routledge.

Ratha, D. and Mohapatra, S. (2013) 'Migrant remittances and development', *The Evidence and Impact of Financial Globalization*, Washington, DC: World Bank pp 121–30.

Saraswathi, T. S., Mistry, J. and Dutta, R. (2011) 'Reconceptualizing lifespan development through a Hindu perspective', in L. A. Jensen (ed) *Bridging Cultural and Developmental Approaches to Psychology: New Syntheses in Theory, Research and Policy*, New York: Oxford University Press, pp 276–300.

Shaw, A. and Charsley, K. (2006) 'Rishtas: adding emotion to strategy in understanding British Pakistani transnational marriages', *Global Networks*, 6(4): 405–21. http://dx.doi.org/10.1111/j.1471-0374.2006.00152.x

Shrestha, S. and Zarit, S. H. (2012) 'Cultural and contextual analysis of quality of life among older Nepali women', *Journal of Cross-Cultural Gerontology*, 27(2): 163–82.

Statham, P. (2020) 'Living the long-term consequences of Thai–Western marriage migration: the radical life-course transformations of women who partner older Westerners', *Journal of Ethnic and Migration Studies*, 46(8): 1562–87.

Thomas, M. J., Mulder, C. H. and Cooke, T. J. (2017) 'Linked lives and constrained spatial mobility: the case of moves related to separation among families with children', *Transactions of the Institute of British Geographers*, 42(4): 597–611.

Ugargol, A. P. and Bailey, A. (2021) 'Reciprocity between older adults and their care-givers in emigrant households of Kerala, India', *Ageing & Society*, 41(8): 1699–725.

Van Willigen, J., Kedia, S. and Chadha, N. K. (1995) 'Personal networks and sacred texts: social aging in Delhi, India', *Journal of Cross-Cultural Gerontology*, 10(3): 175–98.

World Bank (2020) *Migration and Development Brief 32: COVID-19 Crisis through a Migration Lens*, April, Washington, DC: World Bank.

Xu, L., Wu, B., Chi, I. and Hsiao, H.-Y. (2012) 'Intensity of grandparent caregiving and life satisfaction among rural Chinese older adults: a longitudinal study using latent difference score analysis', *Family and Community Health*, 35(4): 287–99.

Yeoh, B. S. A., Huang, S. and Lam, T. (2005) 'Transnationalizing the "Asian" family: imaginaries, intimacies and strategic intents', *Global Networks*, 5(4): 307–15.

8

Interpreting the landscapes of care for older men in Delhi and Kolkata: perspectives from care receivers and caregivers

Selim Jahangir, Ajay Bailey and Anindita Datta

Introduction

The geographies of care literature covers care practices in its many different forms and spatial structures (Milligan, 2017; Hanrahan and Smith, 2020; Power and Williams, 2020), including home-based care negotiations (Button and Ncapai, 2019) in everyday care practices. Recently the landscapes of care or caringscapes have started to be mapped, investigating how different spatial cares are practised and perceived by different people (Meier and Bowman, 2017; Bowlby and McKie, 2019). Care and care relationships are located in, shaped by and shape particular spaces and places that range from local to global (Milligan and Wiles, 2010). Similarly, Lawson (2008) argues that the way care is understood, experienced and practised is shaped by socio-economic and political contexts. McKie et al (2002), while defining 'caringscapes', brought up two important points. First, caregiving is a social practice, is gendered and it is determined by the creative strategies of caregivers (largely women) in both professional and family settings (Power, 2016; Williams and Sethi, 2020). Second, care should be viewed as a fundamentally social, economic and cultural relationship. In addition, it is important to mention that caregiving in the Asian context, particularly in India, is mainly carried out by women, especially spouses and daughters-in-law (Ajay et al, 2017; Ugargol and Bailey, 2020). Female family members, traditionally, are expected to take care of older adults and children (Pillai et al, 2012; Ugargol et al, 2016). The synergy between the gendered nature of caregiving and its spatial dimension essentially engender the contextual caringscapes.

Caringscapes are developed through an individual's involvement with varied social landscapes of care, caregiving roles, employment and social policies, and gendered and generational expectations of care and work (McKie et al, 2002). To understand 'care', one needs to consider all those who are involved in the care relationship because the nature, extent and form of these relationships are affected by *where* they take place (Milligan and Wiles, 2010). Therefore, care is not only interpersonal relations but also people–place relationships. Critically, landscapes of care are both product of and produced by the social and political–institutional arrangements for care.

Ageing, care and geography

Geographers have long been unravelling the complex relationships between people, place and care through different philosophical and methodological frameworks (Schwanen et al, 2012). Geographers in the field of ageing have termed this interdisciplinary body of knowledge 'geographical gerontology' (Andrews et al, 2009). The work of Rowles (1986) and Laws (1995, 1996) has pushed the boundary of geographical gerontology to the understanding of geographies of ageing. The influential works of Harper and Laws (1995) provided the second wave leading towards the specialisation of 'geography of ageing'. Based on the second wave of inquiry the scope and nature of contemporary geographical research on ageing has tremendously expanded (eg, Andrews and Phillips, 2005; Hopkins and Pain, 2007; Cutchin, 2009; Del Casino, 2009; Hardill, 2009; Schwanen et al, 2012). Geographers working on ageing are contributing to our understanding of the delicate relationships between human geography and social gerontology. Currently 'geographies of ageing' incorporates work on ageing across sub-disciplines, particularly in health geography, population geography and social geography (Andrews et al, 2009), whereas studies on geographies of care have been concerned with relationships between people, place and (health) care (Milligan et al, 2007). Geographers working broadly within this field also address the issue of formal and informal caregiving, relationships between paid caregivers and care recipients within new settings and the changing meaning and nature of home (Milligan and Power, 2010; Milligan and Liu, 2015; Wang, 2019), as well as people's relationships with particular parts of the city, voluntary and community care settings, palliative care settings (Andruske and O'Connor, 2020; Croucher et al, 2020). Other studies have considered the impact of transitions particularly in relation to caregivers and older people (Monkong et al, 2020). However, majority of the studies on ageing and care are in Western contexts and very few have been conducted in the Indian context.

Only recently have social scientists and social work professionals have started working on the emerging issues of the living conditions of older adults in different parts of India. The initial studies were mainly focused on examining the issues related to the social, psychological and health problems experienced by older adults and assessing the impact of various schemes meant for the welfare of older persons. Most of the studies were based on secondary data collected on issues like age and sex structure, rural–urban residence, literacy, marital status, work status, dependency status, disability and health status (Ramamurti and Jamuna, 2005 as cited by S. Siva Raju, 2011), whereas the study of ageing through a geographical perspective is rarely found. However, some studies have focused on spatial care practices including institutional care, living arrangements and emotional attachment in India (Ugargol and Bailey, 2018; Pazhoothundathil and Bailey, 2020). In the absence of contemporary work in geographies of ageing couples with changing social and physical contexts of ageing in India, this chapter seeks to interpret the landscapes of care – the spatial expressions of the relationship between the socio-structural processes and structures that shape experiences and practices of care – of older men through the perspectives of care recipients and their caregivers. In this chapter we investigate the landscapes of care or caringscapes of older men living in homes and institutional care centres in two metropolitan cities in India: Delhi and Kolkata. We also explored how care practices are grounded in different spaces over which the older men and their caregivers repetitively engaged in routine activity and (re)shaped caringscapes.

Conceptual framework

Caring relationships can involve varying degrees of emotional attachment in a variety of settings producing complex 'landscapes of care' or 'caringscapes'. Caringscapes develop through an individual's involvement with varied social landscapes of care, caregiving roles, employment and social policies and gendered and generational expectations of care and work (McKie et al, 2002). Therefore, to understand 'care', one should consider care relationships because the nature, extent and form of these relationships are affected by *where they take place* (Milligan and Wiles, 2010). Hence, care combines both interpersonal relations and people–place relationships. Critically, landscapes of care are both the product and produced by the social and political-institutional arrangements for care (see Chapter 11 for the obligations to care for older adults). Landscapes of care are multilayered because they are shaped by issues of responsibility, ethics and morals, and by the social, emotional, physical and material aspects of caring. This includes support, services and the spatial politics of care (Brown, 2003). Hence, caringscapes are embedded in the multilayered genderscapes that are, in turn, shaped by women's lives in spaces that differ widely with respect to their traditional role, degree of mobility, participation in society, agency and autonomy (Datta, 2011).

Here we examine how caringscapes overlap with the genderscapes. Drawing on Appadurai's (1996) concept of the 'scape', Datta (2011) defined genderscapes as a fluid and multilayered space. Akin to genderscapes, caringscapes are complex and dynamic over which care is

Figure 8.1: Conceptual framework caringscapes of older men embedded in multilayered genderscapes

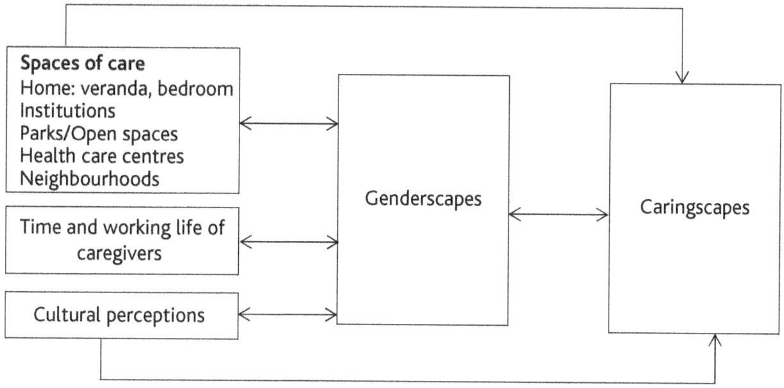

perceived, performed and transformed. It includes institutions, homes and neighbourhoods and is the product of the space over which it is constructed. In addition, due to changing family structure, the living arrangements and care of the older men are also being influenced as the young generation is engaged in working life to meet the essential needs (Ahlin and Sen, 2020). Therefore, there is an increasing trend to shift to the institutions due to lack of caregivers in the home.

Traditionally care for older adults is gender-specific in Indian society, where women are considered the primary caregivers. The responsibility of caregiving goes mainly to wives, daughters-in-law, daughters living at home (Ugargol and Bailey, 2020) and to female caregivers in institutions (Pazhoothundathil and Bailey, 2020). In this study both the home and institutions are overwhelmingly represented by female caregivers. Lin and Wolf (2020) found that adult daughters are more likely to be caregivers to both mothers and fathers than adult sons. They argued that daughters provide more domestic assistance and personal care to older parents, whereas sons perform more traditional roles for men such as home maintenance chores and financial or managerial assistance (Fingerman et al, 2020; Roth, 2020).

Participant recruitment

The study applied a qualitative research design. The methods employed included in-depth interviews, the non-participant observation and field diaries. A total of 79 in-depth interviews were conducted, of which 47 were older men and 32 were their caregivers. Out of these 47 older men, 25 were from Kolkata and 22 were from Delhi. Among the caregivers 17 were from Kolkata and 15 were from Delhi. Participants were selected through purposive sampling and interviews were conducted until data saturation was achieved. The data were collected in the months of June, July and August 2013 in Kolkata and in the months of December 2013 and February and March 2014 in Delhi.

In this study two types of institutional caregivers have been included: those who are paid directly by the care recipient and those who are paid by institutions. We also recruited some paid caregivers who provide care to more than one older adult in the institutions. Seventeen older adults and 13 caregivers have been taken from institutional care centres in Delhi (see Table 8.1). In Delhi, due to constraints in accessing the older adults living at home, five older men and two caregivers have been included (see Table 8.2). The constraints were mainly due to the age and gender of the first author who collected the data. Older adults did not allow the author to interview the *bahu-betiya* (daughters–inlaw and daughters) as it is not culturally acceptable for an unrelated male to talk to the women of the house. In Kolkata 13 older adults and 12 caregivers from institutional care centres (see Table 8.1) and 12 older adults and 5 caregivers from private homes were interviewed (see Table 8.2).

Ethical considerations

The older adults and their caregivers were provided with information regarding the purpose of the study and the interviews. We also sought the participants' verbal consent regarding the recording of the interview and taking of photographs. Participants were allowed to read the introductory part of the in-depth interview guide. Before conducting the interview, the first author had introduced himself with the purpose of the study and produced his university and residential ID to each older adult and their caregivers both in private homes and institutions. In addition, their names and addresses have been kept confidential. In the process of recruiting the participants, ethical issues arose, of which the core issue was the permission for interviewing the participants. The researcher had taken full permission from the New Delhi Municipality Corporation for interviewing the older men and their caregivers living in the institutions in Delhi. In the institutional care centres in Kolkata, we were allowed to interview the older adults and their caregivers with the first author's university card and department letter.

Interviews and observation

The in-depth interviews were conducted in the institutional care centres (commonly known as old age homes in India) and private homes in both cities. An in-depth interview guide was used for the personal interview of the older men and their caregivers. The interview guide was prepared in English but was translated into Hindi and Bengali. There were few participants who

Table 8.1: Profile of participants living in institutions

Name	Age	City	Previous occupation	Caregivers (interviewed)
Brijesh	72	Delhi	Fruit seller	Carer paid by institution
Charanjeet	90	Delhi	Clothes marketing	Carer paid by institution
Jagdal	75	Delhi	Cycle repairing	Carer paid by institution
Kamal	74	Delhi	Car mechanic	Carer paid by institution
Kirti	76	Delhi	Comptroller and Auditor General of India	Carer paid by receivers
Krishna	76	Delhi	Assistant private secretary	Carer paid by receiver
Madan	86	Delhi	Senior account officer	Carer paid by receiver
Manmohan	66	Delhi	Telegram officer	Carer paid by receiver
Narendrapal	62	Delhi	Businessman	Carer paid by receiver
Piyush	79	Delhi	Managerial post in Railway Ministry	Carer paid by receiver
Praveen	64	Delhi	Worked in food company	Carer paid by institution
Rajesh	73	Delhi	Chief telecomms engineer	Carer paid by institution
Ram Mohan	70	Delhi	Work at cold storage	Carer paid by institution
Ramesh	70	Delhi	Handyman	Carer paid by institution
Sunil	70	Delhi	Plant supervisor	Carer paid by receiver
Vishwanath	84	Delhi	Worked in technology company	Carer paid by receiver
Amit	77	Kolkata	Medical representative	Carer paid by receiver
Subhas	65	Kolkata	Businessman	Carer paid by institution
Subodh	65	Kolkata	Security guard	Carer paid by receiver
Sudhir	87	Kolkata	Politician	Carer paid by institution
Sukumar	80	Kolkata	Teacher	Carer paid by receiver
Tushar	75	Kolkata	Doctor	Carer paid by receiver
Anil	86	Kolkata	P.R.O. in Air India	Carer paid by receiver
Elvin	77	Kolkata	Engineer in railways	Carer paid by receiver
Kalipada	77	Kolkata	Printing department	Carer paid by receiver
Panchanan	87	Kolkata	Worked in Bengal club	Carer paid by receiver
Somoresh	88	Kolkata	Typist	Carer paid by receiver
Shakti	61	Kolkata	Rail controller	Carer paid by receivers
Tushar	75	Kolkata	Medical doctor	Carer paid by receiver

Note: All names have been anonymised.

Table 8.2: Profile of participants living in private homes

Name	Age	City	Previous occupation	Caregivers (interviewed)
Anil	86	Delhi	Lab assistant	Married son
Harish	76	Delhi	Administrative officer	Divorced daughter (not interviewed)
Mangat Ram	65	Delhi	Chemist shopkeeper	Daughter in law
Subhramaniyam	75	Delhi	Typist	Wife and daughter (not interviewed)
Sunheri Lal	70	Delhi	Farmer	Sons and daughter in laws (not interviewed)
Abdul Kalam	92	Kolkata	Mechanic	Wife and daughter in laws (not interviewed)
Manju Nath	75	Kolkata	Receptionist,	Wife
Ramesh	72	Kolkata	Transport conductor	Wife and daughter in law
Anwar Ali	68	Kolkata	Worked in bakery	Wife (not interviewed)
Bholanath	68	Kolkata	Central government	Wife (not interviewed)
Bimal	103	Kolkata	Worked in timber storage	Son
Koushik	72	Kolkata	Worked at textile factory	Son and wife (not interviewed)
Biswanath	86	Kolkata	Businessman	Daughter (not interviewed)
Dipankar	74	Kolkata	Consultancy firm	Wife (not interviewed)
Joydeep	79	Kolkata	Worked in Steel Authority of India	Wife
Malay	71	Kolkata	Civil engineer	Wife (not interviewed)
Bapendra	75	Kolkata	Chairman, Co-operative Housing Federation	Wife

Note: All names have been anonymised.

preferred English over the local language for the interviews. For older adults living in private homes, most of the interviews were conducted in park spaces where they go to meet fellow older adults in the afternoons. Parks were selected so that they could share their everyday life experiences away from their family members. Some of the older adults living in homes who were unable to walk properly were interviewed in a separate room. The interviews of the institutional care receivers were conducted in their personal rooms and in open spaces at the institutions. Additional information was collected through observation as it was felt that interviews alone could not reveal the differences of what the participants actually do and what they say (Hennink et al, 2020). It also helped to cross-check the information shared by the participants in their interviews on particular issues, such as behaviour towards each other. These observations were noted down in the field diary during the field study and incorporated while explaining the contexts.

Data analysis

This study is based on the personal interviews data that were digitally recorded and transcribed into Bengali and in Hindi. All the transcribed data were translated into English. The interviews were analysed with the help of WeftQDA, a software package for qualitative data analysis. This software helped to develop codes and categories from the participants' stories. Then, each of the code families was described comparing different statements and quotes made by the participants. After that, these descriptions were contextualised further with the observation data. The main code families that emerged in the study were perceptions of care, caregivers, medical care, economic care and perception of the younger generation by the present older adults. For this chapter, the code families such as perceptions of personal care, emotional care, medical and economic care and cultural perception of care have been used to explain the context. These perceptions have come out of both the deductive as well as inductive methods of data collection. Perceptions such as personal care, economic care and medical care have been collected through the deductive method, whereas perceptions relating to emotional care and cultural perception of care emerged through the inductive method. The results are analysed with the narratives of the care recipients and the caregivers and their emotional attachments and relationships with the people and place.

Caringscapes of Delhi and Kolkata: narratives of care recipients and caregivers

In this study the caringscapes or the landscapes of care involve the perceptions of care and the perceived appropriate location of care for older adults. Here the caringscapes are mapped and inferred based on the narratives of the care receivers and the caregivers in both the spaces, that is, in institutional (public) spaces as well as in homes.

Perceptions about care and its transactions over varied space

In their in-depth interviews, the participants expressed their varied perceptions of care or *Dekhbhal* (Hindi) or *Dekhasona* (Bengali). Both these terms encompass physical, social, economic and emotional care. Older men perceived that meeting their needs was the care they expected. These needs ranged from small tasks such as bringing tea, exhibiting good behaviour and showing sympathy, to higher-order needs such as food, health care, clothing, cleaning, financial support and emotional attachment. All these care activities take place over spaces which range from home to neighbourhoods. Within homes, there are certain spaces where older adults spend more time and develop emotional attachment with those micro spaces. Similarly, in the institutions the older adults also nurture emotional attachment with different types of cherished possessions including material and memorial aspects that act as sense of co-presence (Pazhoothundathil and Bailey, 2020), thus creating unique caringscapes in the older adults' immediate surroundings. The caringscapes, in turn, also produce different meanings of care embodied with perceptions and cultural practices.

Perception of personal care or *seva/seba*

Personal care is perceived to be the most sensitive and is seen to be accompanied with emotional attachments to the receivers and givers. This is known as *seva* in Delhi and *seba* in Kolkata. It includes assisting the older adults with personal hygiene or physical care including bathing and dressing, and with activities of daily living including meal preparation and feeding. Personal care and supportive social relations play a major role in emotional well-being and physical health (Gyasi et al, 2020; Reynolds et al, 2020). In this study the older adults perceived that *seva/seba* have more emotional attachments with each other when compared to *dekhbhal* or *dekhasona* because *seva* or *seba* are associated with personal care including touching and massaging the body. Older men perceived that such kind of personal care is only given by the family members, specifically daughters and granddaughters, which reflect the gendered nature of such care practices. The older adults perceived that geographical distance is not a barrier for care since their children, particularly daughters, can provide care from distance. The older adults living in the institutions also perceived that they get emotional support and care when their daughters visit them.

> 'I have my daughters as well who also take care of me. They know how to take care of daddy. From their childhood days they know what I like and what I don't. Even after marriage they call me every day from their in-law house. I am so lucky with my daughters. My younger daughter is a service holder, and she brought Horlicks and gave me. They called their mother every day that whether I am regularly taking it or not because I forget to take. I cannot disagree. They are doing lots for us.' (Shyam Prakash, 79, institutional care receiver, Delhi)

Older adults living in institutions viewed material care including providing clothes and other gifts as not being *real* care. They perceived that the *real* care can only be provided by own children or family members, preferably spouses or daughters. Here, the care receivers reflected that *seva/seba* has emotional attachment which gives them life satisfaction (Lin et al, 2020). But for the institutional care receivers *seva/seba* means spontaneous care from caregivers. Some of the older men living in institutions perceived home as the best place for care but lack emotional and personal care from their children (Chapters 9 and 10 present different experiences of older adults and motivations to choose an old age home). The images of care practices that embodied different roles and responsibilities also shape the caringscapes of the older men as these are rooted in the real spaces.

> 'Actually personal opinion comes from core of my heart. The care which own blood can give we cannot expect from anybody else. I get only economic care. If I need they are ready to give me financial care, rest religious, social, emotional it is all missing. You must have an emotional touch you must have an ethical touch, with your family members. You must interact with them daily on the dining table or whenever or whenever you get time you must interact.' (Brijesh, 76, institutional care receiver, Delhi)

On the other hand, most of the caregivers saw older adults as demanding, and that they have to pay heed to all those demands so that the older adults would not feel deserted and neglected. The results revealed that older men want more time from their caregivers and the institutional caregivers cannot spend extended amounts of time with each individual older man. Instead, they sit on the veranda or in open spaces where the older adults and caregivers talk mostly in the mornings and the evenings. Due to time constraints, the caregivers in institutional care centres manage to support the older men in various creative ways in everyday care practices. Caregivers mentioned that they are more careful about the health of the older adults and that is why they try to ensure that they have a proper diet.

> 'If I feed someone, I will consider that as care. Someone asks me to do something, I do that; it will be a care. If I cook something for them, they become happy. I rub oil in their heads or offered them tea. For me these things are care. I give medicine with hot water three – four times in a day then he gains some energy.' (Madhabi, 42, institutional caregiver, Kolkata)

Cultural perception of care

By 'cultural perception of care', the care receivers and caregivers refer to the practice of traditional forms of care. Historically, family members used to care for the older adults unconditionally – there were no substitutes. One of the care receivers, Manjunath, (see Table 8.1) perceived that in the past the older adults had been shown respect which he thought was missing in current society. Some of the societies in rural India guaranteed power, honour and respect to the older adults (Pongiya et al, 2011). One of the major reasons for caring for older adults with veneration and respect lies in the fact that the children would become the heir of the property, land in particular, after the death of the older adults. Older men in their interviews had in general negative perceptions on the cultural care they received and they provide varied reasons for it such as 'lack of *sanskar* [cultural values]', 'fault in cultural upbringing', 'modernity', 'women's work participation' and 'independence and liberty'. Both the older men and their caregivers perceived that the care was much better in the past than in present times. This traditional form of care was viewed to be emotionally closer than what they received now. Chirkov et al (2005) found that cultural care is positively associated with life satisfaction.

'We would really look after our parents, love and respect them. We would take care of them before they would ask us to do it for them. But now, we have to tell them if we want to be looked after. We could understand what our parents would need and accordingly we would give them that before they even asked us.' (Manjunath, home care receiver, Kolkata)

'See I have taken care of my father and mother with great respect. I used to take care of them before they would ask to do for them. But now, I have to tell them if I want to be looked after.' (Sunheri Lal, home care receiver, Delhi)

The older adults perceived that it is the cultural upbringing of children that will determine whether they will receive care from the next generation and this upbringing encompasses the cultural landscape. Hence, the caringscapes of older adults are fashioned out of the cultural landscapes of Indian society. The predominance of women in care practices has constructed stereotypical notion that care is women's work and, hence, the caringscapes are also perceived to be gendered in nature.

Health care

As older adults are more likely to develop chronic health conditions, they need more health care with increasing age (Dey et al, 2012). In India older adults who are above 65 years spend on average 1.5 times more on health care compared to those in the 60–64-year age category (Mahal and Berman, 2002). Some of the participants, therefore, have given more significance to health care than other aspects of care. It has also been found that those who prioritised health care are either suffering from some ailment or condition, or that they are satisfied with their basic needs of food and shelter. On the other hand, it can be said those who are from relatively poor families prioritised the personal care, that is, food and family attachment, leaving aside health care. Even health insurance for Indian older adults is limited by low coverage of populations. According to the National Family Health Survey (2004–05) only 10 per cent of households in India had at least one member of the family covered by any form of health insurance (IIPS, 2007). Previous studies have established that older adults who were in government service, such as the civil services and railways, receive free medical services and feel secure about medical care (Acharya and Ranson, 2005; Pati et al, 2019). This study, in addition, found that the older adults go alone to health centres or hospital for their regular check-ups. Meanwhile, some of the older adults who were not getting free treatment were quite concerned about their health care and dependent on their children's help in this aspect of care.

'And for medical treatment I go to a doctor (whom my son told to take care of me) who is our family doctor. He advised me to go through thorough check up in every two or three months.' (Kamal, home care receiver, Delhi)

'For me the most important care is health care because I have blood pressure, then I do have a sleeping problem. I have to take the tablet before I have to go for sleeping. I cannot have a proper sleep. For this type of care the medicine is required which my daughter used to bring for me. When I ask for medicine she immediately bring it for me. If I say that this medicine has finished she immediately brings that.' (Malay, 71, home care receiver, Kolkata)

In an exceptional case one of the institutional care receivers in Kolkata responded that for health care he himself makes the medicine from medicinal plants. He reads a lot about medicinal plants for his health as he has very little faith in modern medicines. During the interview he showed his belongings which mostly consist of books and he did not forget to show his bed which was full of medicinal books (see Figure 8.2). He even kept the books under his bed. According to him these are the things which he considers as resources and part of everyday life. This also shows the place attachment of the older adults and the role of books, constituting the part of their landscape of care.

On the other hand, the home caregivers are not so concerned about the medical care of the older adults. Participants revealed that they do not wait for their children's help when they need to go for a medical check-up. In some cases the older adults go alone as they do not want to become a

Figure 8.2: Institutional care receiver with his belongings in Kolkata

burden to their children. It was also reported that the family members only accompany the older men when they need to travel far for treatment or to attend appointments for a serious illness. The caregivers perceived that they do not want to take leave from their job to accompany their parents to appointments for minor treatments.

'See for medical treatment we go for the University Health Centre. He can go health centre alone but whenever he needs to go outside then I accompany him.' (Suresh, home caregiver of Anil, Delhi)

'I buy my own medicine. I have my money to buy them but those are not available here. My sons do not do those works. Since my medicine is not available here I have to go outside and get them. The medicine alone costs me 800–1000 rupees in a month.' (Bholanath, 68, home care receiver in Kolkata)

Economic care

Traditionally the family provides economic support to older adults in India (Rajan et al, 2020). The interviews reveal that the older adults drawing pensions consider that economic assistance as just one part of care. For them it is merely a means of surviving; care has other aspect to it, which are more important than this.

> 'Not at all. Money cannot provide you care. You cannot purchase care by money; money is not everything. You need money but it cannot solve my care.' (Anil, home care receiver, Delhi)

On the other hand, there were some older men who considered economic care as the most important element, as other parts of care – such as living arrangements – are dependent on this economic support. Previous research (Bongaarts et al, 2001; Aguila et al, 2020; Mudrazija et al, 2020) on the link between living arrangements and economic care also supports the importance of economic independence. Mahajan and Ray (2013) mentioned that between 60 and 75 per cent of all older adults in India are economically dependent on family members – usually on their children. Here, once more, the gendered nature of care for older adults in terms of economic care reflects the prevailing pattern of caregiving. Many older participants reported that their sons are primarily providing the economic care to them.

> 'My sons do, especially my younger son have done a lot. I had undergone an open surgery at Apollo. My son had spent his money then.' (Manju Nath, home care receiver, Kolkata)

Home caregivers are of the view that it is their duty to provide economic support to the older men as they are living a retired life. Children stated that their parents brought them up and now it is time to return the favour in terms of economic support, along with other forms of care.

> 'We give the money, otherwise who else will give. They are leading a retired life; there is nobody else to look after them other than us. We do this.' (Madhabi, home caregiver of Ramesh, Kolkata)

On the other hand, institutional caregivers perceived that economic support is secondary, and that other aspects of care are more important. Nowadays, most of the older adults have their own source of economic support but for them that holds little meaning, as they seek closeness of family members and other relatives.

> 'People come to my NGO and say that they can give monetary help, but they can't devote time. All that the older adults need is someone to attend to them and talk to them. Money is secondary matter.' (Veena, institutional caregiver, Delhi)

Depending on their socio-economic status, older adults decide on the location for their care or living arrangements (see Chapter 10 on pathways into care homes). Some of the older adults who are economically better off shifted to high-quality institutional care centres, whereas most of the older adults prefer to stay in government-run institutions. Older adults also develop emotional attachments with the caregivers at the institutions and consider them as family, even sharing their thoughts with them. Therefore care practice has become a normative experience. Care of older adults living in homes, however, still depends on the caregiver's income and other benefits. When a caregiver gives up a job or reduces their work hours, the economic care of the older adults is affected. Besides, the quality of everyday care of older adults living in institutions also depends on their own economic circumstances. Therefore, the economic context operating at the individual to wider society level and in public or private spheres (Wiles and Rosenberg, 2003; Milligan, 2009) shapes the varied landscapes of care.

Discussion and conclusion

In this chapter we have sought to engage critically with some of the geographical debates around care of older men through their interconnected socio-economic and emotional aspects in the prevalent gendered nature of care practices. This is consistent with previous studies that documented the gendered nature of care practices in India, wherein care responsibilities are primarily borne by women (Pazhoothundathil and Bailey, 2020; Ugargol and Bailey, 2020). Such caregiving 'burden', primarily on informal family caregivers (especially women), is embedded in sociocultural norms, wherein caregiving is an obligation for women (Raschick and Ingersoll-Dayton, 2004). A number of substantial studies (see Bauer and Sousa-Poza; 2015; Mosquera et al, 2016; Ugargol and Bailey, 2018) have suggested that such caregiving burden has an adverse impact on the mental health and well-being of the informal caregivers. On the other hand, Mackenzie and Greenwood (2012), contended that caring has positive experiences as well, such as sense of gratification and notion of altruism among the informal home caregivers. These mixed notions of care practices made older adults' care dynamic and complex and, thus, substantiated the gendered nature of caringscapes by entrenching into cultural norms.

We made an attempt to understand the complex spatialities of care and care relationships through 'landscapes of care' in a subjective manner. The micro-level landscapes of care such as the hospital room, the home, open spaces/parks and the neighbourhood, underpins that the care does not only operate at inter-personal level but also at spatial level. These caringscapes are rooted in real space and encompass lived spaces from the micro to macro, that is, from homes and institutions to neighbourhoods, cities and countries. Recent studies on new geographies of care practices (see Kofman and Raghuram, 2015; Strauss, 2020) argued that care work is growing increasingly global and is being commodified. Besides, a number studies revealed how these interpersonal and global care relations are shaped by power relations and have fashioned care policies, particularly in economically more advanced societies with a higher proportion of older adults (Connell and Walton-Roberts, 2016; Strauss and Xu, 2018; Schwiter, Brütsch and Pratt, 2020).

It is evident that the caringscapes are shaped by the perceptions of 'care' and dyadic care relationships between the caregivers and care receivers embedded in their social and cultural settings. As Wiles and Rosenberg (2003) argue, care practices shape and are shaped by the social and physical characteristics of the numerous interconnected scales of different geographical locations and places that caregivers negotiate in their everyday lives. The current transformations of care practices globally, and subsequent policy interventions at individual and welfare state level, are giving rise to context specific caringscapes (Power, 2016). Caringscapes in the Indian context are deeply rooted in filial obligation and intergenerational dependence where older adults are entitled to receive care from children in exchange for the care they had provided to their children (Gupta et al, 2009; Ugargol et al, 2016). Once again this illustrates that the practice of intergenerational reciprocal care is strongly gendered and involves inequalities of power. Here, the care relationships between older men and their caregivers are situated within wider socio-economic contexts which influence the power relations between them (Milligan and Wiles, 2010; Kennedy, 2016; Power, 2016).

The results also demonstrated how intergenerational property inherent rights determine the care practices and power relations. Given the privilege of their property inherent rights and contribution to raise the children in India, the older men perceived that it is their right to receive care as the wealth will eventually be transferred to the children. On the other hand, the emotional attachment also comprises the affective dimension of caringscapes, since both the older adults as care receivers and their informal family caregivers traditionally engaged in reciprocal care practices. Hence, it is necessary for researchers and policy makers to understand the 'caring situation' in which the care is practised. Therefore, social and ethical contexts embedded in the cultural landscapes are a prerequisite for the broader framework of the caringscapes.

References

Acharya, A. and Ranson, M. K. (2005) 'Health care financing for the poor: Community-based health insurance schemes in Gujarat', *Economic and Political Weekly*, 40(4): 141–50.

Aguila, E., Park, J. H. and Vega, A. (2020) 'Living arrangements and supplemental income programs for older adults in Mexico', *Demography*, 57(4), 1345–68.

Ahlin, T. and Sen, K. (2020) 'Shifting duties: becoming "good daughters" through elder care practices in transnational families from Kerala, India', *Gender, Place and Culture*, 27(10): 1395–414.

Ajay, S., Kasthuri, A., Kiran, P. and Malhotra, R. (2017) 'Association of impairments of older persons with caregiver burden among family caregivers: findings from rural South India', *Archives of Gerontology and Geriatrics*, 68: 143–8.

Andrews, G. J. and Phillips, D. R. (2005) 'Geographical studies in ageing: progress and connections to social gerontology', in G. J. Andrews and D. R. Phillips (eds) *Ageing and Place: Perspectives, Policy, Practice*, New York: Routledge, pp 7–12.

Andrews, G. J., Milligan, C., Phillips, D. R. and Skinner, M. W. (2009) 'Geographical gerontology: mapping a disciplinary intersection', *Geography Compass*, 3(5): 1641–59.

Andruske, C. L. and O'Connor, D. (2020) 'Family care across diverse cultures: re-envisioning using a transnational lens', *Journal of Aging Studies*, 55: 100892.

Appadurai, A. (1996) *Modernity at Large: Cultural Dimensions of Globalization*, Minneapolis: University of Minnesota Press.

Bauer, J. M. and Sousa-Poza, A. (2015) 'Impacts of informal caregiving on caregiver employment, health, and family', *Journal of Population Ageing*, 8(3): 113–45.

Bongaarts, J. and Zimmer, Z. (2001) 'Living arrangement of older adults in the developing world: an analysis of DHS household survey', *The Journals of Gerontology: Series B*, 57(3): 145–57.

Bowlby, S. and McKie, L. (2019) 'Care and caring: an ecological framework', *Area*, 51(3): 532–9.

Brown, M. (2003) 'Hospice and the spatial paradoxes of terminal care', *Environment and Planning A*, 35: 833–51.

Button, K. and Ncapai, T. (2019) 'Conflict and negotiation in intergenerational care: older women's experiences of caring with the old age grant in South Africa', *Critical Social Policy*, 39(4): 560–81.

Chirkov, V. I., Ryan, R.M. and Willness, C. (2005) 'Cultural context and psychological needs in Canada and Brazil: testing a self-determination approach to the internalisation of cultural practices, identity and wellbeing', *Journal of Cross Cultural Psychology*, 36(4): 423–43.

Connell, J. and Walton-Roberts, M. (2016) 'What about the workers? The missing geographies of health care', *Progress in Human Geography*, 40(2): 158–76.

Croucher, K., Gilroy, R., Bevan, M. and Attuyer, K. (2020) 'The mobilities of care in later life: exploring the relationship between caring and mobility in the lives of older people', *Ageing and Society*, 41(8): 1788–809.

Cutchin, M. P. (2009) 'Geographical gerontology: new contributions and spaces for development', *The Gerontologist*, 49(3): 440–4.

Datta, A. (2011) 'Natural landscapes and regional constructs of gender: theorizing linkages in the Indian context', *Gender, Technology and Development*, 15(3): 345–62.

Del Casino, Jr., V. (2009) 'Ageing and the "new" social geographies of older people', in V. Del Casino Jr. (ed) *Social Geography: A Critical Introduction*, Chichester: Wiley-Blackwell, pp 238–63.

Dey, S., Nambiar, D., Lakshmi, J. K., Sheikh, K. and Reddy, K. S. (2012) 'Health of the elderly in India: challenges of access and affordability', in J. P. Smith and M. Majmundar (eds) *National Research Council (US) Panel on Policy Research and Data Needs to Meet the Challenge of Aging in Asia*, Washington, DC: National Academies Press, pp 371–86.

Fingerman, K. L., Huo, M. and Birditt, K. S. (2020) 'Mothers, fathers, daughters, and sons: gender differences in adults' intergenerational ties', *Journal of Family Issues*, 41(9): 1597–625.

Gupta, R., Rowe, N. and Pillai, V. K. (2009) 'Perceived caregiver burden in India: implications for social services', *Affilia*, 24(1): 69–79.

Gyasi, R. M., Phillips, D. R. and Amoah, P. A. (2020) 'Multidimensional social support and health services utilization among noninstitutionalized older persons in Ghana', *Journal of Aging and Health*, 32(3–4): 227–39.

Hanrahan, K. B. and Smith, C. E. (2020) 'Interstices of care: re-imagining the geographies of care', *Area*, 52(2): 230–4.

Hardill, I. (2009) 'Introduction: geographies of aging', *The Professional Geographer*, 61(1): 1–3.

Harper, S. and Laws, G. (1995) 'Rethinking the geography of ageing', *Progress in Human Geography*, 19(2): 199–221.

Hennink, M., Hutter, I. and Bailey, A. (2020) *Qualitative Research Methods*, Thousand Oaks, CA: SAGE.

Hopkins, P. and Pain, R. (2007) 'Geographies of age: thinking rationally', *Area*, 40(3): 287–94.

IIPS (Indian Institute of Population Sciences) (2007) National Family Health Survey 3, 2005–06: India: Volume I. Mumbai. http://www.mohfw.nic.in/nfhs3/index.htm

Kennedy, A. (2016) 'Landscapes of care: feminist approaches in global public relations', *Journal of Media Ethics*, 31(4): 215–30.

Kofman, E. and Raghuram, P. (2015) *Gendered Migrations and Global Social Reproduction*, London: Palgrave Macmillan.

Laws, G. (1995) 'Embodiment and emplacement: landscape, representation and identity in Sun City retirement communities', *International Journal of Aging and Human Development*, 40(4): 253–80.

Laws, G. (1996) 'A shot of economic adrenalin: reconstructing the "elderly" in the retiree-based economic development literature', *Journal of Aging Studies*, 10(3): 171–88.

Lawson, V. (2008) 'Geographies of care and responsibility', *Annals of the Association of American Geographers*, 97(1): 1–11.

Lin, I. F. and Wolf, D. A. (2020) 'Division of parent care among adult children', *The Journals of Gerontology: Series B*, 75(10): 2230–9.

Lin, Y., Xiao, H., Lan, X., Wen, S. and Bao, S. (2020) 'Living arrangements and life satisfaction: mediation by social support and meaning in life', *BMC Geriatrics*, 20: 1–8.

Mackenzie, A. and Greenwood, N. (2012) 'Positive experiences of caregiving in stroke: a systematic review', *Disability and Rehabilitation*, 34(17): 1413–22.

Mahajan, A. and Ray, A. (2013) 'The Indian elder: factors affecting geriatric care in India', *Global Journal of Medicine and Public Health*, 2(4): 1–5.

Mahal, A. and Berman, P. (2002) 'Estimating baseline health expenditures on the elderly in India'. Draft. Harvard School of Public Health, Department of Population and International Health, Boston, MA.

McKie, L., Gregory, S. and Bowlby, S. (2002) 'Shadow times: the temporal and spatial frameworks and experiences of caring and working', *Sociology*, 36(4): 897–924.

Meier, D. E. and Bowman, B. (2017) 'The changing landscape of palliative care', *Generations*, 41(1): 74–80.

Milligan, C. (2009) *There's No Place Like Home: Place and Care in an Ageing Society* (Geographies of Health), Aldershot: Ashgate.

Milligan, C. (2017) *Geographies of Care: Space, Place and the Voluntary Sector*, London: Routledge.

Milligan, C. and Liu, Y. (2015) 'Place and informal care in an ageing society: reviewing the state of the art in geographical gerontology', *Progress in Geography*, 34(12): 1558–76.

Milligan, C. and Power, A. (2010) 'The changing geography of care', in T. Brown, S. McLafferty and G. Moon (eds) *A Companion to Health and Medical Geography*, West Sussex: Wiley-Blackwell, pp 567–86.

Milligan, C. and Wiles, J. (2010) 'Landscapes of care', *Progress in Human Geography*, 34(6): 736–54.

Milligan, C., Atkinson, S., Skinner, M. and Wiles, J. (2007) 'Geographies of care: a commentary', *New Zealand Geographer*, 63(2): 135–40.

Monkong, S., Krairit, O., Ngamkala, T., Chonburi, J. S. N., Pussawiro, W. and Ratchasan, P. (2020) 'Transitional care for older people from hospital to home: a best practice implementation project', *JBI Evidence Synthesis*, 18(2): 357–67.

Mosquera, I., Vergara, I., Larrañaga, I., Machón, M., del Río, M. and Calderón, C. (2016) 'Measuring the impact of informal elderly caregiving: a systematic review of tools', *Quality of Life Research*, 5(25): 1059–92.

Mudrazija, S., Angel, J. L., Cipin, I. and Smolic, S. (2020) 'Living alone in the United States and Europe: the impact of public support on the independence of older adults', *Research on Aging*, 42(5–6): 150–62.

Pati, S., Swain, S., Knottnerus, J. A., Metsemakers, J. F. and van den Akker, M. (2019) 'Health-related quality of life in multimorbidity: a primary-care based study from Odisha, India', *Health and Quality of Life Outcomes*, 17(1): 116.

Pazhoothundathil, N. and Bailey, A. (2020) 'Cherished possessions, home-making practices and aging in care homes in Kerala, India', *Emotion, Space and Society*, 36: 100706.

Pillai, V. K., Levy, E. and Gupta, R. (2012) 'Relationship quality and elder caregiver burden in India', *Journal of Social Intervention: Theory and Practice*, 21(2): 39–62.

Pongiya, U. D., Murugan, S. and Subakanmani, S. (2011) 'Evaluation of degree of depression in geriatric population – a community study', *Indian Journal of Gerontology*, 25(2): 150–9.

Power, A. (2016) *Landscapes of Care: Comparative Perspectives on Family Caregiving*, London: Routledge.

Power, E. R. and Williams, M. J. (2020) 'Cities of care: a platform for urban geographical care research', *Geography Compass*, 14(1): e12474.

Rajan, S. I., Shajan, A. and Sunitha, S. (2020) 'Ageing and elderly care in Kerala', *China Report*, 56(3): 354–73.

Ramamurti, P. V. and Jamuna, D. (2005) 'Will legislation help the care of older persons?', *Journal of International Institute on Ageing*, 16(1): 15–18.

Raschick, M. and Ingersoll-Dayton, B. (2004) 'The costs and rewards of caregiving among aging spouses and adult children', *Family Relations*, 53(3): 317–25.

Reynolds, R. M., Meng, J. and Dorrance Hall, E. (2020) 'Multilayered social dynamics and depression among older adults: a 10-year cross-lagged analysis', *Psychology and Aging*, 35(7): 948–62.

Roth, A. R. (2020) 'Informal caregiving and network turnover among older adults', *The Journals of Gerontology: Series B*, 75(7): 1538–47.

Rowles, G. D. (1986) 'The geography of ageing and the aged: towards an integrated perspective', *Progress in Human Geography*, 10(4): 511–39.

Schwanen, T., Hardill, I. and Lucas, S. (2012) 'Spatialities of ageing: the co-construction and co-evolution of old age and space', *Geoforum*, 43: 1291–5.

Schwiter, K., Brütsch, J. and Pratt, G. (2020) 'Sending granny to Chiang-Mai: debating global outsourcing of care for the elderly', *Global Networks*, 20(1): 106–25.

Siva Raju, S. (2011) 'Studies on ageing in India', Institute for Social and Economic Change, Bangalore United Nations Population Fund, New Delhi Institute of Economic Growth, Delhi.

Strauss, K. (2020) 'Feminist economic geography', in A. Kobayashi (ed), *International Encyclopedia of Human Geography* (2nd ed), Oxford: Elsevier, pp 43–6.

Strauss, K. and Xu, F. (2018) 'At the intersection of urban and care policy: the invisibility of eldercare workers in the global city', *Critical Sociology*, 44(7–8): 1163–87.

Ugargol, A. P. and Bailey, A. (2018) 'Family caregiving for older adults: gendered roles and caregiver burden in emigrant households of Kerala, India', *Asian Population Studies*, 14(2): 194–210.

Ugargol, A. P. and Bailey, A. (2020) 'Reciprocity between older adults and their care-givers in emigrant households of Kerala, India', *Ageing and Society*, 41(8): 1699–725.

Ugargol, A. P., Hutter, I., James, K. S. and Bailey, A. (2016) 'Care needs and caregivers: associations and effects of living arrangements on caregiving to older adults in India', *Ageing International*, 41(2): 193–213.

Wang, M. S. (2019) 'Is home the best place for aging? The complex landscape of eldercare', *Social Work in Public Health*, 34(4): 330–42.

Wiles, J. and Rosenberg, M. (2003) 'Paradoxes and contradictions in Canada's home care provision: informal privatisation and private informalisation', Special Issue, Health and Well-Being in Canada, *International Journal of Canadian Studies*, 28: 63–89.

Williams, A. and Sethi, B. (2020) 'The predicament of caring: work interferences and health of family caregivers of persons with multiple chronic conditions', *Gerontology and Geriatric Medicine*, 7 July: 6.

9

The role of cultural meaning system and place attachment in retaining home ownership while residing in retirement homes in Kerala, India

Nikhil Pazhoothundathil, Ajay Bailey and Inge Hutter

Introduction

Home is a place marked by many life course events. When an older adult leaves her/his home and starts to live in a retirement home she/he has to reconfigure their sense and meaning of home. The shift in place of residence is likely to bring about changes in control over a place (home) and the sense of place attachment (Heywood, 2005). Home can be central to many well-being factors for older adults such as care and care reciprocity (Ugargol and Bailey, 2020); domestic routine and rhythm (Lager et al, 2016); social relationship; religious and cultural practices (Mazumdar and Mazumdar, 2005; Bailey et al, 2008); life course events; material possessions; memories and emotional investments (Cristoforetti et al, 2011). Home is also embedded with memories, self-identity, sense of security, cherished possessions and family relations. In the Indian cultural context, older adult care is generally seen as a duty of adult children, which means the primary caregiver is usually the daughter-in-law (Liebig, 2003). Urbanisation and industrialisation have increased the workforce participation of all members of the household. This, coupled with migration of children, results in the non-availability of caregivers within the household (Nair and Kumar, 2017). As a result of these changes, formal care services for older adults have begun to receive considerable attention, especially in urban areas. Institutions providing geriatric care such as old age homes have become a source of formal care services as an alternative for traditional informal care services (Kalavar and Jamuna, 2011; Gupta et al, 2014; Bhattacharyya and Chatterjee, 2017; Mayer, 2017; Pathania et al, 2019). According to Müller (2019) relocation of housing is a complex decision-making process as changing the housing environment allows older adults opportunities for self-reflection and emotional regulation. Unlike in the Western context, this study shows that older adults living in for-profit care homes make efforts to retain and maintain their old home, as home is culturally as well as emotionally relevant in older adults' lives.

This chapter focuses on three questions: i) what motivates older adults to retain their (previous) home while currently residing in retirement homes?, ii) how do older adults maintain their previous homes? and iii) how these motivations help to maintain place attachment?

Ageing and institutional care

The study is based in Kerala, India. According to the 2011 Census, 8.5 per cent of the total Indian population are older adults (aged 60+) (Registrar General of India, 2011). The share of older adults in India in 2015 was 9 per cent, which is expected to grow to 10 per cent in 2020, 20 per cent in 2050 and 33 per cent by end of this century. The oldest-old group (80+) is expected to grow faster than any other age group (United Nations, 2019). As per the 2011 Census, the proportion of older adults (60+) in Kerala is 12.6 per cent (Registrar General of India, 2011). Among the Indian states Kerala is the most rapidly ageing state with 97 older adults per 100 children (Subaiya and Dhananjay, 2011).

According to the traditional Indian system the last two of the four *ashramas* (stages of life) – Vanaparsta and Sanyasa – are connected with later life. In the Vanaprasta stage (retirement) life is marked by a transition phase towards spiritual life, where a person has handed over household duties to the next generation (see Chapter 7 for obligations linked to each stage). In the Sanyasa stage (renounced life), the last stage of the *ashrama* system is marked by the renunciation of material desires with more specific focus on spiritual life (Mazumdar and Mazumdar, 2005). From this perspective, later life can be seen as a process of reducing one's responsibilities and expectations, especially in relation to the home. According to Izuhara (2000), the residential choices of older adults are influenced by family tradition and social norms. The concept of formal care system was introduced by colonial administrators and missionaries during eighteenth century with special focus on poor and homeless older adults. Compared to previous decades, institutional care services for older adults are now receiving considerable attention and importance. Even though in India only a small proportion of older adults use institutional services, the tendency of seeking institutional services is growing and more demand for geriatric care institutions is expected in the coming years when Indian society moves towards further socio-economic and demographic changes. According to the UNFPA study conducted in seven major states in India, 6 per cent of older adults live alone and 16 per cent of them live with a spouse (UNFPA, 2011). India is experiencing rapid population ageing, which will result in the growth of the older adult population in both relative and absolute terms. This is predicted to increase the need for formal care services for these older adults (see Chapters 8 and 10). It is evident from the studies that old age homes are more concentrated in such regions that are characterised by more rapid rates of population ageing (HelpAge India, 2009; Samuel et al, 2016; Nair and Kumar, 2017; Johnson et al, 2018). According to Help Age India (2009), 14 per cent of the total old age homes in India are in Kerala and the state is characterised as a demographically leading state having 12.6 per cent of the population aged 60+ (Registrar General of India, 2011). According to the Social Justice Department (2019), there are in total 614 care homes registered in the state of Kerala, which include 599 non-government care homes (which include both non-profit and for-profit care homes) and 15 government care homes.

Home and cultural meaning system

The concept of home has been extensively used in connection with theories of place attachment and place identity. Place attachment is defined as the emotional bond between person and place and place identity is concerned with the process of forming places as part of one's self-identity irrespective of the qualities or evaluation of those places (Moore, 2000). Home is seen as the place which satisfies people's psychological as well as physiological needs (Maslow, 1955). Based on the literature on meaning of home, Clapham (2011) argues that the well-being of a person is associated with identification and embodied activities. Hence, physical, material and social worlds all play a significant role in promoting the well-being of older adults. Place attachment operates at both the individual and the group level. At the individual level, attachment relates to personal memories, personal experiences and gains. This kind of place attachment helps to create a stable sense of self (Scannell and Gifford, 2010). According to Easthope (2004) a place (home) is constantly linked with physical, social, cultural and emotive worlds. The meaning of home and its material function change according to the changes in life stages of older adults. A study of older women living in congregate houses – a type of multi-occupancy housing in which individuals have a private bedroom but share a common dining room and other facilities with other residents – (Leith, 2006) reveals that older adults are able to conceptualise and evaluate their life situation in response to their environments and try to make a rational judgement according to the available resources and environments.

Any disruption in the physical, social, cultural or emotive attributes will affect the well-being of older adults. When any such changes occur, older adults are likely to adopt coping strategies to mitigate the effect of the change (Cristoforetti et al, 2011). In a study of older adult widows, Cristoforetti and colleagues (2011) found that, in response to loneliness due to the loss of a spouse, older adults use coping strategies such as relocation and personalisation of possessions in order to ensure a sense of continuity, psycho-physical and social well-being. According to Coolen (2008, p 62) 'the meaning of dwelling is believed to lie in the relationship between the features of the dwelling on the one hand and people's goals and intentions on the other'. For example, Hansen and Gottschalk (2006) found that changes in the life stage of older adults, in terms of shrinking the household size and poor health, motivate older adults to seek a better dwelling place. Through a dialectical perspective place attachment is involved in 'movement and rest' and 'inward and outward' aspects. The inward aspects of a place refer to being part of a place like home where individual and familial relations take place and are separated from rest of the world. Outwards refers to the external world. Similar to interpersonal relationship, place attachment is maintained through proximity-seeking behaviours, where closeness of places provides a sense of safety and comfort, if the place is positively constituted. If proximity is not possible, this sense of place can be achieved through symbolic representation (Smith and White, 2004; Scannell and Gifford, 2014).

The meaning of home varies according to culture. In the Indian cultural context home is considered as the central place to perform various *sevas* (care), that is, culturally bounded duties and services to fulfill intergenerational care expectation and obligation. During adulthood an adult couple is primarily responsible for taking care of their children. When the adult couple become older, they are supposed be taken care of by their children. According to Mayer (2017), expectations about ageing are culturally shaped and influence the way people organise their daily lives and social bonding. The transfer of family property from older adults to their next generation is considered as an important life course event marking the fulfillment of familial obligation driven by social and cultural norms. It has been argued that individual reasoning, perceptions and interpretations are derived from cultural schemas (d'Andrade, 1992; Vaisey, 2009; de Haas and Hutter, 2019). Cultural schemas are shared beliefs which shape individual's perceptions, attitudes and expectations (d'Andrade, 1992; Strauss and Quinn, 1997). Cultural schemas are hierarchically organised and have the ability to instigate action. According to Strauss and Quinn (1997, p 26), when the cultural belief becomes a part of an inner sense of a being they become goal driven and acquire motivational force'. Higher-level schemas, which function as goals, are considered to have high motivational force. Middle-level and lower-level schemas generate goals in interaction with higher-level schemas (d'Andrade, 1992). Cultural schemas are divided in to the following four major functions: representational, constructive, evocative and directive functions (Rutagumirwa, 2018). The representational function involves defining knowledge and beliefs about the world which help individuals orient themselves in the social world. Constructive functions create cultural entities which people adhere to. Evocative functions evoke feelings and emotional reactions. The directive function appears as a need or obligation to do something. For older adults in India, the motivation to retain and maintain their home for the next generation is driven by the cultural schemas of 'age role expectation' or 'care obligation'. Fulfillment of the care obligation will bring a sense of satisfaction. Additionally, schemas such as love, nostalgia and pride also motivate older adults to retain their home and maintain a sense of place attachment.

Various studies emphasise the importance of possessions in later life for promoting a sense of continuity, comfort and security (Sherman and Dacher, 2005; Cooney, 2012; Meijering and Lager, 2014; Stevens et al, 2019; Coleman and Wiles, 2020; Pazhoothundathil and Bailey, 2020). According to Seo and Mazumdar (2011), the use of cherished possessions is culturally embedded. The authors further emphasise the importance of cultural values, values, traditions and preferences in older adults' lives, especially when they are in a displaced space. In this study, we look at how cultural schemas and emotions motivate older adults living in care homes to retain their previous home and what different strategies older adults use to maintain their home.

Study site and profile of participants

The material for this chapter comes from a qualitative study conducted at two retirement homes for older adults located in the Kottayam district of Kerala, India, between June and December 2015. One of them is a faith-based retirement home and the other is a secular retirement home. To maintain the anonymity of the respondents, we use pseudonyms for both the participants and the retirement homes. In this chapter both these homes are named as 'Trinity' (faith-based) and 'Sahya' (secular) respectively. Trinity is generally aimed towards middle-class older adults. This three-storey retirement home is managed by a Christian missionary group led by nuns. A separate chapel is built inside the retirement home and masses and prayers are conducted every day. There are separate staff for cooking, washing and cleaning. Each older adult has their own separate room with attached bathroom and toilet facilities. Older adults residing in this retirement home are from nearby areas. Since there are no nursing care facilities, only able-bodied older adults are accommodated in this retirement home.

Sahya is situated in a hilly village area and is aimed towards upper-middle-class groups and is managed by a trust. Compared to the faith-based retirement home, it is newly built and clearly identified as a secular home. Most of the residents had previously lived abroad as they had worked in countries such as the United States and Hong Kong. This retirement home accommodates both able-bodied and non–able-bodied older adults, as they have nursing care facilities. The home also has a library, a lift, WiFi, vehicles, air-conditioned rooms and a garden. Separate trained staff are deployed in each department for supervising, nursing care, cooking, cleaning, washing, gardening and security. Every week three doctors visit the home to perform medical check-ups.

The participants were recruited with prior permission in both settings. Each retirement home is considered as a case study. To get permission for the study a written request form was submitted to the supervisory board of each institution. Since these retirement home managers are very keen to maintain the privacy of the older adults, it took several days to get the permission for the study from the managers, particularly from the Sahya retirement home. Several visits, phone calls and email communications were made to ensure the permission from Sahya. Before starting the first interview, three visits were made to each retirement home to build a rapport with the older adults. Later we sought separate permission from older adults and caregivers. We did not recruit participants who were sick and could not give consent themselves. Each participant was informed about the research before their participation and their consent was recorded. Photographs were taken with prior permission of the retirement home and participants.

We conducted 24 interviews in these homes. At Trinity 13 individual in-depth interviews were conducted. These interviews included seven females, five males and one caregiver. Among the participants two were couples. All the older adults were economically independent. They were receiving retirement pension because either they themselves or their spouses had worked in government service, especially within Kerala. At Sahya a total of 11 interviews were conducted comprising six female, four males and one caregiver.

Data collection

We conducted in-depth interviews to obtain rich information about the life history, life experiences associated with home and place-making practices of older adults in retirement homes. In-depth interviews help i) to gain a detailed insight into the research issues from the perspective of the study participants and ii) understand the socio-economic and cultural context in which people live (Hennink et al, 2011). Semi-structured interview guides were employed. The interview guide was prepared in English and was translated into Malayalam, the local language. Interviews were conducted at the personal rooms of the older adults. Each interview lasted approximately 90 minutes. Interviews were conducted up to the point of data saturation.

Ethical clearance

Prior to conducting the data collection, the study was submitted for ethical approval and was approved by the Institutional Ethics Review Board of the

University of Groningen. Retirement home authorities and participants were informed about the study objectives and the interview process. Interviews were conducted at the convenience of participants after obtaining informed consent to conduct the interviews and to audio-record the conversations. Photographs were taken with the prior permission of the retirement home authority and older adults. Observations were done without making any disturbance for the personal privacy and community life. Privacy and anonymity were maintained.

Data analysis

The interviews conducted were in Malayalam and later translated into English. Atlas.Ti.7, a qualitative software package, was used for data management and analysis. For analysis we adopted the board principles of grounded theory (Glaser and Strauss, 1967; Glaser, 1978; Strauss and Corbin, 1998; Charmaz, 2006), which involved various stages such as developing codes, defining codes, coding data, describing codes, comparing codes, categorising codes, conceptualising codes and developing theory. Two main cycles of coding were applied (see Table 9.1). In the first cycle of coding, primary codes were developed both inductively and deductively. Primary codes were developed through line-by-line coding of each data set, which enabled the researcher to stay as close as possible to the data. In the second cycle, code families or themes were developed through grouping different

Table 9.1: Themes and codes emerging from data

Theme	Codes
Emotional attachment towards home	Ancestral home, caretaker, family property, feel missing home, feeling happy, connect with native, interpersonal relationship with neighbours, ownership, place attachment and memories, place and role, pride, place wanted to stay.
Reasons to leave home	Changes in care relation, changes in family value, changes in norms, death of spouse, changes in meaning of place, feel insecure, feel loneliness, free from household work, health issues, need for care, retired life, lack of assistance.
Strategies to maintain homes	Caretaker of family property, condition of home, elements of fictive kinship. Interpersonal relationship with extended family members. Interpersonal relationship with neighbours, proximity of possession, visit own home.
Attachment to things and places	Material possession and interpersonal relationship. Place and memories, pets, cherished possessions, possession at home.

primary codes based on common attributes guided by analytic research questions. From the primary codes that we identified, we focused on code families for 'Emotional attachment towards home', 'Reasons to leave home', 'Strategies to maintain their homes' and 'Attachment to things and places' where we employed secondary codes. The data presented in this chapter mainly come from the interview data.

Results

Current living situation

The older adults living at Trinity had primarily worked in India especially in government sectors and were economically independent as most of them were receiving their own or spouse's pensions. The spiritual way of life, associated with the Catholic faith, was one of the important features that attracted the older adults to select this particular retirement home for their retirement life. Trinity is situated close to a hospital and only accommodates older adults who are able-bodied as there is no facility for nursing care. This retirement home is surrounded by a wall which features Bible quotes. Inside Trinity, common rooms are decorated with pictures of Jesus and other Christian figures. The prime administrator is a Catholic nun. Though she is younger than the residents the older adults call her 'mother'. Each day starts with mass at 6am followed by prayers at 12 noon and 6pm. Besides this, older adults pray in their rooms. Community prayer times and dinner time are the main opportunities for older adults to meet each other. Playing cards is the main leisure time activity. As most of the older adults have emigrant children; they occasionally travel abroad to spend their time with children. There is a specified time for visitors. Older adults are free to visit their homes and relatives, but it is recommended that they return to Trinity before the commencement of evening prayer at 6pm.

Sahya, the secular retirement home, has more facilities than Trinity, such as air-conditioned rooms, WiFi, a garden, a library and other services. This retirement home accommodates both able-bodied and non–able-bodied individuals, and they have the facilities and staff to provide nursing care services. Compared to other institutions, it is considered to be more luxurious as most of the residents are retired returning migrants. Indeed, a few of the older adults have US citizenship and they receive a social security pension from the USA. Though each room has separate television facilities, some older adults prefer to watch films in the common TV room. This then becomes an occasion to meet and share time with other older adults. As the older adults give more importance to privacy, visits to other rooms are reported less often. Common meeting points are the garden, the TV rooms, the corridors and the dining hall. The celebration of birthdays is a common practice, in addition to the celebrations of festivals like Onam (a regional festival), Christmas and New Year. Some older adults have their own cars. The retirement home has its own car and driver which can be used by the residents. There is no restriction on visitors. Older adults are free to leave the retirement home, which enables them to visit their homes occasionally. Older adults use modern communication technologies like Skype as well as WhatsApp to communicate with children living abroad, and with friends.

Cultural obligation and emotional attachment towards home

In Trinity, 9 out of 12 participants, and in Sahya 6 out of 10 participants retained and maintained their earlier houses while residing in the care homes. The analysis of the interviews revealed a range of reasons for older adults to retain their homes. One is the older adults' cultural obligation to retain their home for the next generation; another is that older adults are emotionally attached to their homes in various ways. Home was not just seen as a shelter. It is imbued with memories and roles – it is part of their identity. For the older adults, home is a central place where interpersonal relationships are maintained within the household (with husband, children and parents) and people outside the household such as neighbours:

'when I went there yesterday, a special feeling passed through me. I became very happy (…) The plants have grown into big trees of fruits and herbs now. They were planted by my husband. Sometimes I collect the fallen fruits on the ground and take with me here (Trinity) (…) nowadays all of them have built huge mansions. Our home was the only big house there years before.' (Mary)

Home and its surroundings are filled with memories of family members (deceased and living) such as spouses, parents, siblings and children. Given the right kind of support (social, physical and daily needs), the older adults we interviewed would have preferred to have lived in their own homes, rather than a care home. This preference is rooted in their emotional attachment to home and the memories it encompasses. Women were more vocal than men about their emotional attachment to their previous homes, as they had tended to bear the main responsibility for domestic tasks and providing care.

'I used to grow some crops like tapioca and coconut. I was actually hesitant to leave home. My three kids my husband..their souls rest there. But I was forced by everyone. Yet, still I've to take care of my home, no!! … it's quite difficult to leave one's home forever, right!! To leave them, to see decaying, to get our property lost. Still everyone

asked me why and for whom I should cling on to that home all alone
…Yes I miss my home (...) I can take care of the affairs there(home),
and maintain my small farm. I never get a minute to make myself sit
down for a moment there (home).' (Elsamma)

Home is also associated with place identity, family roots and sense of pride.
As such simply transferring home ownership to the next generation will not
fulfil the familial obligation. In the context of international migration, older
adults perceive that it is their cultural and familial obligation to retain and
maintain the home for the next generation as home could act as a source
of pride, place identity and potentially could motivate migrant children to
return to Kerala.

'I feel very bad about leaving my house in which we lived for long and
living here. The house is deserted or else it should have been safely
given to someone to look after. So I feel that it (home) is orphaned.
I am sad about it.... If our son is here. Suppose one day if he wishes
to come back from America. We want to preserve it for him and
grandkids even though they won't come. One day our grandkids can
say they have their home in India. They can be proud of it.' (Philomina)

For some older adults, home is important because of the painstaking efforts
they had to take to build the home. Even though ownership status was
transferred to the next generation, older adults felt greater attachment towards
a particular home, because they constructed it with their own earnings. They
perceive/look upon their home as their child. Many of the older adults had
invested their lifelong economic savings in these homes.

'Of course the house at Madras … There were two houses. I had one
built for each children. Then the son in America said he doesn't need
a house. So we sold it. And one is remaining. Another son and family
stays there.. It was I who had constructed the house. Like a mother
give birth to her baby, I had gone through various pain and struggles
to make it. I delivered my home, like a mother. Ha ha. So, there I have
more attachment to them.' (Nainan)

For an older adult like Omana, who has lived most of her life outside
Kerala, home and its immediate surroundings have helped her to reconnect
with her identity after returning to Kerala. It is the respectful behaviour of
neighbours, the beautiful surroundings and the concern shown towards her
that make her feel more welcome. Omana, for the most part of her life, was
an urban dweller and was used to the anonymity that comes with living in
modern metro cities. After the death of her husband and the migration of

her children, she found new bonds and attachment to a small village where her house is located.

'On my birthday on March 1st in 1999 we moved to the house (..) And then, while we were residing there, we were on top of a hill. When looked sideways we could see many other hills stretching away. such a beautiful place and we had such a beautiful life. On the second or third day, I just went out on the hill for a walk; there was a poor house down there. One lady was standing at their gate. She asked me, "Amma (mother), what are you up to?" I replied, "I was going for a walk." As I walked a little further, an old man asked me, "Amma (mother) where is your vehicle, do you want me to call a vehicle?" That moment, I will tell you, honestly, I thought, "This is my identity, this is who I am, I come from here, and this is my home" it was so stronger feeling and it was such a happy feeling, because we stayed in Mumbai, we stayed in Hong Kong, we stayed in Ethiopia and all we hardly knew everybody. We don't even remember their names and they don't even remember our names. Now this is a person who knew me for two days and called me 'amma'(mother).' (Omana)

Home is the place embedded with various emotions such as love, pride, identity and sense of belonging, as well as memories of people and events that motivate older adults to retain their homes while they reside in a retirement home.

Reasons for leaving home

Older adults prefer home as their first choice of residence over any other alternatives. We asked in the interviews about their motivations for leaving their home and choosing a retirement home as their residence. Participants mentioned a range of reasons such as lack of security, health issues, loneliness, migration of children, discrimination at home, loss of a spouse, weather issues and older adult abuse (see also Chapters 8 and 10). However, feeling lonely due to the loss of a spouse or migration of children and health issues were the main reasons behind the decision to move to a retirement home. But for some older adults there was no single reason, rather it was the cumulative effect of multiple reasons that made them make the decision to move into a retirement home.

When older adults feel that they are not getting the care expected from the family, they experienced distress. Sometimes this led to feelings of being discriminated against. Feelings of discrimination seem to be prominent among those older adults who were single and did not have any children.

'After my brother's death I stayed in my home for two years. My friends, who are Nuns, they told me it was not good to stay in my home. They thought that, I am unmarried and problems might arise with my sister-in-law and her children. That I might be a burden to my sister-in-law. I should move to an old age home. It's their way of thinking. I never thought like that at first. But after my brother's death, after sometimes I felt uneasiness in my sister in law's behavior. Once we went to visit a relative, she (relative) wondered who will take care of me when the time comes. I took care of my parents. My sister-in-law and her daughter kept quiet. They could have been said that, they will. Could have been just said … they didn't. I noted that. So I decided to come here. Such occasions. To be frank I felt discriminated. I haven't said this to anyone.' (Alice, unmarried older adult)

The ability to live alone at home in later life rests on a person's functional health and sense of safety (van den Hoonaard, 2009). Some older adults think that it is not safe to stay alone at home because of security reasons. In the interviews older adults mentioned instances of murder and robbery of older adults residing alone at home in nearby villages. They also read about similar incidents happening in and around Kerala in newspapers. For example, during the fieldwork, we found numerous news reports: *The Hindu*, a widely read daily newspaper, reported on 22 January 2015 the murder of an older adult couple in Pathanamthitta district by a migrant labourer who stayed at a deceased older adult's outhouse. Another paper, *Madhyamam*, reported on 10 July 2015 that two older adults were found dead with stab injuries at their residence at Perambra in Kozhikkodu district around 8.30 pm on Thursday. Police source said the accused committed the crime while he was attempting to loot the house. Such horrifying incidents motivated some of the older adults from middle- and upper-class backgrounds to move to retirement homes.

'My only daughter left after her marriage. After that also I stayed there (home) for some time along with a servant, then I fell ill. Ah. … its chikungunya. After that we could not find a servant for some time. We have some difficulty in getting a servant? … Then how can we live alone. Then I slept alone for a few days. A neighbour used to come at night for company. She doesn't have husband and children. Then the two of us. … We will leave the lights on till morning. Because, we now read such things in paper. The thieves and the murder. So, then our fear is over our life.' (Molly)

Sometimes cultural norms associated with marriage and preferred place of residence led to older adults living alone at their home. For example, in the case of Mathew: though he had three daughters, none of them and their husbands were prepared to stay with him. As per Syrian Christian cultural family norms, after marriage the girl should reside at the husband's home and take care of her parents-in-law. Cultural norms of adoption in Syrian Christian families allow parents who do not have a son to adopt a son-in-law and family and retain residences. As all three of Mathew's sons-in-law were also the only sons for their own parents, the possibility of adoption was not possible.

> 'Let me explain. I've got three daughters. There's a custom of adoption. Here, the son in-law will be adopted by the family of the daughter after the marriage. That is, instead of sending the daughter to husband's home, son in-law is supposed to stay at wife's family, after marriage. That's followed in the absence of a son in the family. But, all three of them disagreed with this system. All of them were the youngest ones of their families. So boys were not ready to leave their families. Some sentimental feelings, you know. We stayed at home. We (with wife) prayed, again prayed and finally took a decision.' (Mathew)

Mathew also felt that he had no special attachment towards his home, though his daughters, grandchildren and relatives felt that their ancestral home needed to be maintained. The ancestral home was the pride of the family members. These expectations also put additional pressure on the older adults to retain and maintain the ancestral homes.

> 'Seven years ago, when I left my home and sold my property, everyone blamed me that I did some kind of foolishness, that I don't love my family. My children and grandchildren were actually sad about this. And they won't find their mother's house there anymore. I told them, that there's no need get sentimental about it. At the time of our departure, we must leave behind whatever we have. We won't take anything with us. My cousins blamed me. I ruined Tharavad (ancestral home). They were also born and bought up there (ancestral home).' (Mathew)

Health-related issues motivated older adults to leave their homes. Severe health issues, such as heart attacks or strokes, which happened at home, made the older adults to think twice about staying alone at home. Since they were not co-residing with anyone at home, they would find it difficult to reach a hospital in time. Therefore, the older adults feared that their life would be at risk if they remained at home. When a husband is shifting his place of residence from home to retirement home, his wife also moves with her husband to the retirement home.

'No he wasn't so happy at first. He was a little sad because that house belonged to him. So it was not so easy to give up soon. One incident took place when we were in home. My husband fell ill. We were alone. (...) they (neighbors) were not always available. So it was very difficult for us to get help from them. As we called them for help they'd find reasons to avoid us. I called four or five of our neighbors. None of them responded. Finally, Achayan (here husband) himself drove to the hospital. We survived that day. It led us to decide that living alone wouldn't work out good.' (Theresa)

Ageing, changes in the role within the household and not feeling safe were reasons to push people to seek other residences. An example of this is Ninan, who was once the head of the household. After his wife's death he felt lonely at home. Being alone at home he had the feeling that he was becoming a watchman at home. Additionally, misunderstandings with his daughter-in-law further motivated him to leave home and move into a retirement home nearby, enabling him to remain close to his siblings and other relatives in his home village.

'It was after my wife died and I became lonely that... I felt so. Yet I lived alone for some 7–8 years. Then as I got older, as I reached 80–85 ... It could be anytime. Then in emergency cases ... How many people die alone! My own father-in-law, he was at home, alone, and when the children came home, he was lying there, dead. How many such incidents take place. Then, thieves. The problem of thieves... We are sitting alone. To think so, the situation has come as this. To live alone after wife died... If they(son and daughter-in-law) leave at 8am, they would come by 5 only. We sit alone bored at home, then thieves would come and murder us (...) She(daughter in law) likes to have me stay there (home) only. Then I can be a watchman for the house. (laughs). Isn't it any different from being a watchman?. Having an old man ... With her, such a slight misunderstanding (...) There's another thing, I have allergy. Dust allergy. There in Madras dust is increasing day by day (...) So, considering it all, here is a secure place to be in.' (Nainan)

Older adults who have the experience of living abroad are exposed to new styles of living arrangements. The values of independent living and a focus on individual well-being also motivate older adults to choose retirement home instead of living with their children. For example, Omana. She does not want to stay with her daughters as she wants to live independently. At the same time, she is old and not able to stay alone at her home. Her children, being concerned of her safety, recommended her to stay at a paid retirement home. Hence, it is the collective decision of the entire family.

'After he (husband) passed away my daughter took me away to the US. And I came back in the meanwhile my daughter-in-law had been in need of me to stay with her. I had told that I would live alone. I wanted a place of my own. They wouldn't let me stay alone in Peerumedu (home). So we had to lock it up at Peerumedu.' (Omana)

The narratives show that there are a range of reasons that motivated older adults to leave their homes. The death of a spouse, migration of children or cultural norms regarding the place of residence after marriage, kept older adults alone in their homes. This intensified the feeling of being alone and created a sense of insecurity. Health issues and the quest to live independently also motivated older adults to leave their homes and take up residence in a retirement home.

Older adults' strategies to maintain non-resident homes

Older adults residing in retirement homes take a range of efforts to maintain or care for their non-resident home. Methods to maintain homes are i) letting out the home for rent, ii) allowing a trusted person to reside in the home without rent, iii) visit often to take care of the house, iv) asking relatives or neighbours to take maintain the home, v) appointing a staff for the purpose vi) transferring the ownership of house to a very close blood relative (siblings, nephews/nieces or other extended family members).

Since older adults are very much concerned about their home, they want a trusted person to take care of it for them. At the same time, older adults who had bad experiences with a person who rented their home, later allowed a trusted person to stay at their home, free of charge. The influence of religious leaders and family friends is a crucial element in this decision making. Older adults were always concerned about how to protect their home. One of the strategies is to give their home to others for a temporary period but on a rent-free basis. Since it is not for monetary benefit, they would usually give it to a trusted person.

Here, in the case of Pushpa and her husband, they gave their house for rent for an initial period. Later they found that the person was not keeping their home in an acceptable way, so later they gave it to a group of nuns, based on the recommendation of a priest from their church. Now they are happy that the nuns are looking after their home.

'The house is in custody of nuns. They will keep it clean. Now it's not for rent. First it was rented but they used it roughly and the maintenance was costly. Nuns who came in service of the church were searching for a home. The priest (congregation priest) recommended it. It's for two years. Now they are living there. Sometimes he (husband) goes there.' (Pushpa)

For those older adults who have given their home for rent, it is not the monetary benefit that is important but the assurance that their house is being looked after and cared for by the new residents. The joy and assurance that their house was in good hands motivated older adults to share their furniture and other kitchen utensils.

> 'Now it's (home) rented (...) it's very close to here (Trinity). So I do visit home once in a while. ... They are very good people, maintain our home very well as their own. That is important more that the rental amount. So I rent it them for a small amount which they can't get anywhere near.' (Molamma)

Those older adults who were single, transferred their ownership of their home to close blood relatives, such as siblings. Since they don't have an offspring to transfer their wealth to, they are happy to pass their home to a close blood relative. Cultural norms regarding the transfer of wealth also play a role in this decision making. Following cultural practice, wealth and property of those who are unmarried transfers to their closest blood relatives, such as siblings, nephews and nieces.

> 'The house and property in Kottayam was in the name of me and my brother. But I, Why should I have it! I gave it to him without his consent.' (Alice)

Due to fear of letting their house go to ruin or being misused by tenants, older adults took the responsibility of visiting the house to keep it clean and tidy. Even though no one was actually living there, older adults who could afford to hire domestic helpers and therefore found staff to take care of their home, properties and pets.

> 'I had given it for rent to a man. He has left now. My home has reached such a pathetic condition! It looked like an uninhabited place. He has turned it upside down. So far as my children are abroad, it's my responsibility to take care of my home, no! That's why I visit there, even if I'm not well.' (Mary)

> 'It is still there. It is being maintained still. Two staffs are maintaining it and we are giving them salary too. ... We used to go once in a while. ... Even if it is here, we have two people. They are even more dependable than our son. We have a driver. We helped him to start a taxi service. They all see me as their own father. I see them as my own children. ... We trust them. They have our house key with them.' (Jacob)

Emotional attachment towards their home motivated older adults to retain home ownership. The above narratives show that older adults deploy different strategies to retain and maintain their home.

Attachment to things and places left at home

Possessions left behind at home by older adults range from photographs to plants and pets. Older adults are ready to share their possessions like kitchen utensils, furniture and electronic equipment such as TV and air conditioning with tenants.

> 'I kept some of our possessions like photos, TV, washing machine in a separate room. It's closed and key is with me. I allowed them to use our furniture. Since they already have TV and washing machine they don't want ours.' (Molamma)

Older women in the study reported how attached they were to the domestic possessions they had left behind. Theses possessions, such as cooking utensils, were an integral part of their daily rituals when they lived with the whole family. Due to this feeling of attachment, more women in the study felt sad over the unutilised condition of their kitchen utensils at home. So, they were ready to give them to others who were needy, especially to poor neighbours who respected them. Home possessions also included trees planted by family members. They were happy to take fruits from these trees back to their retirement homes after making a visit home, but not because they wish to have it; it simply evokes the memory and emotional attachment they feel towards their spouse and home.

> 'I'm a bit worried when I think about the utensils at home. There are many of them. How can I maintain all of them when I am here (Trinity)! But I'm planning to give some of them to some poor people. There are others. There are some slum people near our home. They're so friendly and helpful. Poor dears! I plan to give them to those poor ones. They call me "Mummy". ... The plants have grown into big trees of fruits and herbs now. They were planted by my husband. Sometimes I collect the fallen fruits on the ground and take it with me here.' (Mary)

Those older adults who have pets at home depended on others to take care of the animals and their home surroundings. Generally it is a neighbour who does this, and in return this favoured neighbour receives recompense in the form of money and kind. In this way, the older adult is keeping and strengthening his or her interpersonal relationship with the neighbourhood.

Even with the absence of human inhabitation, older adults like to create an atmosphere of home by keeping a pet there.

'We have our dog at home. … There is a neighbor to take care of it. We have asked them to do so. We give them some money and our ration card (a document to avail groceries such as rice, wheat, sugar and kerosene at a cheaper price through public distribution system) so that they buy rice from ration shop and give food to the dog.' (Stephen)

'My Yoshi (pet dog) is at home … he became very old … I appointed a person to take care of all his needs, my home and properties. He will feed my Yoshi. One more thing. I have a big sword at home. Made up of brass. It's quite old too.' (Omana)

Older adults are keeping cherished possessions in the form of photographs, paintings and artistic works as these evoke the memory of beloved and deceased family members connected to their home. Since they are very emotionally attached to these photographs and paintings, the presence of such possessions often brings back the memory of their late family members. In the case of Alice, a single retired older adult former teacher, she likes to keep her parents' and brother's photo inside her cupboard at her home. When she looks into it, she feels sorrow about her present condition of loneliness. Thus, she doesn't want to look at these photos in front of others; she only wants to keep them with her as memories of her parents and brother. Sometimes possessions can be outside the home too. For example, Kurian considers the resting place of his parents and wife, at his church near home, as a valuable possession in his later life. During his occasional visit at home he used to visit his family plot near the church. Generally, Syrian Christians in Kerala have their own family tombs near their family church.

'My wife was an artist. She used to do paint and some good embroidery works. Now in her absence, I feel they are very precious in rest of my life. I have brought one of her painting here (Trinity). And placed it in the wall of our room. Rest of the paintings were kept at my home safely … My wife and my parents are resting in peace there. So naturally I go there every month … Yes, they (personal belongings of deceased wife) are well preserved there (home), although it was rented to nuns.' (Kurian)
'I have photos of my parents and siblings. Some of them I took with me here. Some of them I kept in my almarah at home … now a days, especially after my brother death, I don't like to look into it. I feel sorrow. They all (parents and siblings) have gone. I am the only remaining (sobs).' (Alice)

Older adults' emotional attachment towards home extends to material and non-material possessions in the home. The unutilised condition of their possessions evokes sorrows among older adults. This motivates them to share these possessions with others. Rearing pets at home can be considered as a strategy to avoid the feeling of their homes being uninhabited.

Discussion

The well-being of older adults living in retirement homes and its relation to place attachment have not been sufficiently incorporated both in theorisation as well as empirical understanding in the Indian context. This chapter has examined the motivations and practices of older adults living in retirement homes in India to retain their homes as a possession.

Older adults' first preference of residence is always their home. This study shows that health issues, a need for assistance, a lack of security, migration of children, loneliness due to loss of a spouse and a wish to live independently are the major reasons for older adults to seek an alternative source of residence in the form of a retirement home. This change in place of residence can be regarded as a viable option in response to the environment (Leith, 2006). When they do so, older adults try to secure a suitable retirement home close to their own home. This reflects the proximity-seeking behaviour of place attachment (Scannell and Gifford, 2010) coupled with the choice of residences influenced by family tradition (Izuhara, 2000).

This study shows that there are various reasons for older adults to retaining home ownership while living in a retirement home. Home is a place embedded with memories and emotions (Blunt and Varley, 2004) and owning a home helps to promote autonomy, control, continuity, self-expression and personal identity (Fox O'Mahony and Overton, 2014). Additionally, a sense of homelessness can create distress in terms of lack of autonomy and self-identity (Teo and Chiu, 2016), and hence motivates older adults to retain their home ownership. Traditionally, as per cultural norms in India, home is a place as well as a property, which is intended to be transferred from one generation to the next. By doing so, an intergenerational flow of wealth is executed, and family roots and pride are maintained because the home is a place constantly linked with the cultural and emotive world (Easthope, 2004). This study shows that the concept of home is rooted in the cultural meaning system. Cultural schemas of care and obligation towards the next generation motivate older adults to retain and maintain their homes. Through this, older adults gain a sense of satisfaction in having fulfilled their familial responsibility. Older adults also take responsibility for maintaining the family property, in the absence of their siblings. Memories of their past lives and deceased family members associated with home ties older adults emotionally to their home.

Occasional visits home bring feelings of happiness among older adults. This study shows that older adults in these specific retirement homes are economically independent and have autonomy in decision making. Female older adults are keener to make occasional visits to home and engage in cleaning, gardening and farming activates, even if they suffer physical hardships. These occasional visits give an opportunity to engage in a home-making activities that they usually cannot perform in the retirement homes. These activities ensure a sense of continuity in the older adults' lives. Social ties and interdependence play an important role in maintaining the feeling of home among older adults (Coleman et al, 2016). In order to maintain home, older adults apply different strategies: renting out; seeking help from other family members or neighbours or deploying paid employees. The purpose of renting out their home is not for economic enhancement but to find a suitable person or family to maintain the home and possessions, and for the home to be inhabited. These strategies enable older adults to enter into a new interpersonal relationship or strengthen their already established interpersonal relationship in the absence of migrant children.

The shift in residence brings changes in the meaning of home from shelter to cherished possession. Possessions in the home constitute both material as well as non-material possession, for example, as pets. The presence of pets at home enables older adults to have sense that home remains inhabited. For Miller (1998), home and possessions with a sense of agency motivate older adults to cherish their possessions at home. Moreover, the act of giving up possessions is a painstaking decision, akin to sacrificing a part of one's life (Marcoux, 2001).

This chapter contributes to understanding the ageing process of older adults living in retirement homes in India, which is a relatively new context. As in many other studies (Maslow, 1955; Moore, 2000; Easthope, 2004; Manzo, 2005; Leith, 2006; Clapham, 2011) this chapter also indicates that home is an integral part of making sense of security and identity and is constantly linked with the physical, social, cultural and emotive world. Studies (Sherman and Dacher, 2005; Meijering and Lager, 2014) also proved that cherished possessions promote a sense of comfort, security and continuity. While some studies identify the home as a place of residence, this study identified home as a possession as well as a place of attachment outside the older adluts' current place of residence, which brings feelings of identity, comfort and continuity, and overall promotes the emotional well-being of older adults living in retirement homes.

In the Indian context, place attachment, role of possession and place making practices of older adults in retirement homes are least addressed. This chapter shows that how cultural belief systems, values and emotion motivate older adults to make efforts to retain and maintain their homes as possessions, even if it represents a physical hardship for them to do so. It is done for the benefit of subsequent generations who may have migrated and as a route to maintaining identity and pride.

References

Bailey, A., Channakki, H. R. and Hutter, I. (2008) 'Place making in liminal times: a case study among Karnataka migrants in Goa', in A. Bailey (ed) *Culture, Risk and HIV/AIDS among migrant and mobile men in Goa, India*, Amsterdam: Rozenberg Publishers, pp 171–88.

Bhattacharyya, T. and Chatterjee, S. C. (2017) 'Exploring elder care in different settings in West Bengal: a psycho-social study of private homes, hospitals, and long-term care facilities', *International Journal of Psychological and Behavioral Sciences*, 11(6): 1607–12.

Blunt, A. and Varley, A. (2004) 'Geographies of home', *Cultural Geographies*, 11: 3–6.

Charmaz, K. (2006) *Constructing Grounded Theory: A Practical Guide through Qualitative Analysis*, London: Sage Publications.

Clapham, D. (2011) 'The embodied use of the material home: an affordance approach', *Housing, Theory and Society*, 28(4): 360–76.

Coleman, T. and Wiles, J. (2020) 'Being with objects of meaning: cherished possessions and opportunities to maintain aging in place', *Gerontologist*, 60(1): 41–9.

Coleman, T., Kearns, R. A. and Wiles, J. (2016) 'Older adults' experiences of home maintenance issues and opportunities to maintain ageing in place', *Housing Studies*, 31(8): 964–83.

Coolen, H. (2008) 'The meaning of dwelling features: conceptual and methodological issues', thesis, Delft University Press, Delft University of Technology.

Cooney, A. (2012) '"Finding home": a grounded theory on how older people "find home" in long-term care settings', *International Journal of Older People Nursing*, 7(3): 188–99.

Cristoforetti, A., Gennai, F. and Rodeschini, G. (2011) 'Home sweet home: the emotional construction of places', *Journal of Aging Studies*, 25(3): 225–32.

d'Andrade, R. (1992) 'Schemas and motivations', in R. G. d'Andrade and C. Strauss (eds) *Human Motives and Cultural Models*, Cambridge: Cambridge University Press, pp 23–44.

de Haas, B. and Hutter, I. (2019) 'Teachers' conflicting cultural schemas of teaching comprehensive school-based sexuality education in Kampala, Uganda',. *Culture, Health and Sexuality*, 21(2): 233–47.

Easthope, H. (2004) 'A place called home', *Housing, Theory and Society*, 21(3): 128–38.

Fox O'Mahony, L. and Overton, L. (2014) 'Asset-based welfare, equity release and the meaning of the owned home', *Housing Studies*, 30(3): 392–412.

Glaser, B. (1978) *Theoretical Sensitivity: Advances in Methodology of Grounded Theory*, Mill Valley, CA: Sociology Press.

Glaser, B. and Strauss, A. (1967) *The Discovery of Grounded Theory: Strategies for Qualitative Research*, New York: Academic Press.

Gupta, A., Mohan, U., Tiwari, S. C., Singh, S. K. and Singh, V. K. (2014) 'Quality of life of elderly people and assessment of facilities available in old age homes of Lucknow', *India*, 5(1): 21–4.

Hansen, E. B. and Gottschalk, G. (2006) 'What makes older people consider moving house and what makes them move?', *Housing, Theory and Society*, 23(1): 34–54.

HelpAge India (2009) *Directory of Old Age Homes in India*, New Delhi: Policy Research and Development Department, HelpAge India.

Hennink, M., Inge, H. and Ajay, B. (2011) 'In-depth interviews', in *Qualitative Research Methods*, London: Sage Publications, pp 108–32.

Heywood, F. (2005) 'Adaptation: altering the house to restore the home', *Housing Studies*, 20(4): 531–47.

Izuhara, M. (2000) 'Changing family tradition: housing choices and constraints for older people in Japan', *Housing Studies*, 15(1): 89–110.

Johnson, S., Madan, S., Vo, J. and Pottkett, A. (2018) 'A qualitative analysis of the emergence of long term care (old age home) sector for seniors care in India: urgent call for quality and care standards', *Ageing International*, 43(3): 356–65.

Kalavar, J. M. and Jamuna, D. (2011) 'Aging of Indian women in India: the experience of older women in formal care homes'. *Journal of Women and Aging*, 23(3): 203–15.

Lager, D., van Hoven, D. and Huigen, P. (2016) 'Rhythms, ageing and neighbourhoods', *Environment and Planning A*, 48(8): 1565–80.

Leith, K. H. (2006) '"Home is where the heart is ... or is it?". A phenomenological exploration of the meaning of home for older women in congregate housing', *Journal of Aging Studies*, 20(4): 317–33.

Liebig, P. (2003) 'Old-age homes and services: Old and new approaches to aged care', *Journal of Aging and Social Policy*, 15(2–3): 159–78.

Manzo, L. C. (2005) 'For better or worse: exploring multiple dimensions of place meaning'. *Journal of Environmental Psychology*, 25(1): 67–86.

Marcoux, J.-S. (2001) 'The "Casser Maison" ritual: constructing the self by emptying the home', *Journal of Material Culture*, 6: 213–35.

Maslow, A. H. (1955) *Motivation and Personality*, New York: Harper & Brothers.

Mayer, A. (2017) 'Old age – home? Middle-class senior citizens and new elderscapes in urban India', PhD thesis, Heidelberg University.

Mazumdar, S. and Mazumdar, S. (2005) 'Home in the context of religion for elderly Hindus in India', in G. Rowels and H. Chaudhury (eds) *Home and Identity in Late Life: International Perspectives*, New York: Springer, pp 81–110.

Meijering, L. and Lager, D. (2014) 'Home-making of older Antillean migrants in the Netherlands', *Ageing and Society*, 34(5): 859–75.

Miller, D. (1998) *Material Cultures: Why Some Things Matter*, London: UCL Press.

Moore, J. (2000) 'Placing home in context', *Journal of Environmental Psychology*, 20(3): 207–17.

Müller, H. (2019) 'Then we'll take it along even though we wouldn't take it along'– on the role of spaces and things in transitions into multigenerational cohousing. Presentation at the International Association of Gerontology and Geriatrics European Region (IAGG-ER) Congress: 23–25 May, Gothenburg.

Nair, S. and Kumar, S. (2017) 'Ageing in Kerala: some key issues'. *Indian Journal of Gerontology*, 31(2): 209–38.

Pathania, A., Haldar, P., Kant, S., Gupta, S. K., Pandav, C. S. and Bachani, D. (2019) 'Prevalence of anaemia among elderly persons residing in old age homes in national capital territory, Delhi, India', *Indian Journal of Public Health*, 63(4): 288–96.

Pazhoothundathil, N. and Bailey, A. (2020) 'Cherished possessions, home-making practices and aging in care homes in Kerala, India', *Emotion, Space and Society*, 36: 1–9.

Registrar General of India. (2011) 'Census Report', New Delhi.

Rutagumirwa, S. K. (2018) 'Aging and gender in Tanzania: uncovering the cultural schemas, nexus of identities and the Aging Body, PhD thesis, University of Groningen.

Samuel, R., McLachlan, C. S., Mahadevan, U. and Isaac, V. (2016) 'Cognitive impairment and reduced quality of life among old-age groups in southern urban India: home-based community residents, free and paid old-age home residents', *QJM: An International Journal of Medicine*, 109(10): 653–9.

Scannell, L. and Gifford, R. (2010) 'Defining place attachment: a tripartite organizing framework', *Journal of Environmental Psychology*, 30: 1–10.

Scannell, L. and Gifford, R. (2014) 'Compairing the theories of interpersonal and place attachment', in L. Manzo and P. Devine-Wright (eds) *Place Attachment: Advances in Theory, Methods and Applications*, New York: Routledge, pp 23–36.

Seo, Y. K. and Mazumdar, S. (2011) 'Feeling at home: Korean Americans in senior public housing', *Journal of Aging Studies*, 25: 233–42.

Sherman, E. and Dacher, J. (2005) 'Cherished objects and the home: their meaning and roles in late life', in G. D. Rowles and H. Chaudhury (eds) *Home and Identity in Late Life: International Perspectives*, New York: Springer, pp 63–79.

Smith, J. S. and White, B. N. (2004) 'Detached from their home land: the Latter-Day Saints of Chihuahu, Mexico', *Journal of Cultural Geography*, 21: 57–76.

Social Justice Department. (2019) 'Old age homes in Kerala', http://sjd. kerala.gov.in/DOCUMENTS/Downloadables/OTHERS/30681.pdf

Stevens, D., Camic, P. M. and Solway, R. (2019) 'Maintaining the self: meanings of material objects after a residential transition later in life', *Educational Gerontology*, 45(3): 214–26.

Strauss, A. and Corbin, J. (1998) *Basics of Qualitative Research: Grounded Theory Procedures and Techniques*, Thousand Oaks, CA: Sage.

Strauss, A. and Quinn, N. (1997) *A Cognitive Theory of Cultural Meaning*, Cambridge: Cambridge University Press.

Subaiya, L. and Dhananjay, W. (2011) 'Demographics of Population Ageing in India: Trends and Differentials', BKPAI Working Paper No. 1, New Delhi.

Teo, P. L. and Chiu, M. Y.-L. (2016) 'An ecological study of families in transitional housing – "housed but not homed"', *Housing Studies*, 31(5): 560–77.

Ugargol, A. P. and Bailey, A. (2020) 'Reciprocity between older adults and their care-givers in emigrant households of Kerala, India', *Ageing and Society*, 41(8): 1699–725.

UNFPA (2011) 'Report on Status of Elderly in Selected States of India', New Delhi.

United Nations (2019) 'World Population Prospects 2019', New York.

Vaisey, S. (2009) 'Motivation and justification: a dual-process model of culture in action', *American Journal of Sociology*, 114(6): 1675–715.

van den Hoonaard, D. K. (2009) 'Experiences of living alone: widows' and widowers' perspectives', *Housing Studies*, 24(6): 737–53.

10

Decision-making and choice or *sine qua non*? Care home entry in Tamil Nadu

Vanessa Burholt, R. Maruthakutti and Carol A. Maddock

Background

In India, families are mandated to take care of their older members (Rajan and Mishra, 2011). The Maintenance and Welfare of Parents and Senior Citizens Act (2007) states that parents, grandparents and 'childless' older people who are unable to maintain themselves are entitled to demand and receive income, care and support from children, grandchildren and other relatives who have sufficient resources. Cases (where support is not forthcoming) can be taken to tribunal and can result in the issue of maintenance orders with penalties for non–compliance including fines and imprisonment. Thus, there is a reliance on *informal* social protection, that is, support from kin. However, changes in family structures, family values, migration of family members and a rise in the number of women working outside the home can put increasing strain on families to provide support. Traditional forms of solidarity and collectivism are eroded by market economies: increasing monetisation impacts on forms of reciprocity (Norton et al, 2001), and requirement for a responsive mobile labour force impacts on availability of caregivers (Himmelweit, 2007, Rishworth and Elliott, 2018). Therefore, it is important to challenge the 'realities' of family support systems which may not be as robust as portrayed by policy makers.

Social protection should provide 'a set of public programs designed to mitigate or cope with the adverse effects of risks to income security and physical well-being' (Kapur and Nangia, 2015, p 75). Therefore, in India, we would expect to find welfare policies and programmes that protect individuals against shocks to assets across the life course, and plug any gaps in kin support in later life which may include options to relocate to a care home. However, little is known about older people's decision-making around care and support in later life. This chapter draws on data from 30 in–depth interviews with older male and female residents of nine care homes in three districts of Tamil Nadu and addresses the following questions: i) what are the decision-making routes leading to relocation to a care home? and ii) how does culture and the political economy influence the care choices available to older people? The chapter concludes with some recommendations that could improve the range of choices concerning care in later life.

The traditional family system in India

Historically, different family forms have co-existed in India (eg, joint, nuclear, extended, single parent, dual earners, adoptive families). However, the 'traditional' joint household and extended family has been presented as the mainstay of social life, meeting the social, economic and emotional needs of its members (D'Cruz and Bharat, 2001). In the extended family, value systems are related to familism (prioritising the family over individual needs) and filial piety (emphasising respect and obligations towards meeting parents' needs) (Burholt et al, 2017).

A 'traditional' joint Indian household is typically patrilocal and multi-generational (Chekki, 1996; Breton, 2019). Households may consist of parents, (un)married son(s) and their offspring and unmarried daughters, sharing property and income. Marriage is considered a social duty to the family and the careful selection of a marriage partner can lead to economic, political and social benefits for the family (Chekki, 1996; Nanda, 2019).

In a 'traditional' family, parents expect filial support (Das Gupta, 1999). However, when daughters marry they relocate to their parents-in-law's household (Das, Gupta 1999) and they are responsible for most of the daily household chores (Ugargol et al, 2016). Married couples are expected to have children (Bhambhani and Inbanathan, 2018) and voluntary childlessness is rare. Childlessness is perceived as a curse, and women who cannot bear children, or choose not to have children are stigmatised (Riessman, 2000).

As noted above, a variety of family forms exist in India (D'Cruz and Bharat, 2001). Presently in India, there are more older people living alone and a greater proportion of nuclear households, compared to a decade ago (Sathyanarayana et al, 2014; Dhillon et al, 2016; see Chapters 3 and 4 for new living arrangements and their impact on older adults). Furthermore, migration of family members for work and education has led to extended families living at a distance from each other (Kaushik, 2020), while greater freedom in marriage has impacted on an increase in co-habitation with partners and homosexual partnerships (Kaur, 2019). Despite this, the concept of the 'traditional' Indian household and extended family is the 'ideal' that is used to underpin the government's expectations concerning the informal social protection of older people. This normative set of relationships is socially constructed and sanctioned by the Government of India. Any deviation from the traditional family norm may result in a shortfall in kin support in later life and contribute to the decision to relocate into a care home.

Cultural political economy and the sustainable livelihood framework

Relocation to a care home is shaped by a variety of factors. Firstly, an older person's assets (eg, access to kin support, socio-economic or health status) may affect the decision to relocate. Secondly, the choice of a 'provider' is likely to be influenced by desirability, affordability, availability and accessibility of care (Puthenparambil and Kröger, 2016). Desirability is likely to be swayed by cultural values and norms (see Chapters 7 and 8 on norms of care and caregiving), while affordability, availability and accessibility will be influenced by the political economy. The analysis of the influence of the cultural political economy on the 'choice' to relocate to a care home is situated within a sustainable livelihood framework.

> Livelihood comprises the capabilities, assets (including both material and social resources) and activities required for a means of living. A livelihood is sustainable when it can cope with and recover from stress and shocks and maintain or enhance its capabilities and assets both now and in the future. (Chambers and Conway, 1992, p 6)

The sustainable livelihood framework takes into account the relationships between shocks, livelihood assets (financial, human, natural, physical and social), transforming structures and processes, and the impact on livelihood outcomes. Human assets comprise skills, knowledge, health, ability to work and ability to look after oneself. Social assets comprise networks of family, friends and neighbours and membership of community groups. Financial assets include savings and income from employment and other sources. Natural assets include land and water, while physical assets include housing and sanitation. The sustainable livelihoods framework (see Figure 10.1) takes into account how access to assets assist older people to navigate shocks that they have no control over (such as loss or decline in physical or cognitive function). The relationship to care is evident when human assets are depleted, for example when a shock (such as poor health) means that an older person is no longer able to work, and/or to look after themself. In this respect, the livelihood model takes into account access to other personal or familial financial assets to offset a lack of income from employment, and/or social assets and the availability of caregivers to provide support.

Within the livelihood model transforming structures include public, private and civic organisations, and transforming processes include policies, legislations, institutions, conventions and culture (such as norms, values and beliefs), which, taken together, constitute a complex system that determine access to assets and power, and influence vulnerability to shocks.

The interaction between a person's assets and the cultural political context impacts on livelihood outcomes. For older people in the face of depleted human assets, and with few or no other assets to draw upon, a possible 'livelihood outcome' is residential relocation into an aged care facility to receive basic support including housing, food, health and personal care.

This chapter examines the underlying cultural framework that has influenced (and sustains) social protection in India (see Chapter 11 for a list of social protection programmes). Applying a cultural political economy lens, it considers the extent to which decision-making trajectories that conclude with relocation to a care home are based on access to a range of options and choices or borne out of necessity. The analysis of interviews pays attention to i) the practices that allow the social welfare system to function alongside ii) the beliefs and values that legitimise these practices (Sewell, 1999) within the context of the sustainable livelihood framework.

Data and methods

Sample selection

Care homes were purposively selected from three southernmost districts in Tamil Nadu: Thoothukudi, Tirunelveli and Kanyakumari. Forty-two care homes were identified: 13 in Thoothukudi, 11 in Tirunelveli and 18 in Kanyakumari. The ratio of fee-paying to free care homes in each district, and the size of the care homes was used to inform the sampling strategy and to obtain a sample of 10 people in each district.

Data collection

As the study was exploratory, a qualitative interview method was selected to elicit information on decision-making leading to relocation to aged care facilities. Face-to-face semi-structured in-depth interviews with residents in the care homes were conducted in Tamil by PhD scholars (Dr R. Anitha, Dr S. Ponni and Dr R. Hemalakshmi) from the Department of Sociology at Manonmaniam Sundaranar University, Tirunelveli, Tamil Nadu. The interviews were recorded and transcribed. They were translated by a third party into English and anonymised. Pseudonyms are used throughout the chapter.

Data analysis

Framework analysis was used to analyse the data (Ritchie and Spencer, 2002). A preliminary framework comprising top level themes was applied to a few transcripts and categories (sub-themes) were identified and refined. The refined thematic framework was systematically applied to the textual data.

Schematic diagrams indicating the (numbered) sequence of shocks to assets, transforming structures and processes and livelihood outcomes were developed and used alongside the charted material to capture the commonalities of experience across cases (Ayres et al, 2003). Recurring themes were used to group interviews.

Chronological explanatory summaries of interviews were created to communicate the complexity of experiences (Polkinghorne, 1995). Transforming structures and processes were rarely derived directly from the transcripts, but required higher-level interpretive analysis, which is elaborated upon in the discussion section.

Two exemplars from each group illustrate how contrasting positions (eg, socio-economic and/or marital status) converge in care home entry, but influence 'choice sets' available to participants (eg, entering paid versus free aged care facilities). The exemplar methodology has been used for centuries to represent complex concepts, for example *Nicomachean Ethics* by Aristole in 350 BC used exemplars to help explain wisdom and the inter-relationship between ethics, virtues and character (Bronk et al, 2013). This methodology is an appropriate way to develop a deeper understanding of care in relation to sustainable livelihood framework, and how culture and the political economy influence the care choices available to older people (Burholt et al, 2020). In order to understand the complexity of the interrelationships between assets (in particular the availability of social assets such as family care and support, to alleviate shocks to financial and human assets) and transforming structures and processes (culture and social protection) we have selected narratives of older people that exemplify the particular theme we are describing (eg, never married or childless) in a highly developed manner (Bronk et al, 2013). The exemplar narratives are not selected to be 'typical' but instead incorporate features experienced by other participants in a concentrated sequence of events. The exemplars unite the 'psychologically real' influence of cultural norms and values and the processual influence of social protection on actions and experience and illuminates their respective influence on the care trajectory that are apparent in others' narratives, but in a more moderate way.

Results

Deviations from the 'traditional' joint household and extended family

Cultural deviations from the 'traditional' joint household and extended family impacted on care availability in later life and were observed for a majority of the care home residents (25 out of 30). These were related to having never married, having married but bearing no children or daughters only or experiencing conflictual, neglectful or abusive relationships with relatives.

Never married or childless

Marriage is considered a cultural obligation to the family. However, five interviewees had never married because of culturally constructed normative constraints relating to disability (*n*=2), being orphaned (*n*=1) and based on the researchers' perception that there was (a high likelihood of) undisclosed homosexuality (*n*=2). All five unmarried participants were childless. Additionally, four (once-) married participants had no offspring, thus deviating from the norm in India.

Areesha (never married, 63) was from a wealthy family with five siblings and lived in the 'biggest house in the village'. She had vitiligo since childhood and her mother never arranged for her to marry because of her culturally informed beliefs about beauty and health (Chaturvedi et al, 2005).

> 'My mother was afraid. This [skin] would be very thin. I had plenty of hair and was good looking. A village administrative officer was proposed to me. But my mother was doubtful. She was apprehensive that he was willing to marry me only for the jewels and that he would desert me later. So she didn't marry me off.' (Areesha, 63)

Areesha did not inherit any land as her widowed mother was cheated out of her property by a relative. Areesha's siblings passed away. She lived alone in rented accommodation but had local friends from the church congregation. Following a road traffic accident Areesha's vision deteriorated. She had been collecting her pension from an uncle's house, but as her sight waned and her relative moved, her source of income ceased.

> 'I was getting ₹1,000 [per month; 100 Indian rupees = approximately £1]. I had well-to-do relatives at [neighbourhood in district]. It was their address that I gave for getting ₹1,000. Later they sold that house. [...] I stopped getting that amount.' (Areesha, 63)

Areesha's neighbours informed two local professional women that she was 'living a life of hardship'. The gap between older people's needs and state welfare provision is sometimes met by philanthropic middle/upper class women who act as donors and informal social workers (Pushpa, 2001). These women became Areesha's non-kin carers, buying groceries and paying her rent. Once Areesha's eyesight prohibited her from cooking the women secured her a place in a fee-paying care home.

Deepak (widowed, 68) had been a daily-wage earner (ie, irregular daily paid work on construction sites or in agriculture) since the age of 23. Deepak's siblings were also daily wage earners. Deepak was married, but his wife had asthma and a cough. The latter may have been due to tuberculosis

Figure 10.1: Livelihood framework and care home trajectory for never married or childless participants, Areesha and Deepak

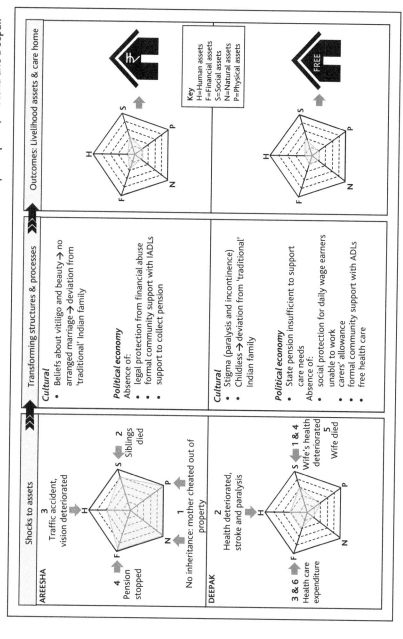

(TB) which can result in infertility in women (Rao, 2018) as they did not have any children.

> 'One could get just enough to make ends meet. And whatever I earned was spent on the treatment for my wife. She had asthma and cough. I had to spend a lot for her treatment. If you got work on the day, you could get your wages and with that you could buy medicines and spend for household expenses. That's all.' (Deepak, 68, widowed)

At the age of 50, Deepak had suffered a stroke and one year later was paralysed and unable to work.

> 'Blood started flowing from my nose and mouth. After a year, I became impaired and bedridden. For one year my wife was supporting me to move around. But then my limbs became so weak that I couldn't walk any more.' (Deepak, 68, widowed)

Deepak's wife looked after him until her health also deteriorated. Their only source of income was donations from visitors which they used to pay village children to fetch water and groceries, and sweep the house. Eventually, Deepak's wife was admitted to intensive care where she spent several months before passing away. Deepak sold their home to pay for her hospital treatment and subsequently lived near his brother's house.

> 'I don't have a house of my own to dwell in. I don't have even a cent of land. I was there just like a street dweller. [...] I was lying there like a dog. It was a kennel covered with a tarpaulin.' (Deepak, 68, widowed)

Deepak's brother bathed him and washed his clothes. However, he frequently worked away and during these periods Deepak's other relatives would not provide any care. A local boy brought Deepak food from a hotel and disposed of the contents of Deepak's 'bedpan'.

> 'There are lots of problems in taking care of such a person like me. [...] They don't want to see me lying down like this. They [show me] disdain. [...] I have become unwanted by all. I have relatives [...] But there are none to look after me. All have just neglected me.' (Deepak, 68, widowed)

A neighbour suggested that the Deepak would be better off in a care home:

'Looking at my condition, he called a medical representative and discussed with him. That medical representative said that there was a cloister […] and that there was a Sister who could help. […] She made a recommendation for me and brought me here.' (Deepak, 68, widowed)

Areesha and Deepak had different socio-economic positions that contributed to diverging experiences earlier in their lives, but ultimately, the long-term impact of childlessness was similar. In later life both were dependent on non-filial support that exceeded cultural expectations. Without formal community care, neither had a choice other than to relocate to a care home to receive support. Whereas Areesha was able to purchase her care, Deepak lived in a home for destitute older people.

Daughters as a source of support in later life

Nine participants did not have access to any filial support. Their situation was similar to childless participants as once daughters marry they migrate to become part of their spouse's family and are unavailable as caregivers to their parents.

During her childhood Maalia (widowed, 65) was abused by her stepmother and moved to a children's home: 'I went on my own, not able to bear the tortures of my stepmother.' Maalia married, but was abandoned by her husband when she was six months pregnant. Shortly after giving birth, Maalia sent her daughter to be cared for in an 'orphanage' while she moved into a women's refuge. She started work in the kitchen at the care home she had lived in as a child. The facilities (orphanage, women's refuge, care home) were in a cluster that were run by the same organisation.

When her daughter reached marriageable age, Maalia borrowed ₹3,000 from the proprietors for her wedding.

She [my daughter] was brought up here and she was married off here. They [the organisation] selected the groom and conducted the wedding. They did well with proper wedding gifts. But that scummy guy is doing like this [is an alcoholic].' (Maalia, 65, widowed)

Maalia earned ₹500 per month in the kitchen and the organisation kept her salary to pay off her debt. Her repayments continued for 22 years until she burned her leg in an accident in the kitchen and needed significant health care expenditure for treatment. A priest paid ₹27,000 for her hospital fees and Maalia continued to work to pay off the increased debt. Eventually, in need of an eye operation that she was unable to afford, and incapacitated, she asked to move to the older people's care home within the cluster of facilities.

Figure 10.2: Livelihood framework and care home trajectory for participants with only daughters, Maalia and Nihal

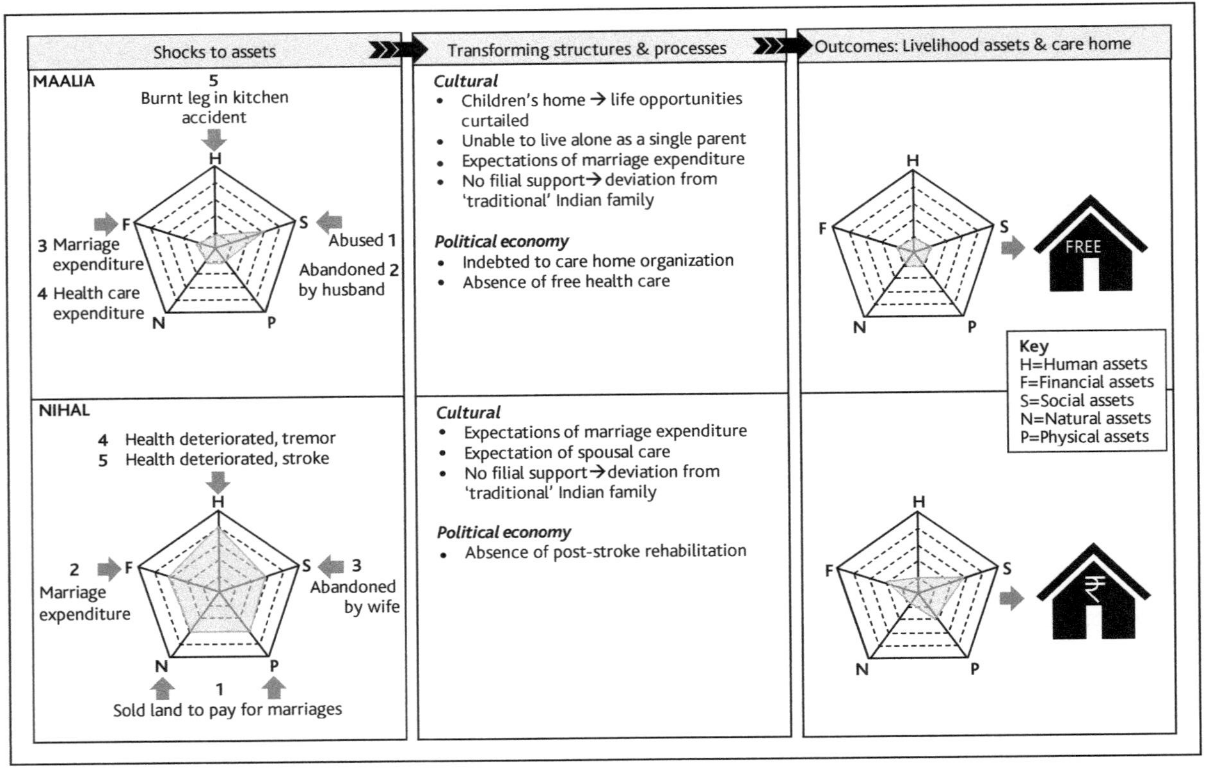

She was unable to ask for financial or physical help from her daughter who was struggling to take care of her own children, and she questioned the viability of the Act that mandated this support.

> 'They took me to the government hospital. They said that I should undergo an operation. But I didn't have any money. I begged the doctor to leave me at the home [for older women]. They say that the children should take care of [older people]. How can she [my daughter] help me? She could give me some ₹5 or ₹10. She is doing housemaid work.' (Maalia, 65, widowed)

Nihal (married, age unknown) had two daughters. He worked abroad in the construction industry for 25 years and regularly sent remittances back to his family. After the marriages of both daughters a substantial debt was accrued and Nihal accused his wife of financial impropriety. During the ensuing argument Nihal physically abused his wife which resulted in separation.

> 'For the money I had given, there shouldn't have been any debt. But she had incurred a debt of ₹350,000. So we had the dispute. […] We did everything characteristic of a fight – hitting, pushing and pulling. Our children had to intervene. Then my wife went away and didn't return.' (Nihal, married)

In order to clear the debts Nihal sold his wife's jewellery. He returned to work abroad 'to compensate for what we lost'. However, within a year he came back to India, unable to work having acquired a tremor. Initially, his wife looked after him during his hospital treatment, but quickly moved back in with her daughter. Once he was discharged from hospital, Nihal lived alone until he had a stroke. While he was unconscious he was moved to a care home by his son–in–law, who paid for his care. Despite having abused his wife, he expected her to provide him with care:

> 'She [my wife] should take care of me in a helping manner. Let her be as a helping hand at this old age, giving some hot water or porridge. This is what one could expect in old age.' (Nihal, married)

While Maalia's daughter was unable to provide any kind of support, Nihal's daughter was unwilling to provide physical care, but financially supported her father. Nihal did not expect any more from his daughter who had already transgressed normative roles by providing a home for her mother (a refuge from abuse), but still expected his wife to fulfil her 'duty' of care to him.

Conflictual, neglectful or abusive family relationships

Of the 30 participants interviewed, eight reported financial abuse (including seizing land and property), six reported physical abuse, seven were neglected and four were abandoned. Three reported multiple forms of abuse. Seven participants who were not classified as childless or having only daughters (see above sections 'Never married or childless' and 'Daughters as a source of support in later life'), had family relationships that were conflictual, neglectful or abusive (see also Chapter 8 for methods older men use to adapt behaviours to avoid abuse).

Varsha (widowed, 75) had one son and three daughters. She worked on the saltpan as a daily wage earner. Varsha looked after herself until her health deteriorated substantially and she was neither able to work nor manage her activities of daily living. She moved into rented accommodation with her son. However, a typical argument with her daughter-in-law (her primary caregiver) (Jamuna, 2003) led to the abrogation of the relationship with her son and homelessness. Although Varsha had three daughters, she felt unable to live with any of them.

> 'You should not go and live in your daughter's house, especially when you have a son. Won't the son-in-law question it? Your daughter may want you to be with her. But will your son-in-law think the same way? We should not disturb the life of our daughter.' (Varsha, 75, widowed)

Varsha was turned down for a pension three times. Without a home, filial support or income, Varsha's daughter admitted her to a home for destitute older people.

Padma (widowed, age unknown) received a very good dowry from her parents, 'when I got married, my parents adorned me with a heap of jewels'. She sold her jewellery when she was widowed and bought 38 cents of land (1 cent is $\frac{1}{100}$ of an acre – 40.5 m^2 or 435.6 ft^2).

Padma had five children: three daughters and two sons. At the request of her eldest son, she gave 8 cents of her land to help fund her niece's dowry/wedding. She lived with her youngest son but was neglected. She was provided with a 'bed' of coconut husks in his shop and given insufficient food. Padma wanted to live with her youngest daughter and was willing to give her 30 cents of land in return for providing her with care. In order to avoid 'losing' the land to their sister, Padma's sons deceived her into signing over the land to them.

> 'When another daughter wanted to take the 30 cents [of land] in return for caring for me until my last days, my two sons took me to the church one day and got signatures. I didn't know what it was for.

Figure 10.3: Livelihood framework and care home trajectory for participants with conflictual, neglectful or abusive family relationships, Varsha and Padma

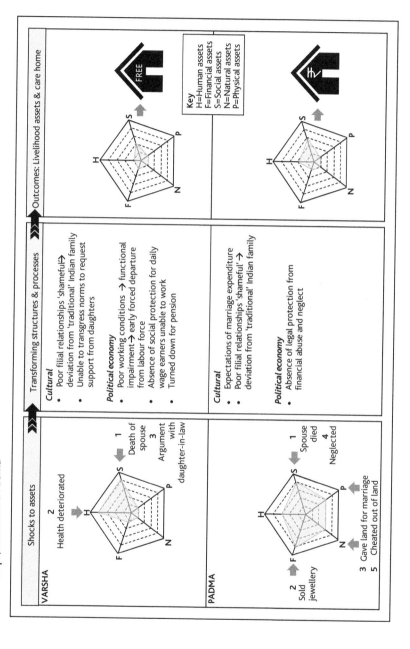

After coming here [care home] only then I came to know that they cheated me.' (Padma, widowed)

Following the acquisition of her land, Padma's sons tied her hands and legs and left her at the care home. One son pays for her care.

Varsha and Padma had familial relationships that deviated from the 'respectful' norm. Whereas an argument left Varsha without a home or filial support, Padma was abused and cheated out of her land. Despite differences in the type of relationship deficits, neither had a choice over relocation to a care home. Padma's higher socio-economic position resulted in placement in a fee-paying care home, whereas Varsha moved to a care home for destitute older people. Padma was financially abused and forcibly (physically abused) and relocated into a care home, whereas Varsha was evicted and destitute because of poor family relationships and her unwillingness to transgress cultural norms.

Discussion

The timing and nature of the shocks to livelihoods impacted on decision-making pathways and outcomes for older care home residents. Shocks to human assets (the capacity to work and care for oneself) were the most significant events that fuelled a move to a care home and were influenced by deteriorating health, injury or retirement. Income was curtailed by exclusion from the workforce, but financial assets were also affected by expenditure on relatives (eg, marriage of daughters), health procedures, hospitalisation and the inability to secure a pension. In some instances the impact of a shock to financial assets was mitigated by drawing on alternative familial resources where these existed, or by liquidating natural and physical assets through the sale of land or property. Without alternative sources of income (eg, savings) financial support from the family was essential in order for an older person to avoid destitution. However, families were not always the source of financial support, there were also examples of financial abuse where monetary, physical and natural assets were seized from older people by relatives. As the state relies on *informal* social protection, social assets were extremely important as a source of basic necessities (eg, food and housing), personal and health care, safety and financial security in later life. Shocks to older people's social assets included abandonment, ill health or death of spouse, arguments and abuse.

Overall the majority (26 out of 30) of the care home residents lacked filial support, and/or were economically destitute due to a variety of livelihood shocks. Avoiding destitution is dependent on financial transfers from family or social protection by the state (Shankardass, 2020). When older people are deemed ineligible for help because they transgress norms of the 'ideal family' (eg. having only daughters) or other cultural practices (eg, clean, healthy, heterosexual, socially compliant), they may be both rejected from supportive relationships and excluded from state support (Harriss-White, 2005). Additionally, families and households may have few financial assets to draw upon. In these contexts, caregiving and financial support is perceived as 'unaffordable'. This can be due to the loss of productive hours through caregiving and the outlay required to meet the resource needs (nutritional, clothing and health care) of an older person. Ugargol et al (2016) found that co-residence facilitates the pooling of resources and plays a crucial role in caregiving and support to older adults. However, in poor households older people are in a weak position to make claims to limited household resources, as consumption may result in an economically productive household member or child going without food or other essential material provisions (Vera-Sanso, 2018). The only option or 'choice' in this situation may be for an older person to move into an aged care facility. These issues are addressed in more detail below.

Cultural processes impacting on care in later life

Cultural processes that create stigma through prejudice and discrimination transformed the experience of many participants. These included reactions to gender, medical conditions perceived as 'disability', homosexuality and class/caste.

Reflecting on the society in which participants from this study were embedded during the 1990s, Seizer noted that 'for most Tamil women there are only two desirable identities which both revolve around her position within a male lineage: one is that of girl-child, living with her father's family, and the other is that of woman-wife, living with her husband's family' (Seizer, 1995, p 98). Consequently, deviations from these cultural expectations influenced life course trajectories and were observed for Areesha and Maalia. For both women, the political economy created a state of dependency and powerlessness in later life resulting in the decision to move to a care home being made for them.

The socio-cultural status of Maalia and Areesha narrowed their life choices. Areesha's vitiligo influenced her marriage prospects, excluding her from creating a supportive network for later life. Maalia's childhood experience of abuse and institutionalisation positioned her with fewer life opportunities than others (Sinha et al, 2016). Her marriage prospects were limited by her social status. Abandoned by her husband, as a single parent Maalia would have lacked access to resources and faced discrimination within the community (D'Cruz and Bharat, 2001). Her life lacked predictability, job security, material or psychological protection. Living in extreme poverty, Maalia would have had little choice other than to abandon her own daughter into the care system (Sinha et al, 2016), reproducing a cycle of poverty and a life of precarity.

Nowadays in Tamil Nadu, women from wealthy families may expect to have a university education and a career. However, for the majority of women, marriage is still a priority (Srinivasan, 2014) and only a few aspire to push cultural boundaries and remain unmarried (Lamb, 2018). The slow pace of cultural change in Tamil Nadu is evident in continued discrimination and violence against women (especially for the most socially disadvantaged) alongside social pressure to conform to subordination, patriarchal domination, domesticity and caregiving service (Rao, 2014). The cultural political economy has not delivered positive transformational opportunities, but instead continues to inhibit the prospects of alternative work–life–care practices for women (Buzzanell et al, 2011). This suggests that modern women who deviate from normative expectations may also experience restricted choices for care and support and limited decision-making power in later life.

Women are not the only people to experience exclusion from full participation in Indian society. People with disabilities or certain health conditions are also discriminated against. For example, incontinence confers cultural stigma on a household. Brinjath and Manderson (2008) noted that odours associated with incontinence influence the social perception of the house. While Lamb (2000) has suggested that in North India 'children clean up parents' urine end excrement lovingly and without complaint when they become incontinent' (p 36), this is neither generalisable across India nor to other family members. For example, some adult children feed older parents infrequently in order to minimise the intimate care work associated with defecation (Meher et al, 2018). Furthermore, in this present study, it was difficult for Deepak to receive help in the community from his family as his paralysis and incontinence impacted on the likelihood of consanguineously distant kin providing care. Stigmatisation as a result of 'bodily pollution' can constrain family functions, such as arranging marriages (Brijnath and Manderson, 2008). In order for the family to continue 'normal' activities, a solution is to relocate the older person to a care home.

The oppression of and discrimination against women, and the prejudices and stigma associated with culturally constructed 'disabilities' and/or deformity (eg, vitiligo, paralysis), or uncleanliness (eg, incontinence) culminated in a process of disenfranchisement for those people perceived to have transgressed cultural norms. Similar sanctions were also applied to those who were unable to bear a child (eg, Deepak), had female children only (eg, Maalia and Nihal), or had dysfunctional relationships with children (eg, Varsha and Padma) as they also deviated from compliance with the normative 'traditional' Indian family. The participants had been excluded from a range of choices for long-term care arrangements and for many, social exclusion had resulted in destitution. Thus, destitution has its foundations in culturally normative practices that punish non-conformity with exclusion from support in later life.

Political economy influencing care in later life
Social protection

Social protection has a role in reducing poverty and mitigating livelihood shocks, by providing income security and support so that people are better able to manage outcomes such as unemployment (including in old age), sickness, and disability. However, many older people in India work until they are no longer able to as they are reliant on generating income from employment (Rajan, 2010). Perversely, the conditions of work for those on the lowest wages (eg, agricultural labourers, brick makers) are particularly arduous or hazardous and can have a negative impact on function, resulting in an early forced departure from the workforce and financial dependency on others (Vera-Sanso, 2006). For example, as a saltpan worker Varsha would have endured particular hardships such as dehydration, with little provision for clean drinking water, toilets and shelter from the heat (Devi, 2017). Consequently, she would have been prone to health problems associated with working in the saltpan, including joint pain, kidney disease and retinal issues (Devi, 2017). The deterioration in Varsha's health led to exclusion from work and dependency on her son. This pattern of hard labour leading to functional impairment or injury and workforce exclusion was observed in other interviewees accounts. Better working conditions would mean that people could remain productive for longer.

Neither Varsha, nor Deepak (a daily wage labourer) received any financial social protection when they were unable to work. Although the National Social Assistance Programme is meant to provide social security benefit for people living in poverty, it is often targeted at particular populations (eg, tribes or scheduled castes). Panchayats (elected village councils) are responsible for distribution, but funds often fail to reach those in need. Social protection for those unable to work would reduce their dependency on others.

Dependency on family support in later life is problematic for older people when relatives have a hand-to-mouth existence or live on the verge of poverty. Lack of time has been cited in other studies as one of the greatest barriers to providing care to older people (Bahtt et al, 2017). Presently, there is no financial support provided to kin carers in India. This is especially important for low-income families (eg, Deepak) in which care-provision entails losing productive labour hours (Brinda et al, 2014).

The Maintenance and Welfare of Parents and Senior Citizens Act (2007) mandated family care. This was supposed to enable older people to claim maintenance and support from children (where this was not forthcoming) through tribunals. In 2018, the Act extended the network of relatives to include grandchildren and other relatives with sufficient resources. Only older people without family, or with families/themselves registered as below the poverty line (BPL) were entitled to claim a pension (Indira Gandhi National Older Age Pension Scheme (IGNOAPS)). However, there are flaws within the social protection system that excludes many older people in need. For example, between half and three-fifths of the poorest households in India are not registered as BPL (Ram et al, 2009; Drèze and Khera, 2017), bureaucratic systems are difficult to navigate and pensions are difficult to secure (Burholt et al, 2020; see also Chapter 11).

The extended network of relatives mandated to provide care are contrary to cultural norms: 75 per cent of older people live with sons and only 3 per cent live with daughters (Sathyanarayana et al, 2014). The government has not acknowledged that the transgression of cultural norms are neither feasible nor acceptable for many. The interviews with care home residents indicated that many of them felt it was culturally unacceptable for older people to live with daughters or relatives, other than sons, and in general, these relatives did not want them living with them. Older people did not want to take relatives to a tribunal, and then live with those relatives or rely on them for financial support. Without taking up these first two options, the amendment to the Act has left many older people without any options other than to declare themselves destitute and seek the support of charitable care homes, as illustrated in Varsha's story.

For those participants able to secure a national pension (₹1,000 per month), this was often insufficient to meet their needs. For example, Deepak's pension was insufficient to pay for support that would allow him to continue to live in the community.

Health and social care provision

Shocks to human assets (the capacity to work and care for oneself) were the most significant events that prompted a move to a care home. These were influenced by deteriorating health and injury, suggesting that the health care sector has a vital role to play in protecting against adverse outcomes. Affordability and accessibility of primary, secondary and tertiary care (eg, for post-stroke rehabilitation, mental health and vision loss) provided obstacles to older people putting them at risk of increasing poor health or catastrophic out-of-pocket expenditure, escalating the challenges that they faced (Brinda et al, 2015, Dash and Mohanty, 2019).

Areesha and Deepak's stories illustrated issues with accessibility to health and social care in India. Areesha was visually impaired but unable to draw on any formal community support for help with instrumental activities of daily living (eg, cooking, cleaning, laundry and managing finances). Deepak did not have access to community continence services or help with activities of daily living (eg, personal care tasks: bathing, getting dressed and toileting). The lack of services associated with personal care may be compounded by the lack of 'respectability' (intersecting with cultural processes) associated with professions that undertake 'dirty work' or 'body work', as these are considered menial tasks typically undertaken by servants in India (Johnson, 2011). Without familial support, older people living alone are reliant on the beneficence of friends and neighbours (or non-governmental organisations). When an individual's needs outstrip the capacity of the benefactor(s), then the only remaining option is to relocate into a care home to receive support.

Around four-fifths (82 per cent) of health care expenditure in India is 'out-of-pocket' expenditure (van Doorslaer et al, 2007). The World Health Organization (WHO) defines 'catastrophic health care expenditure' as an outlay that exceeds 40 per cent of the income remaining after subsistence expenditure (Kawabata et al, 2002). The impact of chronic disease (for the older person, or their spouse) such as TB, and the emphasis on 'cure' within the India health care system (Brinda et al, 2015) resulted in catastrophic expenditure for 40 per cent (n=12) of the participants. For example, to meet the medical costs associated with the hospitalisation of his wife, Deepak sold his house: his out-of-pocket expenditure left him homeless and increased his impoverishment (Brinda et al, 2015, Dash and Mohanty, 2019). The treatment Maalia received for a burn increased her indebtedness to the care facility. It has been estimated that annually approximately 4.9 million older people in India move into poverty because of catastrophic out-of-pocket health care expenditure (Brinda et al, 2015). It is unsurprising that health care expenditure has been cited as a major barrier to families providing care to older people (Bahtt et al, 2017).

Public investment is required to provide increased access to primary health care in the public sector, thus reducing the imperative to seek care from the private sector, and the pressures on out-of-pocket expenditure. The presence of a chronic condition in later life may decrease the likelihood of familial care provision, especially if caregiving increases impoverishment through health care expenditure. Secondary or tertiary services (for care and rehabilitation) for functional and cognitive impairment stemming from chronic diseases (eg, stroke, dementia) also needs investment to increase both the accessibility of services and the specialist skills of staff (Srinath Reddy et al, 2005). This, in turn, could alleviate pressures on kin-caregivers opening up possibilities for older people to live with relatives, or receive care in the community, rather than relying on care home provision.

The legal system

Amongst the function of national legal systems is the preservation of individual rights, the protection of minorities against majorities, and the promotion of social justice. Therefore, a legal system should protect older people from discrimination and harm. There were several examples of shortfalls in the legal system, that if activated, could have positively transformed the experiences of some participants. Participants' narratives suggested that laws need to be strengthened (or enacted) in relation to gender discrimination and abuse in family and care relationships. The prevalence of reported abuse (73 per cent) was greater in our study of care home residents than found in a community sample drawn from Chennai (14 per cent) (Chokkanathan and Lee, 2005) and across India (11 per cent) (Sathya and Premkumar, 2020), suggesting that it poses a significant risk for care home entry. None of the participants had drawn on the legal system to protect them from neglect or abuse, suggesting a lack of awareness, accessibility or acceptability.

There was evidence of institutionalised financial abuse within the care system. Maalia's life was shaped by her desire to provide better opportunities for her daughter (through marriage). While the organisation that provides accommodation for Maalia and her daughter publicly stated that they make every effort to find suitable grooms for female residents, *and* meet all of the associated costs, the wedding arrangements resulted in Maalia's indebtedness to the organisation. This 'indebtedness' was further compounded by health care costs. Legislation may be required to outlaw this hybrid model of 'care' which emulates both the workhouse and debtors' prison of Victorian Britain (Driver, 1993). Overall, the legal system failed to protect Maalia throughout her life from physical abuse, abandonment and financial abuse.

Conclusions

Recovery from shocks to livelihood assets was attenuated or strengthened depending on an individual's cultural socio-economic status and access to assets over the life course. Thus, the process of asset accumulation or decumulation was transformed by cultural norms, discrimination, prejudice and stigma. Although deficits and shocks to assets could potentially be mitigated by political economic structures and processes, our analyses revealed the antithesis, that is, many of these processes reinforced culturally constructed inequalities. Specific features of the political economy failed to provide for the most vulnerable, excluding them from key resources, sufficient protection from harm, and a choice over where they lived, and from whom they received support in later life.

Care choices and care pathways for older people in India could be improved by making changes to social protection, public health and care and the legal system. In particular, the Maintenance and Welfare of Parents and Senior Citizens Act needs to acknowledge that the presence of relatives does not confer the availability of care provision. A majority of care home residents had families that deviated from the social ideal 'traditional' joint family. Cultural norms prevented some participants from drawing on support from daughters or other relatives. In addition to amendments to social protection, the provision of a carers' allowance, accessible and affordable health and community care would ease pressures on family assistance where this is available and provide alternatives for older people without filial support. The legal system also needs to ensure it protects older people from abuse, strengthening dissemination of information to raise awareness of legal action, and improving accessibility for the most marginalised and vulnerable populations.

References

Ayres, L., Kavanaugh, K. and Knafl, K. A. (2003) 'Within-case and across-case approaches to qualitative data analysis', *Qualitative Health Research*, 13(6): 871–83.

Bahtt, A. N., Joseph, M. R., Xavier, I. A., Sagar, P., Remadevi, S. and Paul, S. S. (2017) 'Health problems and healthcare needs of elderly – community perspective from a rural setting in India', *International Journal of Community Medicine and Public Health*, 4(4): 1213–18.

Bhambhani, C. and Inbanathan, A. (2018) 'Not a mother, yet a woman: exploring experiences of women opting out of motherhood in India', *Asian Journal of Women's Studies*, 24(2): 159–82.

Breton, E. (2019) 'Modernization and household composition in India, 1983–2009', *Population and Development Review*, 45(4): 739–66.

Brijnath, B. and Manderson, L. (2008) 'Discipline in chaos: Foucault, dementia and aging in India', *Culture, Medicine, and Psychiatry*, 32(4): 607–26.

Brinda, E. M., Rajkumar, A. P., Enemark, U., Attermann, J. and Jacob, K. S. (2014) 'Cost and burden of informal caregiving of dependent older people in a rural Indian community', *BMC Health Services Research*, 14(1): 207.

Brinda, E. M., Kowal, P., Attermann, J. and Enemark, U. (2015) 'Health service use, out-of-pocket payments and catastrophic health expenditure among older people in India: the WHO study on global AGEing and adult health (SAGE)', *Journal of Epidemiology and Community Health*, 69(5): 489–94.

Bronk, K. C., King, P. E. and Matsuba, M. K. (2013) 'An introduction to exemplar research: a definition, rationale and conceptual issues', *New Directions for Child and Adolescent Development*, 142: 1–12.

Burholt, V., Dobbs, C. and Victor, C. (2017) 'Social support networks of older migrants in England and Wales: The role of collectivist culture', *Ageing & Society*, 38(7): 1453–77.

Burholt, V., Maruthakutti, R. and Maddock, C. A. (2020) 'A cultural framework of care and social protection for older people in India', *GeroPsych: The Journal of Gerontopsychology and Geriatric Psychiatry*, 0: 1–3.

Buzzanell, P. M., Dohrman, R. L. and D'Enbeay, S. (2011) 'Problematizing political economy differences and their respective work-life policy constructions', in D. K. Mumby (ed), *Reframing Difference in Organizational Communication Studies: Research, Pedagogy, Practice*, Thousand Oaks, CA: Sage Publications, pp 245–66.

Chambers, R. and Conway, R. (1992) *Sustainable Rural Livelihoods: Practical Concepts for the 21st Century*, Brighton: Institute of Development Studies, University of Sussex.

Chaturvedi, S. K., Singh, G. and Gupta, N. (2005) 'Stigma experience in skin disorders: an Indian perspective', *Dermatologic Clinics*, 23(4): 635–42.

Chekki, D. A. (1996) 'Family values and family change', *Journal of Comparative Family Studies*, 27(2): 409–12.

Chokkanathan, S. and Lee, A. E. Y. (2005) 'Elder mistreatment in urban India: a community-based study', *Journal of Elder Abuse & Neglect*, 17(2): 45–61.

D'Cruz, P. and Bharat, S. (2001) 'Beyond joint and nuclear: the Indian family revisited', *Journal of Comparative Family Studies*, 32(2): 167–94.

Das Gupta, M. (1999) 'Lifeboat versus corporate ethic: social and demographic implications of stem and joint families', *Social Science & Medicine*, 40: 173–84.

Dash, A. and Mohanty, S. K. (2019) 'Do poor people in the poorer states pay more for healthcare in India?', *BMC Public Health*, 19(1): 1020.

Devi, S. (2017) 'A study to assess the morbidity profile of salt pan workers of Thoothakudi district – a cross-sectional study 2017', MD thesis, The Dr. MGR Medical University, Chennai, Tamil Nadu, http://repository-tnmgrmu.ac.in/10984/1/201500119sabitha_devi.pdf

Dhillon, P., Ladusingh, L. and Agrawal, G. (2016) 'Ageing and changing patterns in familial structure for older persons in India: a decomposition analysis', *Quality in Ageing and Older Adults*, 17(2): 83–96.

Drèze, J. and Khera, R. (2017) 'Recent social security initiatives in India', *World Development*, 98: 555–72.

Driver, F. (1993) *Power and Pauperism: The Workhouse System, 1834–1884*, Cambridge: Cambridge University Press.

Harriss-White, B. (2005) 'Destitution and the poverty of its politics—with special reference to South Asia', *World Development*, 33(6): 881–91.

Himmelweit, S. (2007) 'The prospects for caring: economic theory and policy analysis', *Cambridge Journal of Economics*, 31(4): 581–99.

Jamuna, D. (2003) 'Issues of elder care and elder abuse in the Indian context', *Journal of Aging & Social Policy*, 15(2–3): 125–42.

Johnson, S. E. (2011) 'A suitable role: professional identity and nursing in India'. PhD thesis, London School of Hygiene & Tropical Medicine.

Kapur, D. and Nangia, P. (2015) 'Social protection in India: a welfare state sans public goods?', *India Review*, 14(1): 73–90.

Kaur, R. (2019) 'Family matters in India: a sociological understanding', in P.N. Mukherji, N. Jayaram, and B.N. Ghosh (eds), *Understanding Social Dynamics in South Asia: Essays in Memory of Ramkrishna Mukherjee*, Singapore: Springer, pp 147–59.

Kaushik, A. (2020) 'Elder care from a distance: emerging trends and challenges in the contemporary India', in M.K. Shankardass (ed), *Ageing Issues and Responses in India*, Singapore: Springer, pp 97–113.

Kawabata, K., Xu, K. and Carrin, G. (2002) 'Preventing impoverishment through protection against catastrophic health expenditure', *Bulletin of the World Health Organization*, 80(8): 612.

Lamb, S. (2018) 'Being single in India: gendered identities, class mobilities, and personhoods in flux', *Ethos*, 46(1): 49–69.

Lamb, S. (2000) *White Saris and Sweet Mangoes: Ageing, Gender and Body in North India*, Berkeley and Los Angeles: University of California Press.

Meher, M., Trnka, S. and Dureau, C. (2018) 'Pollution and intimacy in a transcendent ethics of care: a case of aged-care in India', *Ethnos*, 83(4): 744–61.

Nanda, S. (2019) *Love and Marriage: Cultural Diversity in a Changing World*, Long Grove, IL: Waveland Press.

Norton, A., Conway, T. and Foster, M. (2001) *Social Protection Concepts and Approaches: Implications for Policy and Development*, London: Centre for Aid and Public Expenditure/Overseas Development Institute.

Polkinghorne, D.E. (1995) 'Narrative configuration in qualitative analysis', *International Journal of Qualitative Studies in Education*, 8(1): 5–23.

Pushpa, S. (2001) 'Women and philanthropy in India', in K. McCarthy (ed), *Women Philanthropy and Civil Society*, Bloomington and Indianapolis: Indiana University Press, pp 271–86.

Puthenparambil, J. M. and Kröger, T. (2016) 'Using private social care services in Finland: free or forced choices for older people?', *Journal of Social Service Research*, 42(2): 167–79.

Rajan, I. (2010) *Demographic Ageing and Employment in India*, Geneva: International Labour Organization for Asia and the Pacific.

Rajan, I. and Mishra, U. S. (2011) *The National Policy of Older Persons: Critical Issues in Implementation*, New Delhi: United Nations Fund for Population Activities (UNFPA).

Ram, F., Mohanty, S. K. and Ram, U. (2009) 'Understanding the distribution of BPL cards: all-India and selected states', *Economic and Political Weekly*, 44(7): 66–71.

Rao, N. (2014) 'Marriage, violence, and choice: understanding Dalit women's agency in rural Tamil Nadu', *Gender & Society*, 29(3): 410–33.

Rao, V. A. (2018) 'Genital TB and infertility', in K. Rao (ed), *The Infertility Manual*, New Delhi: Health Sciences Publisher, pp 217–28.

Riessman, C. K. (2000) 'Stigma and everyday resistance practices: childless women in south India', *Gender & Society*, 14(1): 111–35.

Rishworth, A. and Elliott, S. J. (2018) 'Aging in low- and middle-income countries: aging against all odds', in M. W. Skinner, G. J. Andrews and M. P. Cutchin (eds), *Geographical Gerontology: Perspectives, Concepts, Approaches*, Abingdon: Routledge, pp 110–22.

Ritchie, J. and Spencer, L. (2002) 'Qualitative data analysis for applied policy research', in A. M. Huberman and M. B. T. Miles (eds), *The Qualitative Researcher's Companion*, Thousand Oaks, CA, Sage, pp 305–29.

Sathya, T. and Premkumar, R. (2020) 'Association of functional limitations and disability with elder abuse in India: a cross-sectional study', *BMC Geriatrics*, 20(1): 220.

Sathyanarayana, K. M., Kumar, S. and James, K. S. (2014) 'Living arrangements of elderly in India: policy and programmatic implications', in G. Giridhar, K. M. Sathyanarayana, K. S. James, M. Alam and S. Kumar (eds), *Population Ageing in India*, Cambridge: Cambridge University Press, pp 74–95.

Seizer, S. (1995) 'Paradoxes of visibility in the field: rites of queer passage in anthropology', *Public Culture*, 8(1): 73–100.

Sewell, W. H. (1999) 'The concept(s) of culture', in V. Bonnell and L. Hun (eds), *Beyond the Cultural Turn: New Directions in the Study of Society and Culture*, Berkeley, CA: University of California Press, pp 35–61.

Shankardass, M. K. (2020) 'Ageing issues and responses in India: a synopsis', in M. K. Shankardass (ed), *Ageing Issues and Responses in India*, Singapore: Springer, pp 1–7.

Sinha, A., Lombe, M., Saltzman, L. Y., Whetten, K., Whetten, R. and Positive Outcomes for Orphans Research Team (2016) 'Exploring factors associated with educational outcomes for orphan and abandoned children in India', *Global Social Welfare*, 3(1): 23–32.

Srinath Reddy, K., Shah, B., Varghese, C. and Ramadoss, A. (2005) 'Responding to the threat of chronic diseases in India', *The Lancet*, 366(9498): 1744–9.

Srinivasan, S. (2014) 'Growing up unwanted: girls' experiences of gender discrimination and violence in Tamil Nadu, India', *The European Journal of Development Research*, 26(2): 233–46.

The Maintenance and Welfare of Parents and Senior Citizens Act (2007) Delhi: Government of India, https://legislative.gov.in/sites/default/files/A2007-56.pdf

Ugargol, A. P., Hutter, I., James, K. S. and Bailey, A. (2016) 'Care needs and caregivers: associations and effects of living arrangements on caregiving to older adults in India', *Ageing International*, 41(2): 193–213.

van Doorslaer, E., O'Donnell, O., Rannan-Eliya, R. P., Somanathan, A., Adhikari, S. R., Garg, C. C., Harbianto, D., Herrin, A. N., Huq, M. N., Ibragimova, S., Karan, A., Lee, T.-J., Leung, G. M., Lu, J.-F. R., Ng, C. W., Pande, B. R., Racelis, R., Tao, S., Tin, K., Tisayaticom, K., Trisnantoro, L., Vasavid, C. and Zhao, Y. (2007) 'Catastrophic payments for health care in Asia', *Health Economics*, 16(11): 1159–84.

Vera-Sanso, P. (2006) 'Experiences in old age: a south Indian example of how functional age is socially structured', *Oxford Development Studies*, 34(4): 457–72.

Vera-Sanso, P. (2018) 'Ageing, poverty and neo-liberalism in urban south India', in A. Walker (ed), *The New Dynamics of Ageing*, Bristol: Policy Press, pp 325–46.

11

Welfare and development programmes for older adults in India

S. Siva Raju

Introduction

The problems and issues faced by India's older population are receiving considerable attention by the government of India. Though concern for the welfare of older adults was recognised from the Third Five-Year Plan onwards, a national old age pension scheme was only initiated by the central government in 1995 during the Eighth Five-Year Plan period. The National Policy for Older Persons (NCOP, 1999), formulated by the Ministry of Social Justice and Empowerment, strengthened government resolve to address the issue effectively. The policies and programmes acknowledge the need to address varied issues for older adults and various attempts have been made to revise the policy for to meet the changing needs of the ageing population in India. Undoubtedly, the existing social security schemes have contributed to improving the quality of life of the older adults, especially those who live below the poverty line. Given the vulnerable sections of older population, such as those who are living below poverty line (BPL), widows, those living with a disability, those working in the informal sector and other marginalised groups, the focus of the government is mainly on delivering welfare by attempting to address their basic needs such as food, clothing and shelter. Accordingly, the governments at central and state levels have programmes and schemes such as the old age pension, widowhood pension, provision for older adults to stay in government sponsored old age homes and other such welfare-oriented measures. This chapter maps the various schemes provided by the government of India for older adults and other schemes which are also open for older adults. In addition to listing these issues the chapter goes a step further to discuss the barriers in accessing these schemes.

However, concerns persist about the awareness among both the community and potential beneficiaries, as well as issues of the accessibility, implementation, utilisation and effectiveness of the programmes (Prasad et al, 2013; UNFPA, 2012). The Building Knowledge Base on Population Ageing in India (BKPAI) study (2011) shows that, in Maharashtra, over two-thirds of the older adults surveyed were aware of the Indira Gandhi National Old Age Pension Scheme (IGNOAPS); and two-thirds of older women were aware of the Indira Gandhi National Widowhood Pension Scheme (IGNWPS), compared to 57 per cent of older men. Less than half (45 per cent) of the older adults, knew about the Annapurna scheme. One finding of major concern is that only 3 per cent of men and women from BPL households receive benefits from IGNOAPS and just a tenth of widows from BPL households benefit from IGNWPS. Utilisation of the Annapurna scheme is almost negligible (less than 2 per cent).

Several programmes, such as schemes addressing financial security through income generation which are implemented not only by government but also by community-based organisations with similar objectives and targeted at the same set of beneficiaries. In the field of health care, government health infrastructure and NGO initiatives through mobile medical vans, health camps and health awareness drives mostly target the same set of people in communities. Similarly, concessions and subsidies implemented by ministries such as the Ministry of Rural Development, Ministry of Finance and Ministry of Social Justice and Empowerment are often planned and executed by different ministries/departments/agencies but have almost similar objectives and target the same groups/areas.

Government schemes and programmes for older adults

Various programmes and schemes for the benefit of older people are in place, which are implemented by different ministries, both at central and state government levels. The Ministry of Rural Development (MoRD), through the National Social Assistance Programme (NASP), targets older adults directly or indirectly to ensure their social security, shelter and employment. In addition, the Ministry of Health and Family Welfare (MoHFW) has launched a National Programme for the Healthcare of Elderly (NPHCE) to meet the health care needs of older people. The Public Distribution System aims at ensuring food security. The Ministry of Finance has made provisions for the benefit of older people by designing special financial instruments and in its income tax rules. The Ministry of Social Justice and Empowerment (MoSJE) is tasked with the implementation of the Maintenance and Welfare Act 2007 and protecting the rights and security of the older population in India. Most of the schemes implemented by different agencies are carried out independently. Due to this there is a possibility of overlapping of target population, wastage of resources, exclusion of genuine beneficiaries and poor coverage and its implementation. Thereby there is a need to have an integrated model of combining these schemes while delivering to the target beneficiaries.

Various schemes, such as the Old Age Pension Scheme, Widow's Pension Scheme and Annapurna Scheme, are directly targeted at older adults. The National Family Benefit Scheme and National Disability Pension Scheme can indirectly benefit older adults and are implemented under the National Social Assistance Programme. In addition, there are schemes run by MoRD, which include Indira Awas Yojana and Mahatma Gandhi National Rural Employment Guarantee Scheme. These schemes provide support in the form of addressing basic needs such as shelter and financial support respectively. The various features of the schemes, including eligibility and entitlements, are explained in the following sections.

Indira Gandhi National Old Age Pension Scheme (IGNOAPS): IGNOAPS is known as Indira Gandhi Rashtriya Vruddhapkal Nivvrutti Vetan Yojna in Maharashtra. Persons aged 60 years and above may claim the benefits of IGNOAPS if they belong to BPL households accordingly to the criteria prescribed by the government of India. As central assistance, the government of India provides a monthly pension of ₹200/– (approximately $3) to persons aged 60 years and above and ₹500/– (approximately $7) per month to those aged 80 and above. The state contributes an equal amount. The average monthly per capita income of an individual in India is ₹11,186 (approximately $160) as per the Ministry of Statistics and Programme Implementation. Implementation of the scheme and disbursement to beneficiaries is the responsibility of the Tehsildar (the Administrative Head of Taluka, ie, developmental block, which is the unit below district level in a state). This implementation of this scheme is undertaken by Tahsildar, Sanjay Gandhi Yojana, of the Taluka, where state contribution is added to it before disbursement to the beneficiaries.

Indira Gandhi National Widow Pension Scheme (IGNWPS): IGNWPS is also known in Marathi (which is the main language in the state of Maharashtra) as Indira Gandhi Rashtriya Vidhava Nivvrutti Vetan Yojna. This scheme provides for a pension of ₹200/– to widows (women only) aged 40 to 65 years who belong to BPL families. In addition, the state contributes ₹400/– per month from Sanjay Gandhi Niradhar Anudan Yojana. To be eligible for this scheme, the claimant must be a resident of the state for at least 15 years.

Sanjay Gandhi Niradhar Anudan Yojna: This scheme aims to provide financial assistance to a wide variety of groups of disadvantaged or underprivileged people: destitute, blind, disabled, orphaned children, those suffering from major illnesses, divorced women, abandoned women, women freed from prostitution, women victims of sexual assault, transgender individuals, etc., who are under 65 years of age and whose annual family

Table 11.1: Government programmes available for older adults in India

Department of Social Justice and Special Assistance	*Old Age homes:*	Currently there are 29 old age homes (government sanctioned), each with capacity of 100 senior citizens. Under this scheme for every older person who is enrolled into the home, the old age home receives ₹930 per month towards their support.
	Shravan Bal State Pension Scheme:	Under this scheme, BPL older adults above 65 years of age are given ₹400 per month, in addition to the amount of ₹200 per month received under the Indira Gandhi Old Age Pension Scheme (central government) ie, a total of ₹600 per month. In addition, the elderly with an annual income less than ₹21,000 are also eligible Eligibility criteria: Destitute. Age 65 and above, 15 years of domicile in Maharashtra and household enrolled as BPL family entitled to the combined pension of ₹600 per month.
Central government schemes		Day care centres, old age homes and multipurpose mobile centres. The schemes are to be implemented by registered voluntary organisations. For implementing these schemes, the voluntary organisation gets 90 per cent of expenditure from the central government, while the remaining 10 per cent has to be met by them. Indira Gandhi National Old Age Pension Scheme: This scheme was initiated in 2010, where BPL older adults who are 65 years and above are entitled to ₹200 per month from the central government. Eligibility criteria: Destitute, age 65 and above and household enrolled as BPL family.
Income tax concessions		For those aged 60 years and over an income tax concession is provided up to ₹2,50,000. For those above 80 years of age an income tax concession is provided up to ₹5,00,000.
Travel concessions and ease of travel		Railway concessions. Men above 60 years of age get 40 per cent concession on railway mail/express fares. Women above 58 years of age get 50 per cent concession on railway mail/express fares. Older adults going in for major surgery and along with one attendant get 75 per cent concession on railway fare. Older adults get 30 per cent concession in fares of Rajdhani, Shatabdhi, Jana Shatabdhi express trains. Separate booking windows at railway stations are provided for senior citizens. Provision of wheelchairs for older adults who require them will be provided with the station master.
Air fare concession		Men above age 65 and women above age 63 can get 50 per cent concession on air fare in Air India (within India).Air India provides concessions for the older adults for international travel. Sahara Airlines gives 50 per cent concession to the those above age 62 years.

Table 11.1: Government programmes available for older adults in India (continued)

Food security	BPL households having older adults above age 60 years are entitled to 35 kg of grain per month. Those above age 65 years receiving no pension are entitled to 10 kg of free grain per month under Annapurna Scheme.
Maintenance	Chapter 3 of Hindu Personal Law and Code of Criminal Procedure, older adults can get maintenance charges from their heir/s.
Maharashtra State Government	
Pensions	Older adults from BPL families are entitled to a pension amount of ₹400 per month from the state.
Tax	Maharashtra government exempts the older adults from professional tax.
Health care	Free treatment for older adults in Municipality and Municipal Corporation Hospitals. Free treatment for the older adults in government hospitals.
Banking concessions	All nationalised and scheduled banks offer 1–2 per cent additional interest rate on medium and long-term deposits for older adults. Those above age 55 years get 9 per cent interest rate for deposits of ₹1000–₹2,50,0000 under 'Senior Citizens Savings Scheme' of postal department. Monthly income scheme of postal department provides 8 per cent returns on deposits and 10 per cent bonus on maturity for older adults.

income is less than are equal to ₹21,000/-. Each beneficiary is entitled to ₹600/- per month. Families with more than one beneficiary are entitled to ₹900/- per month. These entitlements continue until the beneficiary's children reach the age of 25 years or find employment – whichever occurs first. If the beneficiary has only daughters, the entitlements will continue until they reach 25 years old or get married.

Annapurna Scheme: The Annapurna Scheme has been implemented in Maharastra since 1 April 2001. This scheme is completely sponsored by the Central Government National Social Assistance Programme and is implemented by the MoRD. The scheme provides for 10 kg of food grains per month at no cost to destitute aged 65 years and above. The main eligibility criterion for claiming the benefits of this scheme is that the person should not be receiving a pension from the National Old Age Pension Scheme or any state pension scheme. According to BKPAI survey, on 2 per cent of the sample used the Annapurna Scheme.

Schemes indirectly benefiting older adults: In addition to these schemes that are directly targeted at older adults there are various central and state-sponsored schemes that are in operation in the state for providing social security, housing, health and food security benefits to the most vulnerable sections of the population. These are described below.

National Family Benefit Scheme: This scheme is also referred to in Maharashtra as Rashtriya Kutumbha Labh Yojna and is implemented by the MoRD under the National Social Assistance Programme. It aims to provide a lump sum benefit of ₹10,000 to households below the poverty line on the death of a primary breadwinner, aged 18 to 64 years. The scheme is implemented through the office of Tehsildar, Sanjay Gandhi Yojana of the respective Taluka.

Indira Gandhi National Disability Pension Scheme (IGNDPS): Also known as Indira Gandhi Rashtriya Apang Nivvrutti Vetan Yojna in Maharashtra, it is a centrally sponsored scheme and part of the National Social Assistance Programme implemented by the MoRD. The eligibility for the scheme is those who are destitute with severe or multiple disabilities and who do not receive other pension. The eligible age group is 18–79 years.

Pradhan Mantri Gramin AwaasYojana (PMAY): PMAY was earlier known as the Indira Awas Yojna. It is widely acknowledged as the flagship programme of MoRD for providing housing to the rural poor in India. It aims to provide financial assistance of up to ₹95,000/- as a one-time payment to help BPL households own a home.

Ramai Awas Yojna: This is a state government initiative to improve housing security for BPL households from the Scheduled Castes (those communities notified as Scheduled Castes as per provisions contained in Clause 1 of Articles 341 and 342 of the Constitution and have been defined under clause 24 of Article 366 of the Constitution of India). Eligible beneficiaries are provided financial assistance of up to ₹95,000/- to build homes.

Sravanbal Seva Rajya Nivvrutti Vetan Yojna: Sravanbal Seva Rajya Nivvrutti Vetan Yojana is the Maharashtra state government's initiative to provide monthly pension to destitute older adults. The scheme targets destitute older adults aged 65 years and above and who have an annual family income of less than ₹21,000/- or persons belonging to BPL families. The persons should have been a resident of the state for at least 15 years. There is another provision under this scheme in which the state government contributes an additional benefit of ₹400/- per month to the beneficiaries of old age pensioners under IGOAPS (₹200/- per month from the central government). The implementation of this scheme is responsibility of the Tehsildar, Sanjay Gandhi Yojana of the taluka.

Mahatma Gandhi National Rural Employment Generation Act (MNREGA): MGNREGA was launched with the objective of 'enhancing livelihood security in rural areas by providing at least 100 days of guaranteed wage employment in a financial year, to every household whose adult members volunteer to do unskilled manual work'. Employment is to be provided within 5 km of an applicant's residence, and minimum wages to be paid. If work is not provided within 15 days of applying, applicants are entitled to an unemployment allowance. Thus, employment under MGNREGA is a legal entitlement. MNREGA is implemented by the MoRD at the local level though gram *Panchayats* (GPs – gram *Panchayats* are basic village-governing institute in Indian villages). As MNREGA does not specify an upper age limit for employment, older adults can benefit provided they are physically fit for the work allocated to them.

Rajiv Gandhi Jivandayee Aarogya Yojna (RGJAY): Rajiv Gandhi Jivandayee Aarogya Yojna is a universal health care scheme run by the government of Maharashtra for the poor people of the state who hold one of the four cards issued by the government – Antyodaya card, Annapurna card, yellow or orange ration card. The scheme was first launched in eight districts of Maharashtra in July 2012. It was extended to all the state's 35 districts in November 2013. The programme provides free access to medical care in government-empanelled hospitals (numbering 488 at present) for the treatment of 971 types of diseases, surgeries and therapies costing up to ₹1,50,000 per year per family. For renal transplants the limit is ₹2,50,000. The Maharashtra government pays the annual insurance premium of ₹333 per year per beneficiary family to the public sector National Insurance Company. The scheme covers pre-existing diseases and ailments.

RGJAY is a floater scheme, which means that an individual or his/her family members covered by the policy can collectively avail of free medical treatment up to ₹1,50,000 in a year. Renal transplants are treated as an exceptional case and the government provides up to ₹2,50,000, which was increased to ₹3,00,000 in December 2015 per year for the surgery. This includes the cost of medical examinations of both kidney donor and recipient. The government also announced a separate funds for poor patients who need dialysis.

Public Distribution System: Under the Minimum Common Need Programme of the government of India, poor families in the state are provided food grains at subsidised rates since 1 June 1997. BPL families (those holding yellow ration cards) are provided with 35 kg of food grains (wheat and rice) while APL (above the poverty line) families (those holding saffron ration cards) are provided with 15 kg.

The Antyodaya Anna Yojana (AAY) was introduced on 1 May 2001. Under this scheme 35 kg of food grains (wheat at the rate of ₹2.00 per kg + rice at rate ₹3.00 per kg) is distributed to the AAY cardholders. Families claiming the benefits of AAY are from BPL and are selected from the following categories: single widows or terminally ill persons, disabled persons or persons aged 60 years or more without any means of subsistence or societal support. This scheme is supported by the government of India and seeks to benefit ten million of the poorest families. It was launched by the government on 25 December 2000. The eligible families were identified by the respective state rural developments through a survey of people living below the poverty line survey. There are a 23 beneficiary families of Antyodaya Anna Yojana in Baswantwadi village.

Challenges of implementing programmes for vulnerable groups

The multiplicity of schemes has resulted in wastage of resources and failure to achieve synergies. Various evaluation studies have highlighted leakages, inefficiencies and ineffectiveness of programme design for rural development and implementation. For instance, an all-India evaluation of the scheme by the government of India (Ministry of Rural Development), as quoted in Kumar and Anand (2006), found that the working of NOAPS to be satisfactory but the survey conducted by them for the evaluation identified problems such as a lack of awareness, irregular disbursement of pensions, non-cooperation of the authorities in availing of the benefit, pending applications, leakage of benefits to those who did not qualify on the basis of age or means-testing and, to a small extent, bribery.

A general lack of transparency, use of obsolete technologies, poor coordination among agencies, non-participation of the target groups in the planning and execution of the schemes, lack of qualified personnel in adequate numbers and top-down approaches have been identified as some of the major causes of the sub-optimal use of the scarce resources. The government has acknowledged that slow progress in the reduction in poverty, unemployment, food insecurity and environmental degradation are the result of non-convergent and non-participatory planning processes. Development planning process should be sensitive to these challenges. Hence, 'convergence' in the planning, implementation as well as evaluation of the various programmes is now receiving serious attention in the planning of strategies for efficient utilisation of resources as well as improving the reach of these programmes.

One of the ways of enhancing programme coverage is by broadening the beneficiary base to make more older people eligible for benefits from the various schemes, for example increasing the minimum income cut off, inclusion of other social groups, utilising digital technology and so on.

Hence, there is a need to assess ongoing schemes that are targeted at the general population for their suitability for older adults. The objective is to avoid duplication and rationalise the number and type of programmes and schemes. This approach to developing strategies for inclusion of senior citizens in ongoing programmes and schemes and rationalising the number of such programmes to improve their efficiency to address issues of the marginalised is referred to as 'convergence'.

Case Study of Maharashtra: This chapter also presents a pilot project carried out in Baswantwadi village of Osmanabad district in Maharashtra to understand the situation of older people (Raju, 2011). This was followed by an assessment of their awareness of the programmes implemented by both state and central governments for their benefit, and their utilisation. The idea of 'convergence' is seen from two perspectives in this study. Firstly, we see it as a 'strategy' that implies to convergence of existing programmes and schemes reach the older population by facilitating inter-sectoral coordination to avoid duplication by rationalisation of the number and type of programmes and schemes. Secondly, it functions as a strategy to bring together information from government records and match them with the ultimate beneficiaries to see if they converge.

Profile of the older population in Maharashtra: According to the 2011 Census, 9.9 million persons or 10 per cent of the population in Maharashtra are aged 60 years and over. This is a much higher proportion than the country average of 8.5 per cent. Of this 9.9 million, 4.7 million are men and 5.2 million are women. With the increasing gap between female and male life expectancy, the proportion of women in the older population is expected to increase further and this is likely to also lead to an increasing proportion of widows among the older female population. Low levels of fertility and migration of children to large cities is expected to result in widows living alone. Again, due to lack of involvement of either of the spouse in the formal employment sector, these widows are likely to be without any regular income when they stop working/after retirement.

The figures show Baswantwadi village is quite typical of the state. Around two in five older adults in Baswantwadi village are BPL. About 18 per cent of the older population do not have family support and nearly three-quarters must work to sustain themselves. As most of the older population are also illiterate, their only livelihood option is to work in the fields as long as they are able to do so. This is a clear indication of the inadequacy of the social security provided by the current schemes and programmes of the government.

Methodology: The study was conducted in a phased manner in during 2014–15. In phase one, a Census survey of older adults in Baswantwadi village of Osmanabad district of Maharashtra was conducted with the aim to understand the situation of older adults, their needs, their awareness and the use of ongoing schemes. In the second phase of data collection, information about the ongoing government schemes and their implementation was collected from both provider and beneficiaries by conducting in-depth interviews governmental officials at various levels such as different departments of Tehsil office, Child Development Project Officers (CDPOs), Aanganwadi centres, Gram Sevak, etc.

The survey was designed to collect data on the situation of older adults, their awareness and use of various government schemes in the village. A total of 236 older adults were identified and interviewed in the survey. In addition, a total of 26 beneficiary in-depth interviews were conducted presented as case studies about various cases representing different levels of benefits. Multiple stakeholder interviews were conducted with 15 stakeholders at different levels to explore the challenges in implementation of government schemes and programmes from provider side. Details about the ongoing schemes and programmes was obtained from secondary sources of data such as web portals of government of Maharashtra and the district of Osmanabad and by visiting local offices of the Tehsil responsible for implementation of schemes for older adults. Government officials were interviewed to gain an understanding of the implementation of these programmes and schemes and the barriers (if any) in improving their implementation. A critical review of the existing schemes and programmes both direct and indirect targeting older people and the community as a whole with a view to assessing the extent of coverage of older persons with the possibility for their inclusion to address their needs and improving their quality of life.

The survey data were entered in SPSS and analysed using appropriate bi-variate statistical techniques. The qualitative data from providers as well as beneficiaries were analysed using thematic analysis. A few case studies were developed based on in-depth interviews conducted with the older adults to understand their process of availing the benefits of governmental schemes and programmes.

Awareness and utilisation of government schemes: Our findings revealed that nearly all (98 per cent) of the older adults in Baswantwadi were aware of various government schemes and programmes designed for their benefit. Nearly half of them had applied to claim benefits from one or the other scheme; however, less a third actually reported receiving any benefits from one (Table 11.1). On disaggregating the data according to the poverty line status, it is observed that only two in five older people categorised as BPL received any benefits from the schemes. Hence, a large proportion of the poor older adults remain deprived of benefits from the schemes that are meant to support them (Figure 11.1).

Figure 11.1: Awareness of government schemes and their use by older adults in Baswantwadi

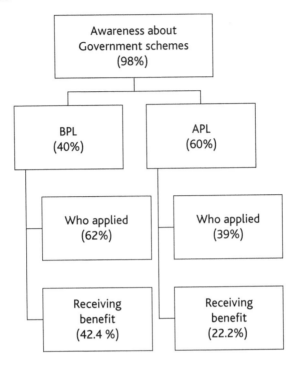

Table 11.2: Awareness of government schemes and their utilisation by older adults according to type of ration card

Economic class based on type of ration card (N)	Awareness about government schemes % (N)	Not Applied for any governmental scheme % (N)	Applied for any governmental scheme % (N)	Benefited from government schemes % (N)
BPL (92)	95.7 (88)	38.0 (35)	62.0 (57)	42.4 (39)
APL (144)	98.6 (142)	61.1 (88)	38.9 (56)	22.2 (32)
Total (236)	97.5 (230)	52.1 (123)	47.9 (113)	30.1 (71)

Application process and utilisation of government-run schemes for older adults: The finding that, despite high awareness, less than half of Baswantwadi's older population had applied for benefits from a scheme (Table 11.2) clearly points to existence of barriers to the progression from awareness to action. A few (about two-fifths) of the older people who did not apply to claim the benefits that they were entitled (as they belong to BPL category) to were asked about the reasons for their not doing so. The purpose of such queries was to understand their perceptions and the challenges

Table 11.3: Distribution of older adults applying, not applying and benefiting from government schemes by type of ration card

Type of ration card (N)	Not applied for any governmental scheme % (N)	Applied for any governmental scheme % (N)	Benefited from government schemes % (N)
BPL (92)	38.0 (35)	62.0 (57)	42.4 (39)
APL (144)	61.1 (88)	38.9 (56)	22.2 (32)
Total (236)	52.1 (123)	47.9 (113)	30.1 (71)

and barriers they may have experienced. To understand the experience of those older persons who applied for but did not receive benefits, we asked them about the challenges and barriers they faced in the process and their perception of not being able to obtain benefits from the programmes. One observation was that the number of older women who reported receiving benefits from the IGNWPS was more than that mentioned in government records. A possible reason for the mismatch is that these women were initially beneficiaries of this scheme; their names were later transferred to the IGNOAPS after they passed 65 years of age. The recipients were not made aware of this change. These findings were investigated further with the help of in-depth interviews of beneficiaries as well as government officials. The objective was to understand the barriers and challenges from the various perspectives of the stakeholders.

Vignettes

Vignette I: older persons who received benefits from government-run schemes

Ramabai (name changed) is a 69-year-old widow. She has not had a formal education and hence, cannot read and write. She had four children. One son passed away few years ago. She lives with two sons and a married daughter and the daughter's extended family. Her sons were educated up to the primary level and are married. Ramabai has 6 acres of land which is farmed by her sons. She holds an APL ration card. She is a beneficiary of *Sravanbal Niradhar Anudan Yojana*.

An ex-gram *Panchayat* member had provided Ramabai with information about this scheme helped her to apply. He even collected and submitted the required documents on her behalf without charging her any money. It took about a year for the approval to come through and Ramabai to start receiving the money. She has received a pension of ₹600 per month for the last four years.

Ramabai has complaints about irregular payments. She receives a consolidated amount every two or three months or sometimes even

Table 11.4: Number of beneficiaries who applied for and/or benefited from various government-run schemes

Ongoing government schemes	Applied % (N)	Benefited % (N)
Indira Gandhi National Widow Pension Scheme (IGNWPS)	10.2 (24)	9.3 (22)
Indira Gandhi National Old Age Pension Scheme (IGNOAPS) & Shravan Bal Nivrutti Yojana	38.3(88)	20.3(48)
MNREGA	30.1 (71)	0.4 (01)
Food grains from Public Distribution System (PDS)	97.5 (230)	97.5 (230)
Indira Gandhi National Disability Pension Scheme (IGNDPS)	0 (0)	0 (0)
National Family Benefit Scheme	0 (0)	0 (0)
Sanjay Gandhi Niradhar Anudan Yojana	0 (0)	0 (0)

more. As the nearest bank (a district cooperative bank) is 5 km away and located in another village, Arli, she has to be accompanied by her grandson whenever she goes to collect her pension. It costs her ₹40/- to visit the bank to collect her pension, but Ramabai is satisfied she is getting some money.

Vignette II: older persons who applied for benefits but did not receive any

Yashwant Shinde (name changed) is a 70-year-old married man with no formal education. He belongs to the BPL category. Mr Shinde said that he had applied for National Old Age Pension Scheme a few years back through a middleman. The broker collected the application form from the Tehsil office at Tuljapur. He provided the necessary document such as proof of age, proof of residence, ration card, voting card and the doctor's certificate to the middleman for submission with the application. The middleman helped Mr Shinde to fill the form and charged him ₹20/- for the application and ₹200 for submitting the documents to the Tehsil office. The doctor's certificate cost an additional ₹200/-. Mr Shinde was assured that the application will be approved and that he would start receiving his pension in two months.

Mr Shinde does not remember the middleman's name. He says that the documents were submitted in the 'Sanjay Gandhi and Indira Gandhi department'. When he enquired at the Tehsil office after two months, he was told that his application had been rejected because his age was shown to be younger than 60 years. Mr Shinde maintains that his age is wrongly mentioned in the voting card, which could be the reason rejection of his application.

Mr Shinde suggests that the department responsible for sanctioning applications should not ask for voting cards because they often carry incorrect information about age. He claims that he knows many people in the village whose age is not correctly mentioned on their voters' card or there is a mismatch of age in the various documents issued by the government (Aadhaar card, voters' card, etc.). Such people also had their applications rejected on similar grounds.

Vignette III: being aware of schemes but not applying to claim benefits

Sharad (name changed), is an 80-year-old farmer. He is also from the BPL category. He has about an acre of agricultural land which has not been cultivated due to the severe drought in recent years. Yet, Mr Sharad has not applied for pension from any of the schemes such as NOAPS or *Shravanbal Niradhar Anudan Yojana*. The reasons are his physical incapacity to do so. His three sons live in Pune and Solapur where they are working as labourers for daily wages. Mr Sharad is not mobile enough to do the application process on his own and his sons do not have the time to help their father. He is also aware of the schemes and knows of people who are getting pensions from them. Besides limited mobility, Mr Sharad says that he has other health problems too, which require medical attention. He is suffering from pain in his eyes and surgery is the only option. He also needs financial assistance for his daily necessities. Mr Sharad wants to apply for pension but will be able to do so only if someone helps him in the process.

Barriers and implementation challenges: Multiple stakeholder interviews were conducted to understand provider's perspectives on the implementation of government schemes and programmes for older adults. The interviewees were from various levels of the administration – from Gram Sevak to staff at the Tehsil office who were involved in the implementation of the schemes, to the Tehsildar at Tuljapur.

Application and documentation: The respondents, who were working in the Tehsildar's office and responsible for preliminary scrutiny of the application said that the primary reasons for rejection of applications are: mismatch (between government records and application) of names, age below the minimum specified for eligibility, incomplete documentation and age mismatch in various documents.

Leakages: There have been cases of older applicants who forged documents taking advantage of their political connections. In many cases, the

Table 11.5: Suggestions from respondents for improving the implementation process through convergence

---

1. **Awareness about application procedures.** There was near-unanimous agreement among the stakeholders that there must greater efforts at spreading awareness about the application procedures so that more people can potentially benefit.

2. **Members of Gram Sabha and Talhati must play more active roles.** As the Talhati and members of the Gram Sabha are aware of the needs of the people and their eligibility, they should be actively involved arranging the necessary documentation and facilitating the application process.

3. **Ease documentation requirements.** There were suggestions that documentation requirements must be so structured that those from rural areas, especially the illiterate and BPL groups, will not have difficulty in complying with them. This will also help them to understand the processes better.

4. **ESHGS in the village.** Despite declining health, most older adults have to continue to work as casual laborers. Government officials and community stakeholders suggested that the older people should be encouraged to form self-help groups for dignity and improved financial security.

5. **Government outreach to help older people.** There were also suggestions that the government officers from the agencies implementing various schemes should visit the villages and identified the needy and help them to claim the benefits. Such an approach will be of considerable help to the most vulnerable and marginalised older adults.

6. **Revision of income limits.** A few respondents suggested the income limit of ₹21,000/- per year should be raised so that more people can benefit.

7. **Universalisation of the pension schemes.** Most of the providers suggested that all older people should be provided with social security irrespective of their caste, class and other conditions. This is essential for realisation of the ideal of true social security for all ages. The rationale for this suggestion is that many older people who may belong to the APL category may have assets which they cannot use for various reasons. For example, these assets may be in the physical possession of their children leaving older people to fend for themselves. Therefore, it is necessary to provide a pension to older people without setting qualifying criteria.

8. **Direct feeding programme for older people.** There was also suggestion, made by a few respondents, for a direct feeding programme for seniors. This could be operationalised in existing Anganwadi centres (rural child care center) where cooked food would be provided to senior citizens along with children and pregnant mothers. Such an arrangement would benefit many senior citizens who live alone and are unable to look after themselves even though may be receiving food grains from the PDS. Another possible benefit of a feeding programme for the older adults is that it can provide work opportunities to those in this group that can work.

---

documentation is complete and such applications are accepted, which denies the really needy who, often, are unable to provide the required documents.

Role of middlemen/brokers: Most older people do not submit their applications directly. Instead, they rely on middlemen or brokers to do the work. Not only do they lose a significant amount of money, which is usually in excess of ₹1,000/-, their applications and documentation are often found to be incomplete and, hence, rejected.

Disbursement of pension: On inquiry into the funds release procedure, the study team found that the money is received every quarter from the collector's office. This happens regularly and there is no backlog in the release of funds. The government regulation clearly specifies that all approved beneficiaries should receive their pensions every month. This is implemented properly at the State Bank of India branch in Tuljapur and no beneficiary having an account with this branch has faced a problem. However, most older people in Baswantwadi have their accounts in a cooperative bank in Arli village, from which many irregularities and instances of malpractice have been reported.

The most vulnerable remain marginalised: The most vulnerable older adults do not get any help or support. Many undeserving beneficiaries use political influence to get the benefits. This results in the exclusion of the most vulnerable. Among the women, especially the widows, most do not have relatives to help them in collecting the required documents help them for claiming the benefits for IGNWPS. Thus, they remain deprived.

Conclusion

From the preceding discussion it is clear that there are specific vulnerable sections of older population especially in rural areas of India, who have no access to various programmes and schemes implemented by government and other stakeholders. In this regard, it should be emphasised that to improve the coverage of programmes and schemes especially of the government sector, there is a urgent need to evolve suitable mechanisms for bringing out convergence across various ministries so that wider coverage of older persons will get the benefit and thereby their care and well-being can be addressed more efficiently. Convergence may be achieved by strengthening inter-sectoral coordination in planning, implementation and monitoring of various ongoing programmes of various ministries and departments. In addition, to convergence in initiatives of public sector, private sector can play a vital role in strengthening the service delivery to improve the lives of older people in India.

Acknowledgements
The author expresses his gratitude to UNFPA, Delhi, for sponsoring the study. The author acknowledges the support received from Dr Nidhi Gupta in conducting the study. Thanks are due to Mr Gandharva Pednekar for his able assistance in the preparation of the chapter.

References

Kumar, A. and Anand, N. (2006) 'Poverty target programs for the elderly in India with special reference to National Old Age Pension Scheme, 1995', *Chronic Poverty Research Centre Working Paper* (2008–9).

NCOP (Office Memorandum of Constitution of the National Council for Older Persons) (1999) No.22-3/99-SD, 10 May, New Delhi: Ministry of Social Justice and Empowerment, Government of India.

Prasad, H. A. C., Sinha, N. K. and Khan, R. A. (2013) 'Performance of major social sector schemes', a sample survey report, working paper no. 2/3013-DEA, Department of economic affairs, Ministry of Finance, Government of India.

Raju, S. (2011) 'Social security for the elderly in India', Thematic Paper 1, Building Knowledge Base on Ageing in India, UNFPA.

UNFPA (2011) 'Status of Elderly in Maharashtra', https://india.unfpa.org/en/publications/status-elderly-maharashtra-2011

UNFPA (2012) 'Report on Status of Elderly in Select states of India, 2011', UNFPA, New Delhi. http://india.unfpa.org/publications/report-status-elderly-select-states-india-2011

12

Lessons and future directions for caregiving research in India

Martin Hyde, Ajay Bailey and K. S. James

Introduction

When discussing this book with colleagues and students, people were generally excited by it and said that there was a real need for such a book. Almost everyone, particularly those in the UK, had a fairly similar argument for why this was important which went something like this: i) the family has traditionally been the main source of care for older adults in India, ii) tradition mandates that daughters–in–law will move in to the family home with their husband and assume caring responsibilities (for all generations), iii) modernisation and migration are destabilising these traditional living arrangements as adult children, in particular women, move for education and/or work, iv) in the absence of any old age social security programs older adults will be unable to get the care that they need and instead face years of disability, depression and loneliness. There is definitely more than a kernel of truth in this accepted narrative about changing living arrangements and care for older adults in India. Families are mandated to take care of their older members through the Maintenance and Welfare of Parents and Senior Citizens Act of 2007. This act empowers any 'senior citizen including parent who is unable to maintain himself [*sic*] from his [*sic*] own earning or out of the property owned by him [*sic*]' to apply for support from their relatives who are then obligated 'to maintain a senior citizen ... so that [they] may lead a normal life'. Failure to do so can result in fines or imprisonment. This Act is often taken to underscore the centrality of the family in India and seen to represent the government's attempt to shore it up in the face of challenges such as migration and modernisation. Again, such concerns are not without merit. As has been noted earlier in the book the scale of internal and international migration in India is staggering. There are estimated to be 450 million internal migrants within India and a further 18 million Indians who live abroad (De, 2019; UNDESA, 2020). Alongside this, as the data presented by James and Kumar (Chapter 3) and Rajan and Sunitha (Chapter 5) show, around a fifth of older adults do not live in households with extended families. For many older Indians this represents the decline of traditional values and is something to be lamented. We see evidence of this in the complaints by the older men in the study by Jahangir, Bailey and Datta (Chapter 9) that the care they receive is poor because of this cultural shift which has resulted in a 'lack of *sanskar*', 'fault in cultural upbringing', 'modernity', 'women's work participation' and 'independence and liberty'.

However, the chapters in this book tell us a much more complex story about living arrangements and care for older adults in India. Rather than being a single, linear narrative, it is a story about the heterogeneity of families, care and migration experiences. The findings presented across these chapters force us to critically question many of the assumptions made about the framing of care provision in India.

Trends in living arrangements of older adults in India

Contrary to the fears often expressed about the decline in traditional living arrangements and the rising number of older adults forced to live alone, the demographic data presented in Chapters 3 and 5 show that, despite a downward trend, multi-generational living still dominates the Indian landscape. The figures from the first round of the Longitudinal Study of Ageing in India (LASI) presented in Chapter 3 show that 68.2 per cent of those aged 60 and over live with their children. Similarly the figures from the Kerala Ageing Survey (KAS) presented in Chapter 5 show that 77.9 per cent of older adults live in households with 3 or more people, and 51.8 per cent live in households with more than five people. Conversely the proportion of older adults living alone remains very low. The figures from LASI and KAS for this are quite similar at 5.7 per cent and 6.3 per cent respectively. Moreover, the data presented in Chapter 3 suggests that this rate has not changed much over the past decade or so: the 2005/06 National Family Health Survey (NFHS) reported 5 per cent of older adults were living alone. Where change is more evident is in the proportion of older adults who are living with their spouse, but not with any children. The KAS data show that this has risen from 11.7 per cent to 15.8 per cent between 2004 and 2019, while the figures presented in Chapter 3 show a somewhat more dramatic rise from 11.7 per cent to 20.3 per cent in 2017/8.

These figures are in line with the evidence presented in Chapter 4 which shows that around one-third of older adults in India expressed a preference independent living, that is, without children. The overall picture from these data is one of stability rather than radical change in patterns of living arrangements. For example, the KAS data show that the average household size for older adults have not changed that much. It was 4.6 in 2004 and 4.3 in 2019. These findings alone are enough for us to begin to question the assumptions about the demise of the traditional family structure in India and the impending crisis of care. However, there does appear to be a significant minority of older adults who are not living in their preferred living arrangements which may be more of a concern for health and well-being. The data from the 'Building Knowledge Base on Population Ageing in India' (BKPAI) show that around one-third of older adults living independently and about a quarter of older adults who co-reside with children would prefer alternative living arrangements. This raises issues about the potential lack of required family support (for those living independently) and the possibility of living abusive or harmful conditions (for those living in co-residence). As noted in Chapter 7 some older adults who co-reside with an adult son reported feeling neglected. Burholt, Maruthakutti and Maddock (Chapter 10) identify domestic abuse (although not always from adult children) as a major risk factor for moving into a care home (73 per cent of their respondents reported experiencing some form of abuse). These figures suggest that rather than trying to reinforce the traditional multi-generational family policy makers ought to be focused on supporting older adults to live in the types of households that they want to live in.

Interestingly, in the context of concerns about the impact of (internal) migration on living arrangements, the evidence from the BKPAI presented in Chapter 3 shows no significant differences in the percentage of older adults living alone or only with their spouse in urban or rural areas. In contrast, the data from Chapter 4 show that preference for independent living is higher for older adults who live in rural areas than in urban areas. Taken together this partially explains the findings that older adults living independently in urban areas have statistically significantly higher likelihood of discordant living arrangements than those in rural areas. Conversely older adults in urban areas who co-reside with family members are much less likely than their rural counterparts to report discordant living arrangements. Again the findings on concordance raise a number of interesting questions and force us to re-examine some basic assumptions about the standard narrative of family and care in India. Intuitively one would expect that older adults in urban areas were more likely to be able to live independently due to the greater proximity of amenities and services compared to rural areas. Moreover, one would expect that the higher costs of property and rents in urban areas would make it more difficult for multi-generational families to live together. As we have seen in Chapter 7 some older adults in rural areas are able to build properties for their children close to their home, which allows them to live independently at home, but to have family close by should support be needed. In urban areas space and costs restrictions might mean that it is difficult to build new buildings for offspring or to be able to ensure that different generations of the same family would be able to find places to live close to one another. In that case it would make sense to try to all live under one roof. More research is needed here to look at the residential patterns of older adults and their families in urban areas and the ways in which residential planning in India's cities might be adapted to allow for different generations to live in proximity to one another, for example the development of mixed residential areas with houses/apartments developed for different age groups.

Alongside the urban–rural results, the inter-state differences are interesting. The figures show quite wide variations, which again cautions us against assuming a single narrative about changing living arrangements and care in India. However, there does not appear to be a strong relationship between the level of population ageing within a state and the proportion of older adults living alone or with their spouse. In the BKPAI data Tamil Nadu clearly stands out as having the highest rates of older adults living alone (16.2 per cent) and living with a spouse (27.7 per cent) among the states covered in the study. It has also undergone relatively rapid population ageing with around 11 per cent of its population aged 60 and over in 2011 (Kathirvel, 2017). However, the neighbouring state of Kerala, which has comparable levels of population ageing, namely 12.6 per cent in 2011 (Press Trust of India, 2014), had a markedly different pattern of living arrangements with just 3.6 per cent of older adults living alone and 11.1 per cent living with a spouse. Interestingly the figures for Tamil Nadu appear to change quite dramatically by 2014/15, falling to 6.3 per cent living alone and 19 per cent living with spouse only. These figures are more in line with those for the other states, however the rate of older adults living alone is still more than double what it is in Kerala at that time. Although this is a very simplistic comparison between just two states, it shows that an increasing proportion of older adults living in households without their adult children is not an inevitable consequence of population ageing.

Moreover, the evidence presented throughout the book shows living arrangements and the availability of care are not the same for all sections of Indian society equally. Instead they are closely bound up with gender and socio-economic position. The figures from the KAS show that women are much more likely than men to be living alone. In 2019 8.2 per cent of women were living alone compared to 3.3 per cent of men. Some of the shift to one-person households seems to be driven by widowhood. Some 16 per cent of those who were in two-person households in 2004 were in one-person households in 2019. Widowhood also has a clear impact on the sorts of living arrangements older adults want. As Syamala, Supriya and Sebastian show in Chapter 4, widows living independently were much more likely than married people to want to co-reside with family members. However it is also likely that some of these are men or women who have never married or had children, such as the case of Areesha, presented in Chapter 10.

Socio-economic factors also impact on living arrangements. However, contrary to the assumption that multi-generational living is more common among poorer sections of society, as those in more advantageous situations are able to provide for themselves, the data from both the BKPAI and the NFHS show that poorer and less educated older adults are more likely to be living alone. These findings appear to match of the findings on living arrangement concordance which show that better-educated older adults who are living independently would prefer to co-reside with other family members, while higher-educated older adults who already co-reside with family are more likely to report concordance between their desired and actual living arrangements. For both cases household wealth also matters. Those in wealthier households, whether living independently or with family members, were more likely to report concordance. This suggests even where older adults do co-reside, they want to be able to maintain (some) economic independence. Yet, as the data presented in Chapter 3 on the economic dependency of older adults in different types of households shows a higher proportion of older adults who live with their children are economically dependent on them (79.2 per cent) compared to older adults who do not reside with children (69.2 per cent) or who live alone (53.1 per cent). Hence, it could be that poorer older adults who reside with their children may feel unable to contribute to the household or, worse, feel that they have no autonomy.

Moreover, poverty intersects with gender as poorer older women are the group who are most likely to live alone (see Calvi, 2020). As shown in the comparison between the experiences of Areesha and Deepak in Chapter 10 access to financial resources can (partially) mitigate the lack of family support. Although the lack of familial and formal community support meant that both had to relocate to a care home to receive support, Areesha's better financial position allowed her to purchase private care, whereas Deepak had to move into a home for destitute older people.

The impact of living arrangements on the health and well-being of older adults

Just as the evidence on the patterns of living arrangements, actual or desired, revealed a rather unexpected and more complex reality of the circumstances of older people in India so too do the findings on the impact of different living arrangements on the health and well-being of older adults. Most striking is the evidence that living arrangements do not appear to be associated with the health or well-being of older adults. The results presented in Chapter 3 show that there were no significant differences in the rates of disability or subjective well-being for older adults living alone, with other older adults or co-residing with children/grandchildren. This finding is remarkable as it suggests that older adults who live alone do not have greater care needs than those who live with other family members. These results are supported by the Cox regression analysis performed in Chapter 5, which show that older adults living alone did not have a significantly higher risk of death compared to those who lived in households of five or more. Even when we look at the evidence for concordant living arrangements we see that even after controlling for a wide range of socio-demographic factors concordant living arrangements for either independent living or co-residence were not significantly related to self-rated health. Taken together, these findings suggest that older adults who live alone have excessive morbidity or mortality compared with those who co-reside with other family members and that this cannot be explained by possible selection effects – those in better health are able to look after themselves and are therefore able to live alone. Once again, this evidence forces us to reconsider the assumptions around living arrangements and care for older adults in India (see Samanta et al, 2015; Ugargol and Bailey, 2018).

Reconceptualising care in the context of changing living arrangements

One possible explanation for this seemingly counter-intuitive set of results is that the focus on household living arrangements is too narrow to understand the family care and support of older adults in India. Several chapters in the book demonstrate that care is provided and received by older adults across widespread networks. As Ugargol and colleagues show in Chapter 6 on care arrangements for older adults in Goa, we need to move beyond thinking about intergenerational care arrangements as being solely delivered through the traditional household structure in which the younger generation, notably sons and daughters-in-law, continue to reside with older parents after marriage. Instead, we need to consider all forms of care arrangements that enable continued intergenerational resource flows between children and older parents irrespective of whether they co-reside, reside nearby or are geographically dispersed. Their fantastic study shows that living apart from children does not necessary preclude exchanges of support between generations. While they clearly show that co-residence with a wide range of family members (ie, not exclusively sons and daughters-in-law) is one way in which families can support each other, they also show that this is not the only way. Families are able to continue to provide care by building or buying properties that are close to one another, for example within the same city, village, sometimes sharing the same courtyard. An excellent example of the latter strategy is Margaret who built three properties, one for each of her sons, around the courtyard of her home. This way Margaret is able to maintain her independence while also being able to access the support of her sons and daughters-in-law. Likewise, the adult children are able to live independently, rather than all in the same house (which as was also shown in the chapter can create tensions), while sharing any caring responsibilities between them so no one family feels over-burdened. A somewhat similar case was presented by Bailey and colleagues in Chapter 7, in which an older adult built two apartments next to his house which he rented out to his daughters. As with Margaret, by creating two separate apartments the older adult was able to retain their independence and when needed could still call on his daughters and their families for support.

The impact of migration on living arrangements and care in India

One of the key issues that underpinned the idea behind this book was to explore the ways in which migration has impacted on older adults in India. As noted above a common argument is that migration has undermined the traditional extended family formation in India, leaving older adults without social support or care (Bailey et al, 2018; Ahlin and Sen, 2020; Muhammad and Srivastava, 2020). Given the aforementioned scale of migration, it is not hard to see where this idea comes from. Moreover, as the main reasons for migration (both international and internal) are for education and employment it tends to be younger people who make up the majority of these migrants. Hence, the sheer scale of movement and the age profile of migrants is assumed to impact on older adults. Indeed, based on the analysis of nearly a decade's worth of data on the living arrangements of older adults in India James and Kumar (Chapter 3) conclude that the decreasing proportion of older adults who co-reside with their adult children and/or grandchildren is primarily due to the migration of adult children to find employment. Hence, contrary to the modernisation hypothesis that wealthier older adults would be more likely to live independently – and do not co-reside with children as they have greater access to resources – James and Kumar found that it was those in the lower socio-economic groups who were more likely to live alone. This suggests that a lack of employment opportunities in the local area and/ or the inability of the older adults to financially support their adult children, forces the children to migrate for work.

However, while migration seems to be a key driver of the changing living arrangements of older adults in India, the findings from other chapters in the book do not indicate that this has necessarily led to a diminution in the care that older adults received. Instead, the picture that is presented is one of changing, dynamic forms of care through combinations of co-residence and various forms of non-co-resident care arrangements, such as close proximity residence and distant but 'embedded' households. As Bailey, James and Hallad argue in Chapter 7, care relations are translocal and include older adults in migrant households, their adult children (co-residing or migrant children), grandchildren, caregivers and non-kin social networks. Indeed, Chapters 6 and 7 provide examples of adult children who have moved away, often to other cities in the same state, who regularly return to visit and provide care for their older parents. For example, Madeleine who receives frequent visits from her two daughters who live nearby as well as from her other daughter who lives over 600 km (and a 12-hour drive) away in another state. Even when children have migrated abroad, they continue to provide support to their parents. This can be direct support, as in the case of Basil who, despite working in an offshore oil rig in Africa returns home every second month to visit his older parents; alternatively, it can be through more indirect measures of support through the use of technology. Margaret, in Chapter 6, describes how she is able to stay in regular contact with her non-resident children via Skype. These sorts of interactions are evidence of the growing 'global householding' of care for older adults in India.

Another key issue that is revealed in the interviews with older adults is that these translocal care networks are reciprocal and that older adults are active agents, not merely passive recipients. This reciprocity takes many forms. As noted previously some of the older adults had bought property for their children so that they could live close by, but that all parties could retain a level of independence (and interdependence). Elsewhere, older couples with children living abroad had travelled to the countries to provide care during and after childbirth. Alternatively daughters or daughters-in-law had returned from abroad to give birth in their hometown and to be cared for by their family. As Bailey, James and Hallad observe, in Chapter 7, this was seen as one of the key life course responsibilities of the parents to the daughter. This last point demonstrates the importance of the concept of 'linked lives', described in Chapter 2, when understanding the impact of migration on older adults in India. As Bailey, James and Hallad show (Chapter 7), in their examination of the life course model through conceptualisation of life stages in Hinduism, rather than seeing the migration of adult children as a threat to the well-being of older adults, many older adults see the successful migration of their children as positive outcome of their life course obligations.

Care homes

Another key contribution of this book is to present a more detailed and nuanced understanding of care homes in India. While many people think that care homes are a recent phenomenon in India, Pazhoothundathil and colleagues note, in Chapter 9, that there is a much longer history. In fact they were set up under British colonial administrators and missionaries as far back as the eighteenth century with special focus on poor and homeless older adults. Accurate estimates on the current number care homes in India is difficult as there is no comprehensive register (Datta, 2017). Nonetheless, the number of care homes is believed to have increased rapidly over the past few years and is expected to continue to rise. A report by Tata Trusts (n.d.) estimated that there were around 1,150 care facilities across India with the capacity to accommodate around 97,000 residents. The report goes on to state that they expect there to be an eight- to tenfold increase in these numbers over the coming decade (Tata Trust, n.d.). However, this growth of care facilities is seen in very much the same way as the perceived decline in multi-generational co-residence. Admission to a care home has traditionally been seen as a failure of both the family and the older adult to ensure proper care and support in later life (Medora, 2007; Lamb, 2013). This negative view of care homes is evidenced by how few older adults say that they would want to live in such facilities. As was shown in Chapter 4, the results of the BKPAI data show that just 0.3 per cent of those aged 60 and over expressed a preference to live in a care home. As Jahangir and colleagues show in Chapter 8, part of this reluctance to enter care homes could be due to the belief that care, *seva* or *seba*, involves touching and massaging the body and that this should only be done by family members. As several of the older male respondents in this study noted care homes, or more precisely, care home staff cannot provide the same level of care as that which can be obtained from the family members because they do not have the same emotional attachment. Another issue is that, as with the history of care homes in other countries, the image of modern care homes is tarnished with their perceived association with institutions set up for the sick and destitute (see Townsend, 1981, for a critical view of care homes in the UK as an extension of the Poor House). On the face of it many of the pathways in to care homes described by Burholt and colleagues in Chapter 10 show why people might continue to have these negative views. Clearly poverty and poor health were major factors for many of the respondents who ended up in care homes. For example, Deepak had a stroke which ultimately left him paralysed and unable to work. This situation was worsened when he had to sell his house to cover medical treatment for his wife. Hence, with no money, no home and living 'like a dog [in] a kennel covered with a tarpaulin', he was admitted to a charity run care home. Likewise, Maalia, who was already in debt due to borrowing money for an operation on her burnt leg, lost her sight and was unable to continue working. As a result she was taken in by a religious care home. In both cases the confluence of poor health (or rather catastrophic health care expenditure) and poverty combined to force Deepak and Maalia into care. This image of care homes as only being for the infirm and destitute is not helped by evidence that many residential facilities (both government and private-run) have a poor record for hygiene, safety, dignity or the privacy of older residents (Tata Trusts, n.d.). However, this is only one story about care homes in India. The chapter by Pazhoothundathil and colleagues show a very different vision of life in care homes. The two homes covered in this study are well resourced with a wide range of facilities such as separate en-suite rooms, a library, WiFi, vehicles, air-conditioned rooms, a garden and well-trained staff. Residents seem to have active lives – they can use their cars or those of the home, they travel abroad to visit family or talk to them via the computer/tablet. This more positive view of care homes fits with findings from a broader study of care homes in Kerala and Tamil Nadu which found that residents generally reported high levels of satisfaction as most of the care homes had facilities such as an ambulance for emergencies, a duty doctor, etc., and the staff held periodical meetings to discuss any problems or issues with the residents. Interestingly, this study also found around a quarter of care home residents in Kerala reported that they had chosen to move into the home (Anil and Hemamala, 2018). As with research on care homes around the world it would appear that the real issue is not with care homes per se but the quality of the care facilities and whether it was the resident's choice to move in or not. The Tata Trust (n.d.) have made a number of recommendations for improving the care home sector in India. These are:

- A set of minimum standards to be mandatorily implemented across all senior living facilities;
- A voluntary accreditation process for higher standards;
- Shelters for the destitute should be supported by the government to improve facilities and upgrade their service quality to recommended minimum standards;
- Implementation and review through a combination of a third-party independent regulator and voluntary ombudsmen or equivalent from civil society;
- Training and certification of sector workers;
- Training of ombudsmen through accreditation body;
- Establishment of model care homes for older adults.

However, as Burholt and colleagues argue in Chapter 10, the choice to invest in developing good care facilities for older adults is a political choice. The current emphasis in Indian politics on maintaining the co-resident or extended family unit as the sole source of care provision for older adults potentially mitigates against a more thorough and constructive set of policies designed to ensure good care facilities for those who want or need them.

Conclusion: supporting choice and diversity

This has been a fascinating book to work on. The chapters cover a wide range of issues, drawing on different methodological and conceptual tools, to give us unparalleled insights into these key debates around living arrangements and care for older adults in India. The narrative that emerges across these chapters is one that challenges the assumed wisdom about the demographic, industrial and social change on older adults. Firstly, contrary to the apocalyptic forecasts about the demise of the traditional family we see that the majority of older adults continue to live in multigenerational households and many prefer to do so. However, there are also those who do not want to live in such households. As we have seen in several chapters in the book, mandating families to look after older adults can create many problems for both the older adults (eg, being forced to live with abusive relatives, and their children, or risking poverty to financially support their parents when they already earn so little). Moreover, many older adults value their autonomy and do not want to live in the same houses as their children. Just with any issue relating to ageing in any country a 'one-size-fits-all' policy will not work. However, this argument is even more true in a country of 1.2 billion people. The findings throughout this book paint a picture of incredible diversity in the attitudes, preferences and living conditions of older adults in India. A central message from that narrative is that recognising the diversity of living arrangements of older adults in India and supporting them to live in the kind of household that best suits them is essential to ensure that all older adults can enjoy a healthy and happy later life. However, choice is dependent on access to resources. The ability to purchase or rent accommodation close to your children or to build apartments next to your house is limited in a country where over 100 million people live in extreme poverty and 90 per cent of the workforce is employed in the informal sector. As we have seen in Chapter 11, there are numerous welfare programmes intended to support older adults. However, there also appear to be just as many obstacles to accessing them. Moreover, one does not simply become poor on reaching a certain age. The cases described in Chapter 10 show the importance of supporting people throughout the life course, for example with good jobs and affordable health care, so that when they reach later life they do so in good health and with financial resources.

References

Ahlin, T. and Sen, K. (2020) 'Shifting duties: becoming "good daughters" through elder care practices in transnational families from Kerala, India', *Gender, Place and Culture*, 27(10): 1395–414.

Anil, D. and Hemamala, K. (2018) 'Perceptions on service quality: a study of old age homes in Kerala and Tamil Nadu'. MATEC Web of Conferences. EDP Sciences, https://doi.org/10.1051/matecconf/201817205003

Bailey, A., Hallad, J. and James, K. S. (2018) '"They had to go": Indian older adults' experiences of rationalizing and compensating the absence of migrant children', *Sustainability*, 10(6): 1946.

Calvi, R. (2020) 'Why are older women missing in India? The age profile of bargaining power and poverty', *Journal of Political Economy*, 128(7): 2453–501.

Datta, A. (2017) 'Old age homes in India: sharing the burden of elderly care with the family', in R. S. Irudaya and G. Balagopal (eds) *Elderly Care in India*, Singapore: Springer, pp 77–93.

De, S. (2019) 'Internal migration in India grows, but inter-state movements remain low', World Bank Blogs, https://blogs.worldbank.org/peoplemove/internal-migration-india-grows-inter-state-movements-remain-low

Kathirvel, D. (2017) 'Demographic trends of elderly in Tamil Nadu', *IMPACT: International Journal of Research in Applied, Natural and Social Sciences*, 5(10): 1–8.

Lamb, S. (2013) 'In/dependence, intergenerational uncertainty, and the ambivalent state: perceptions of old age security in India', *Journal of South Asian Studies*, 36(1): 65–78.

Medora, N. P. (2007) 'Strengths and challenges in the Indian family', *Marriage and Family Review*, 41(1–2): 165–93.

Muhammad, T. and Srivastava, S. (2020) 'Why rotational living is bad for older adults? Evidence from a cross-sectional study in India', *Journal of Population Ageing*, 1: 1–18.

Press Trust of India (2014) 'Kerala population ageing fast: survey', https://www.business-standard.com/article/pti-stories/kerala-population-age ing-fast-survey-114091800463_1.html#:~:text=Kerala's%20total%20pop ulation%20as%20per,rate%20of%202.3%20per%20cent

Samanta, T., Chen, F. and Vanneman, R. (2015) 'Living arrangements and health of older adults in India', *Journals of Gerontology Series B: Psychological Sciences and Social Sciences*, 70(6): 937–47.

Tata Trust (n.d.) 'Report on old age facilities in India'. https://www.tatatru sts.org/upload/pdf/report-on-old-age-facilities-in-india.pdf

Townsend, P. (1981) 'The structured dependency of the elderly: a creation of social policy in the twentieth century', *Ageing and Society*, 1(1): 5–28.

Ugargol, A. P. and Bailey, A. (2018) 'Family caregiving for older adults: gendered roles and caregiver burden in emigrant households of Kerala, India'. *Asian Population Studies*, 14(2): 194–210.

UNDESA (United Nations Department of Economic and Social Affairs, Population Division) (2020) International Migration 2020 Highlights (ST/ESA/SER.A/452), https://www.un.org/development/desa/pd/sites/www.un.org.development.desa.pd/files/undesa_pd_2020_international_migration_highlights.pdf

Index

Page numbers in **bold** refer to tables;
page numbers in *italics* refer to illustrations;
'n' after a page number indicates the endnote number.

health and social care provision 8, 202–3, 235
legal system 204, 205
livelihood framework 187–8, 189, *191*, *194*, *197*
never married or childless 190–3, *191*, 200
political economy influencing elder care 7–8, 200, 201–4, 236
qualitative approach 188
social protection 8, 186, 188, 201–2
Tamil Nadu 7, 185, 188, 236
caringscapes 140–1, 154–5
ageing, care and geography 141–2
development of 142
gender and 140, 142
older men's care 142, 147, 148, 150, 155
people–place relationships 141, 142–3
see also older men's care
Carp, A. 44
Carp, F. M. 44
caste 1, 128–9, 199, 201, 215
Census (2011) 12, 69, 93, 121, 162, 218
Chatterjee, E. 3
Chaudhuri, A. 81
childcare 13, 14, 18, 19
co-residence and 70, 90, 109, 130–2, 133, 234
childlessness 186, 190–3, *191*, 200
China 17, 48–9, 63, 80
Chirkov, V. 150
Clapham, D. 163
co-residence 26
abuse and neglect of the elderly 62, 88, 102, 103, 196, 198, 229
benefits of 62, 70
childcare and 70, 90, 109, 130–2, 133, 234
co-residence concordance 49, 53–5, *54*, **55**, **60**, 231
co-residence as preferred living arrangement option 5, 46, 51, 62, 231, 237
cultural norm: co-residence as pathway to well-being 5, 38, 40
decline in 19, 46, 233, 235
disability and 35, 75, 80, 81
economic issues 32, 34, *33*, *34*, 231
as expected norm 13–14, 38, 40, 44, 47, 59, 62, 81, 86
health-related issues and 34, 56–7, **60–1**, 80
intergenerational care 88, 89, 100–5
Kerala, 6, 81
Kerala, mortality risk and co-residence in large households 6, 77–8, *78*, *79*, 80
migration and 100, 101, 233
pooling of resources and 199
preferred by elderly males 47, 50

prevalence as living arrangement 50, 62, 86, 90, 228, 236–7
reciprocity 89–90
wealth and 63
well-being and **37**, 38
widowhood and 76, 91, 100–1, 104, 127
Coolen, H. 163–4
Cowgill, D. O. 2
Cristoforetti, A. 163
Croll, E. J. 89
culture/cultural norms
changing cultural norms 48
co-residence as expected norm 13–14, 38, 40, 44, 47, 59, 62, 81, 86
co-residence as pathway to well-being 5, 38, 40
cultural norms and care provision 15
cultural obligation and emotional attachment towards home 169–71, 179
cultural perception of care 149–50
cultural processes impacting on elder care 7, 199–201
cultural schemas 7, 15, 164–5, 179
culture, definition 15
culture, gender and intergenerational care arrangements 7, 90–2
home and cultural meaning system 163–5, 179

D

d'Andrade, R. G. 15
Dannefer, D. 16, 133
Datta, A. 140–60, 228
daughters
as caregivers 2, 91, 143
co-residing with (Goa) 104–5
intergenerational care and 91, 100–1
as source of support and care home entry 193–5, *194*, 196, 202
daughters-in-law
as caregivers 2–3, 14, 62, 91, 102, 119, 140, 143, 161, 173, 227
co-residing with (Goa) 103–4
intergenerational care and 91, 101, 102
De, S. 12
Delhi *see* older men's care
demographic transition 1, 2, 25, 27–8, 40
demographic transition theories 39, 62
EAG states 40n1
impact on older adults 81
individualism 39, 62
Kerala 2, 6, 28, 69, 70, 71, 81
Tamil Nadu 28, 230
variation among Indian states 4, 28
demographics
ageing population 1, 4, 45, 86, 119, 162, 210
female higher life expectancy 3, 39, 77, 80–1, 218